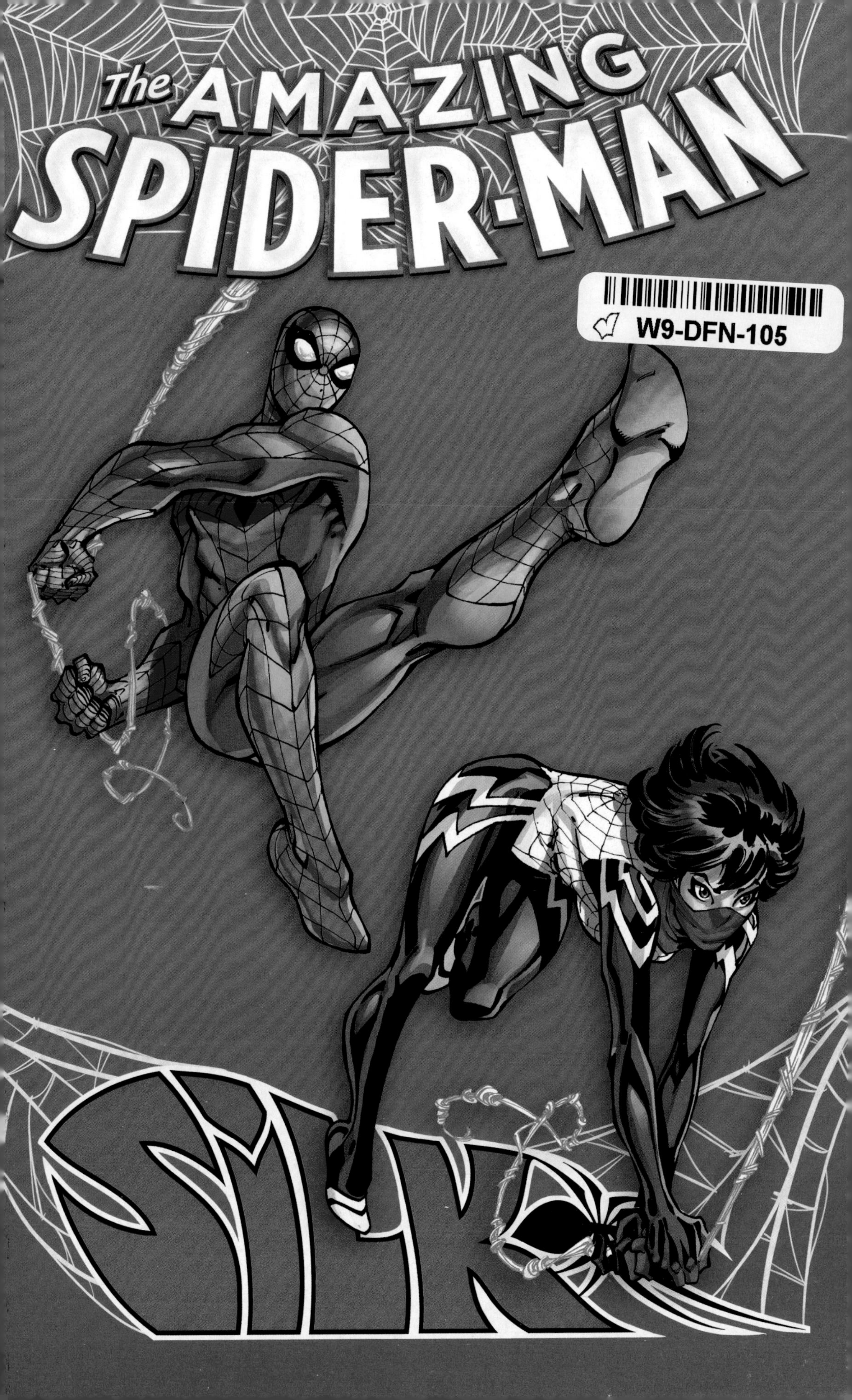
The AMAZING
SPIDER-MAN
SILK

The AMAZING SPIDER-MAN & SILK

THE SPIDER(FLY) EFFECT

ROBBIE THOMPSON
WRITER

GEOFFO
LAYOUTS

TODD NAUCK WITH
TOM GRUMMETT (#2)
PENCILERS

TODD NAUCK WITH
WAYNE FAUCHER (#2)
INKERS

VERONICA GANDINI
COLORIST

VC's CORY PETIT
LETTERER

SCOTT FORBES (#1), **STACEY LEE** (#2), **HELEN CHEN** (#3) AND **RYAN STEGMAN** & **ISRAEL SILVA** (#4)
COVER ART

ANNIE CHENG
PRODUCTION

TIM SMITH 3
PRODUCTION MANAGER

HEATHER ANTOS
ASSISTANT EDITOR

JORDAN D. WHITE
EDITOR

NICK LOWE
EXECUTIVE EDITOR

SPIDER-MAN CREATED BY STAN LEE & STEVE DITKO

COLLECTION EDITOR: JENNIFER GRÜNWALD
ASSOCIATE EDITOR: SARAH BRUNSTAD
EDITOR, SPECIAL PROJECTS: MARK D. BEAZLEY

VP, PRODUCTION & SPECIAL PROJECTS: JEFF YOUNGQUIST
SVP PRINT, SALES & MARKETING: DAVID GABRIEL
BOOK DESIGNER: ADAM DEL RE

EDITOR IN CHIEF: AXEL ALONSO
CHIEF CREATIVE OFFICER: JOE QUESADA
PUBLISHER: DAN BUCKLEY
EXECUTIVE PRODUCER: ALAN FINE

AMAZING SPIDER-MAN & SILK: THE SPIDER(FLY) EFFECT. Contains material originally published in magazine form as AMAZING SPIDER-MAN & SILK: THE SPIDER(FLY) EFFECT #1-4. First printing 2016. ISBN# 978-1-302-90231-5. Publishe by MARVEL WORLDWIDE, INC., a subsidiary of MARVEL ENTERTAINMENT, LLC. OFFICE OF PUBLICATION: 135 West 50th Street, New York, NY 10020. **Printed in Canada.** ALAN FINE, President, Marvel Entertainment; DA BUCKLEY, President, TV, Publishing & Brand Management; JOE QUESADA, Chief Creative Officer; TOM BREVOORT, SVP of Publishing; DAVID BOGART, SVP of Business Affairs & Operations, Publishing & Partnership; C.B. CEBULSKI, VP of Bran Management & Development, Asia; DAVID GABRIEL, SVP of Sales & Marketing, Publishing; JEFF YOUNGQUIST, VP of Production & Special Projects; DAN CARR, Executive Director of Publishing Technology; ALEX MORALES, Director of Publishin Operations; SUSAN CRESPI, Production Manager; STAN LEE, Chairman Emeritus. For information regarding advertising in Marvel Comics or on Marvel.com, please contact Vit DeBellis, Integrated Sales Manager, at vdebellis@marvel.com. Fo Marvel subscription inquiries, please call 888-511-5480. **Manufactured between 7/29/2016 and 9/5/2016 by SOLISCO PRINTERS, SCOTT, QC, CANADA.**

10 9 8 7 6 5 4 3 2 1

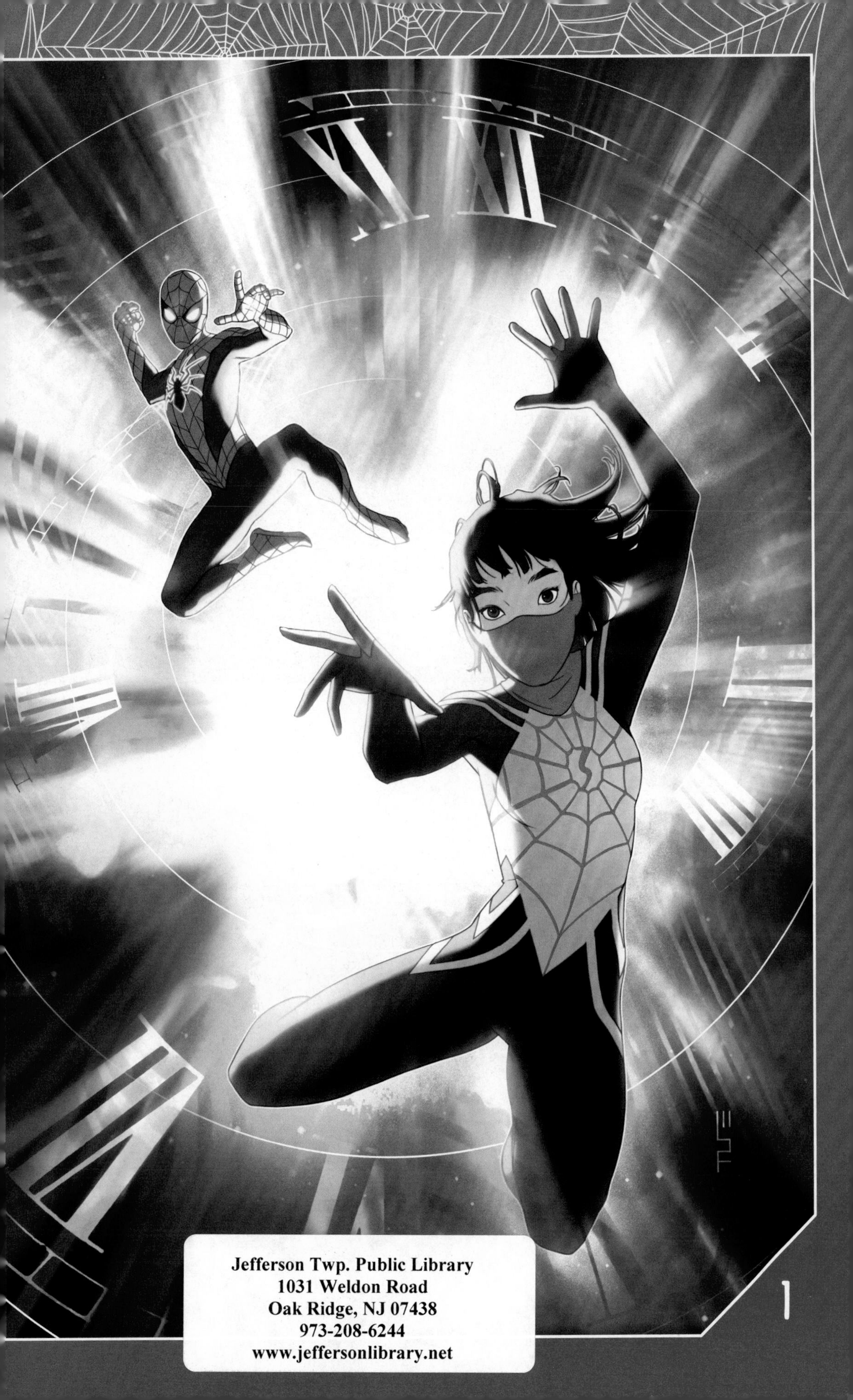

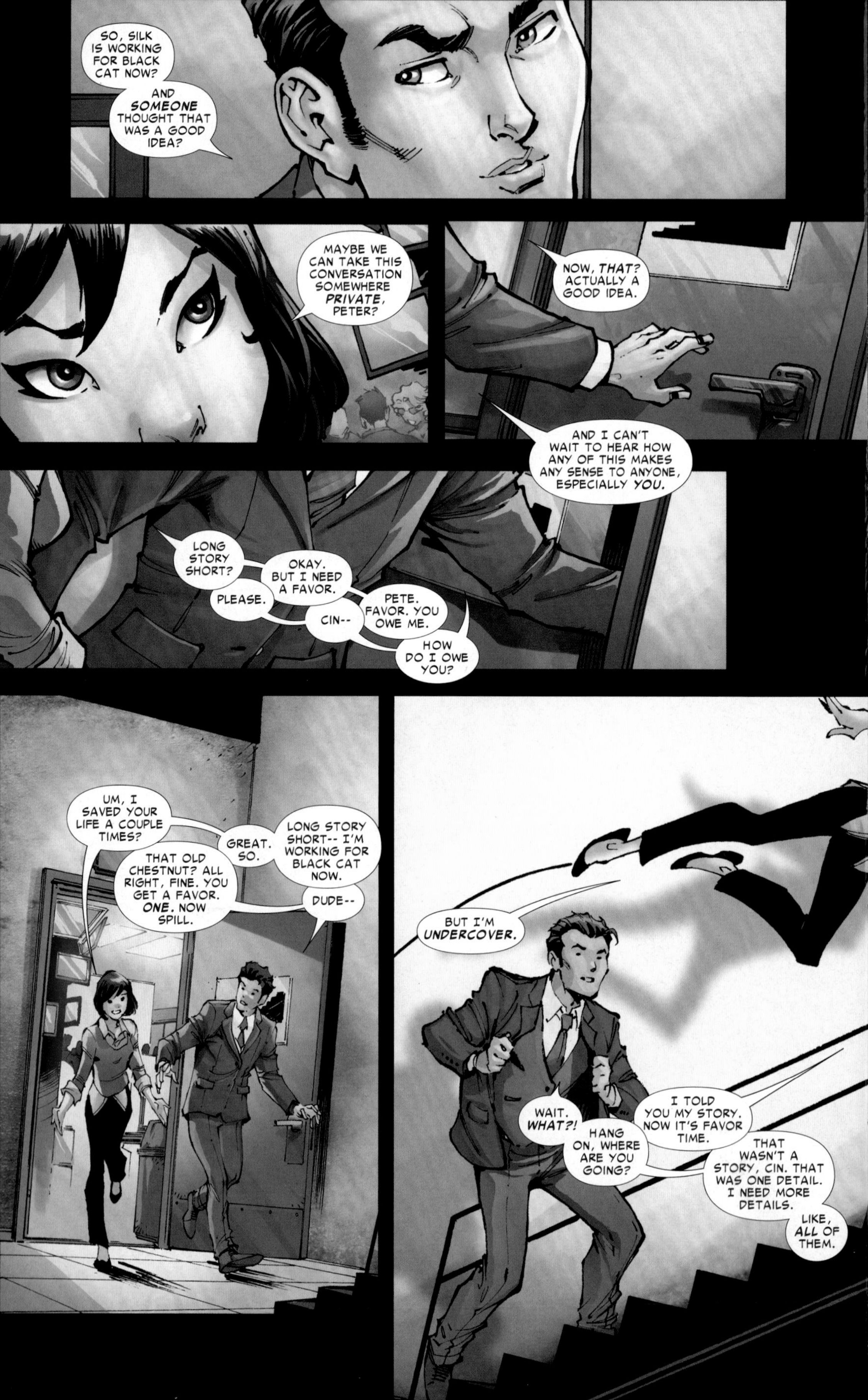
SO, SILK IS WORKING FOR BLACK CAT NOW?
AND SOMEONE THOUGHT THAT WAS A GOOD IDEA?
MAYBE WE CAN TAKE THIS CONVERSATION SOMEWHERE PRIVATE, PETER?
NOW, THAT? ACTUALLY A GOOD IDEA.
AND I CAN'T WAIT TO HEAR HOW ANY OF THIS MAKES ANY SENSE TO ANYONE, ESPECIALLY YOU.
LONG STORY SHORT?
PLEASE.
OKAY. BUT I NEED A FAVOR.
CIN--
PETE. FAVOR. YOU OWE ME.
HOW DO I OWE YOU?
UM, I SAVED YOUR LIFE A COUPLE TIMES?
THAT OLD CHESTNUT? ALL RIGHT, FINE. YOU GET A FAVOR. ONE. NOW SPILL.
GREAT. SO.
LONG STORY SHORT-- I'M WORKING FOR BLACK CAT NOW.
DUDE--
BUT I'M UNDERCOVER.
WAIT. WHAT?!
I TOLD YOU MY STORY. NOW IT'S FAVOR TIME.
HANG ON, WHERE ARE YOU GOING?
THAT WASN'T A STORY, CIN. THAT WAS ONE DETAIL. I NEED MORE DETAILS.
LIKE, ALL OF THEM.

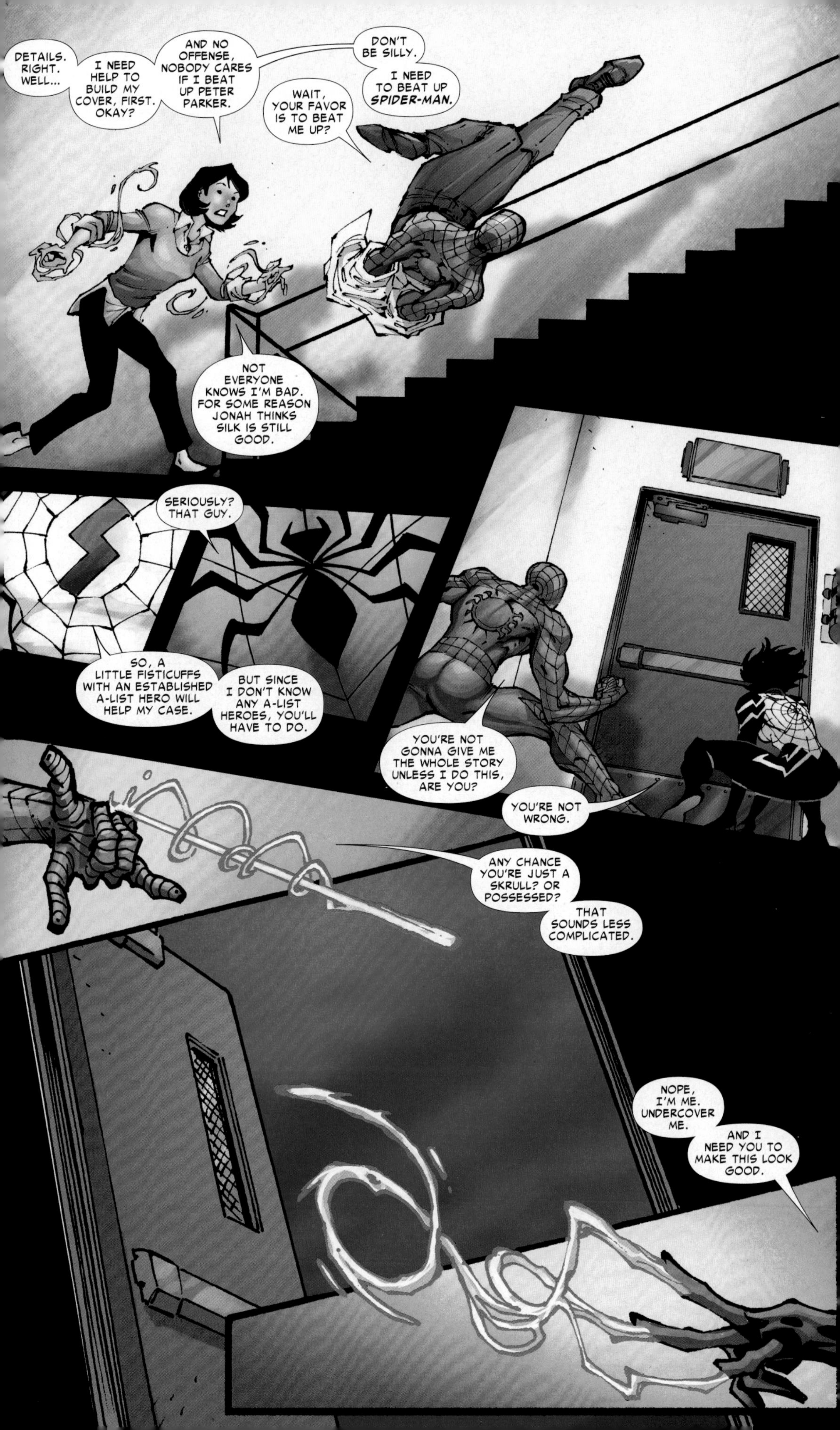

DETAILS. RIGHT. WELL...
I NEED HELP TO BUILD MY COVER, FIRST. OKAY?
AND NO OFFENSE, NOBODY CARES IF I BEAT UP PETER PARKER.
WAIT, YOUR FAVOR IS TO BEAT ME UP?
DON'T BE SILLY.
I NEED TO BEAT UP SPIDER-MAN.
NOT EVERYONE KNOWS I'M BAD. FOR SOME REASON JONAH THINKS SILK IS STILL GOOD.
SERIOUSLY? THAT GUY.
SO, A LITTLE FISTICUFFS WITH AN ESTABLISHED A-LIST HERO WILL HELP MY CASE.
BUT SINCE I DON'T KNOW ANY A-LIST HEROES, YOU'LL HAVE TO DO.
YOU'RE NOT GONNA GIVE ME THE WHOLE STORY UNLESS I DO THIS, ARE YOU?
YOU'RE NOT WRONG.
ANY CHANCE YOU'RE JUST A SKRULL? OR POSSESSED?
THAT SOUNDS LESS COMPLICATED.
NOPE, I'M ME. UNDERCOVER ME.
AND I NEED YOU TO MAKE THIS LOOK GOOD.

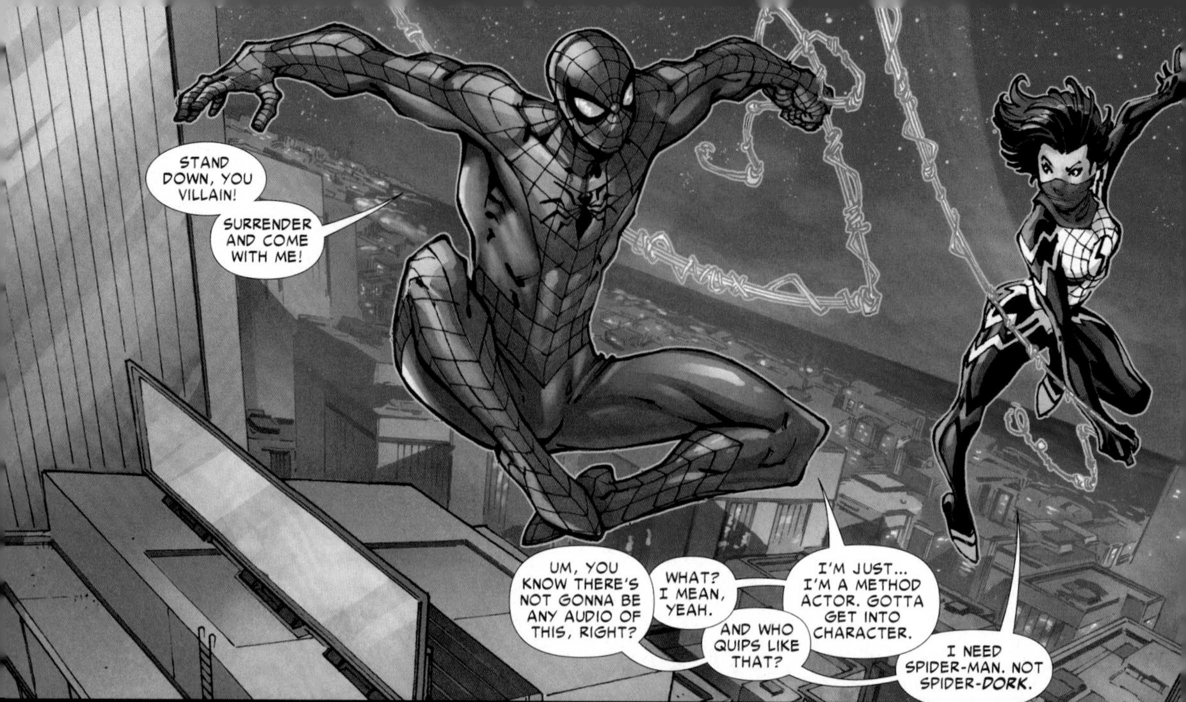
STAND DOWN, YOU VILLAIN!
SURRENDER AND COME WITH ME!
UM, YOU KNOW THERE'S NOT GONNA BE ANY AUDIO OF THIS, RIGHT?
WHAT? I MEAN, YEAH.
I'M JUST... I'M A METHOD ACTOR. GOTTA GET INTO CHARACTER.
AND WHO QUIPS LIKE THAT?
I NEED SPIDER-MAN. NOT SPIDER-DORK.

THE SPIDER(FLY) EFFECT

CHAPTERS ONE & TWO

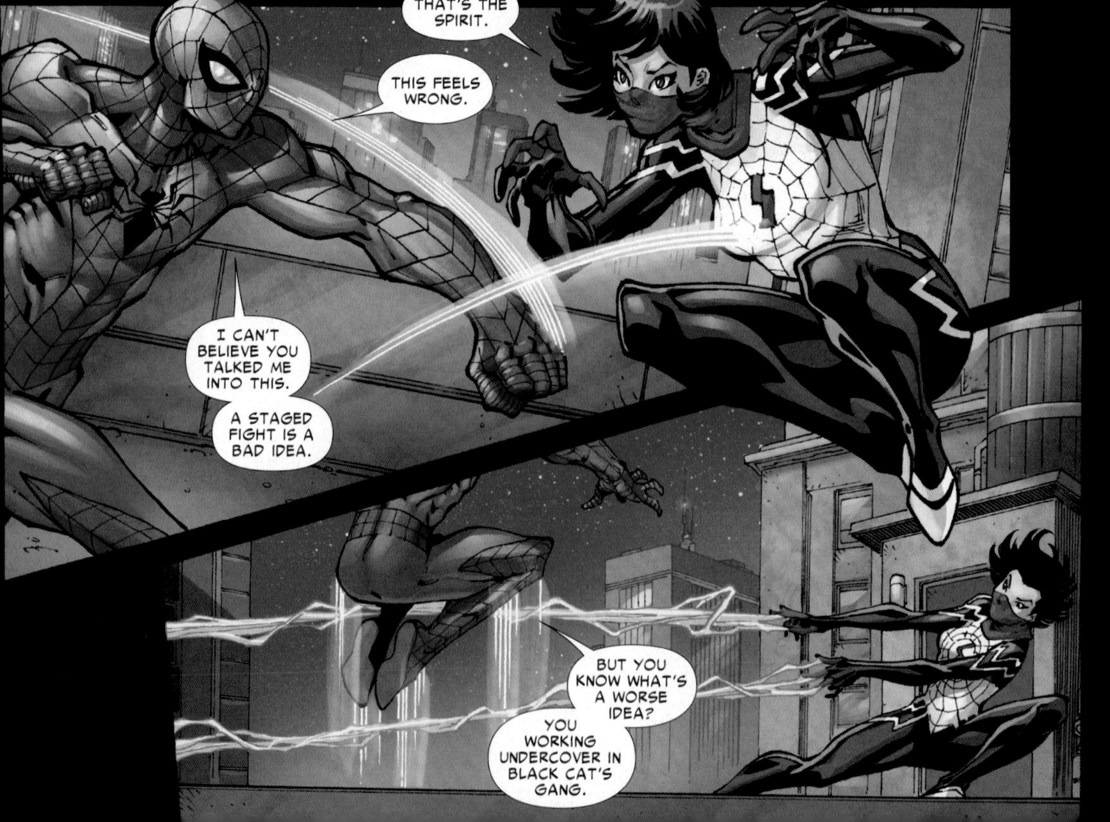
THAT'S THE SPIRIT.
THIS FEELS WRONG.
I CAN'T BELIEVE YOU TALKED ME INTO THIS.
A STAGED FIGHT IS A BAD IDEA.
BUT YOU KNOW WHAT'S A WORSE IDEA?
YOU WORKING UNDERCOVER IN BLACK CAT'S GANG.

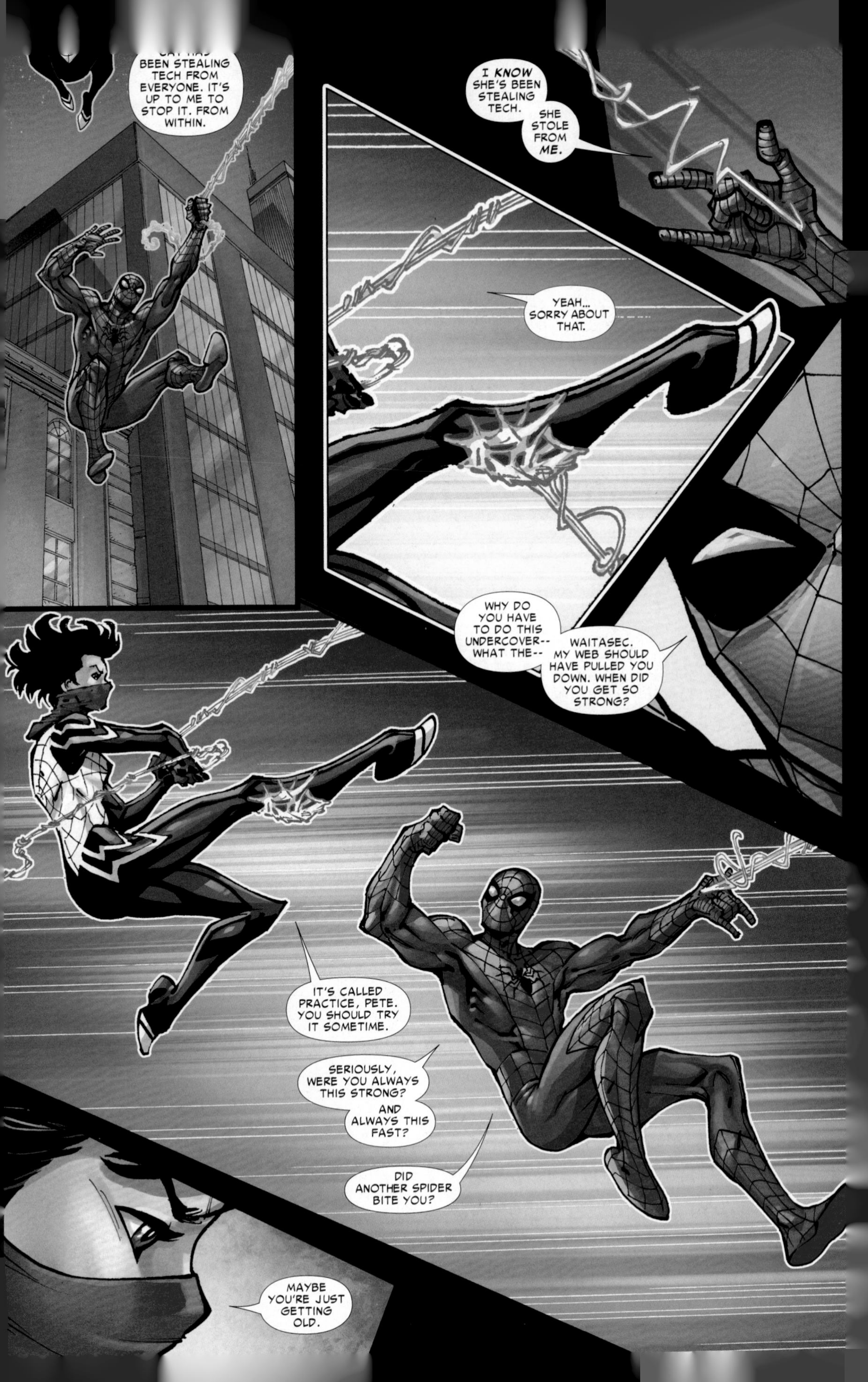
BEEN STEALING TECH FROM EVERYONE. IT'S UP TO ME TO STOP IT. FROM WITHIN.
I KNOW SHE'S BEEN STEALING TECH.
SHE STOLE FROM ME.
YEAH... SORRY ABOUT THAT.
WHY DO YOU HAVE TO DO THIS UNDERCOVER-- WHAT THE--
WAITASEC. MY WEB SHOULD HAVE PULLED YOU DOWN. WHEN DID YOU GET SO STRONG?
IT'S CALLED PRACTICE, PETE. YOU SHOULD TRY IT SOMETIME.
SERIOUSLY, WERE YOU ALWAYS THIS STRONG?
AND ALWAYS THIS FAST?
DID ANOTHER SPIDER BITE YOU?
MAYBE YOU'RE JUST GETTING OLD.

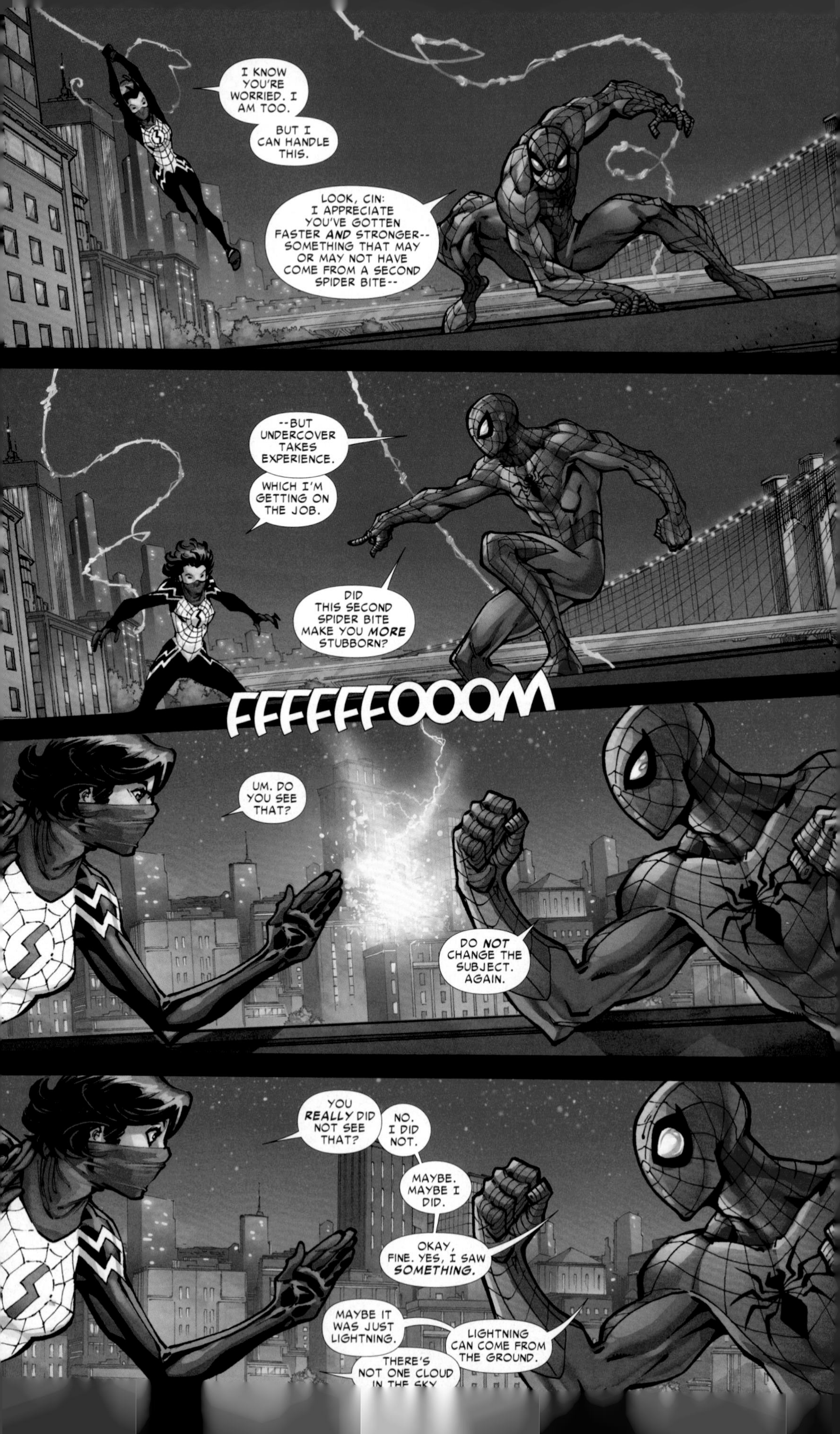
I KNOW YOU'RE WORRIED. I AM TOO.
BUT I CAN HANDLE THIS.
LOOK, CIN: I APPRECIATE YOU'VE GOTTEN FASTER AND STRONGER-- SOMETHING THAT MAY OR MAY NOT HAVE COME FROM A SECOND SPIDER BITE--
--BUT UNDERCOVER TAKES EXPERIENCE.
WHICH I'M GETTING ON THE JOB.
DID THIS SECOND SPIDER BITE MAKE YOU MORE STUBBORN?
FFFFFFOOOM
UM. DO YOU SEE THAT?
DO NOT CHANGE THE SUBJECT. AGAIN.
YOU REALLY DID NOT SEE THAT?
NO. I DID NOT.
MAYBE. MAYBE I DID.
OKAY, FINE. YES, I SAW SOMETHING.
MAYBE IT WAS JUST LIGHTNING.
LIGHTNING CAN COME FROM THE GROUND.
THERE'S NOT ONE CLOUD

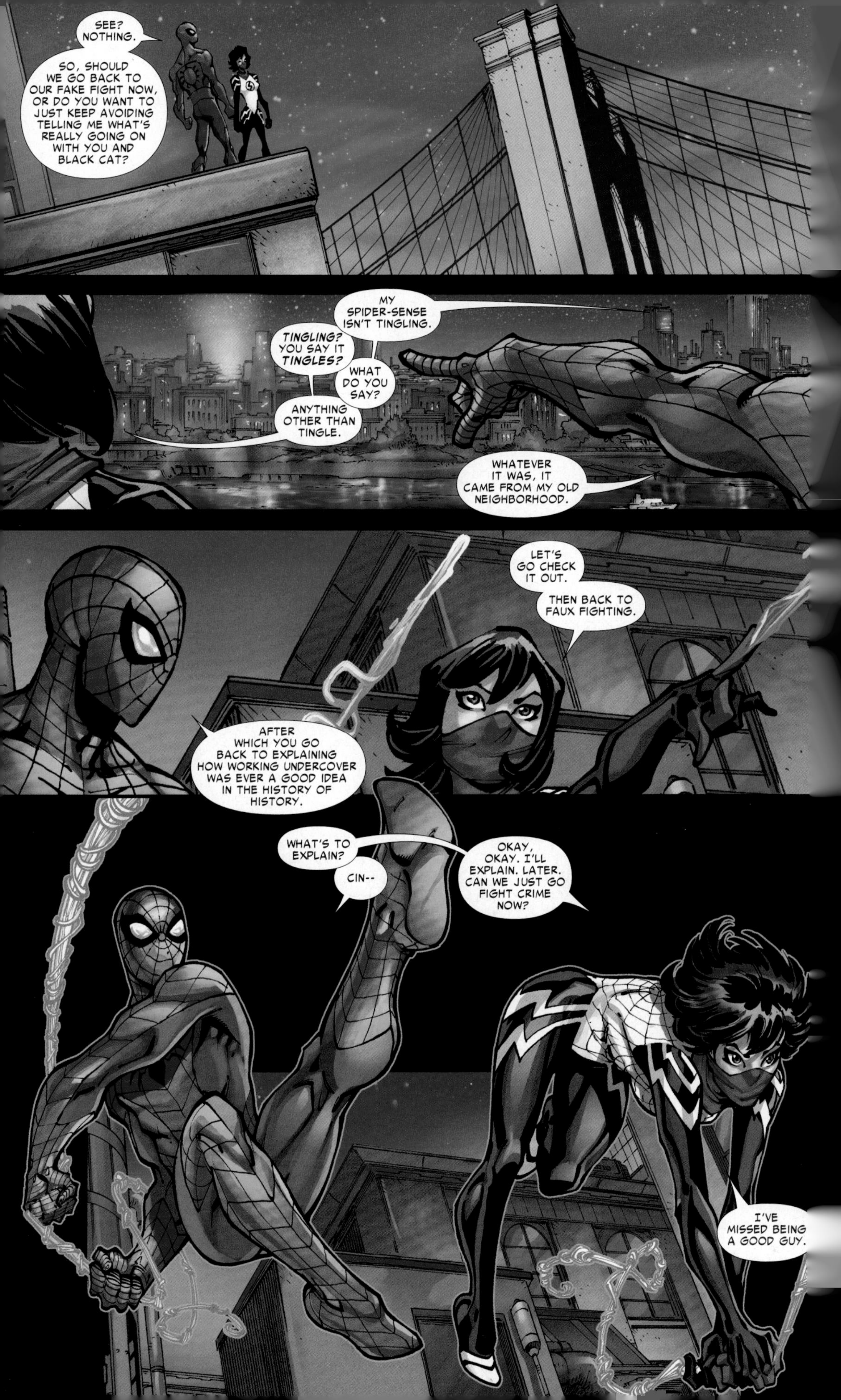
SEE? NOTHING.
SO, SHOULD WE GO BACK TO OUR FAKE FIGHT NOW, OR DO YOU WANT TO JUST KEEP AVOIDING TELLING ME WHAT'S REALLY GOING ON WITH YOU AND BLACK CAT?
MY SPIDER-SENSE ISN'T TINGLING.
TINGLING? YOU SAY IT *TINGLES?*
WHAT DO YOU SAY?
ANYTHING OTHER THAN TINGLE.
WHATEVER IT WAS, IT CAME FROM MY OLD NEIGHBORHOOD.
LET'S GO CHECK IT OUT.
THEN BACK TO FAUX FIGHTING.
AFTER WHICH YOU GO BACK TO EXPLAINING HOW WORKING UNDERCOVER WAS EVER A GOOD IDEA IN THE HISTORY OF HISTORY.
WHAT'S TO EXPLAIN?
CIN--
OKAY, OKAY. I'LL EXPLAIN. LATER. CAN WE JUST GO FIGHT CRIME NOW?
I'VE MISSED BEING A GOOD GUY.

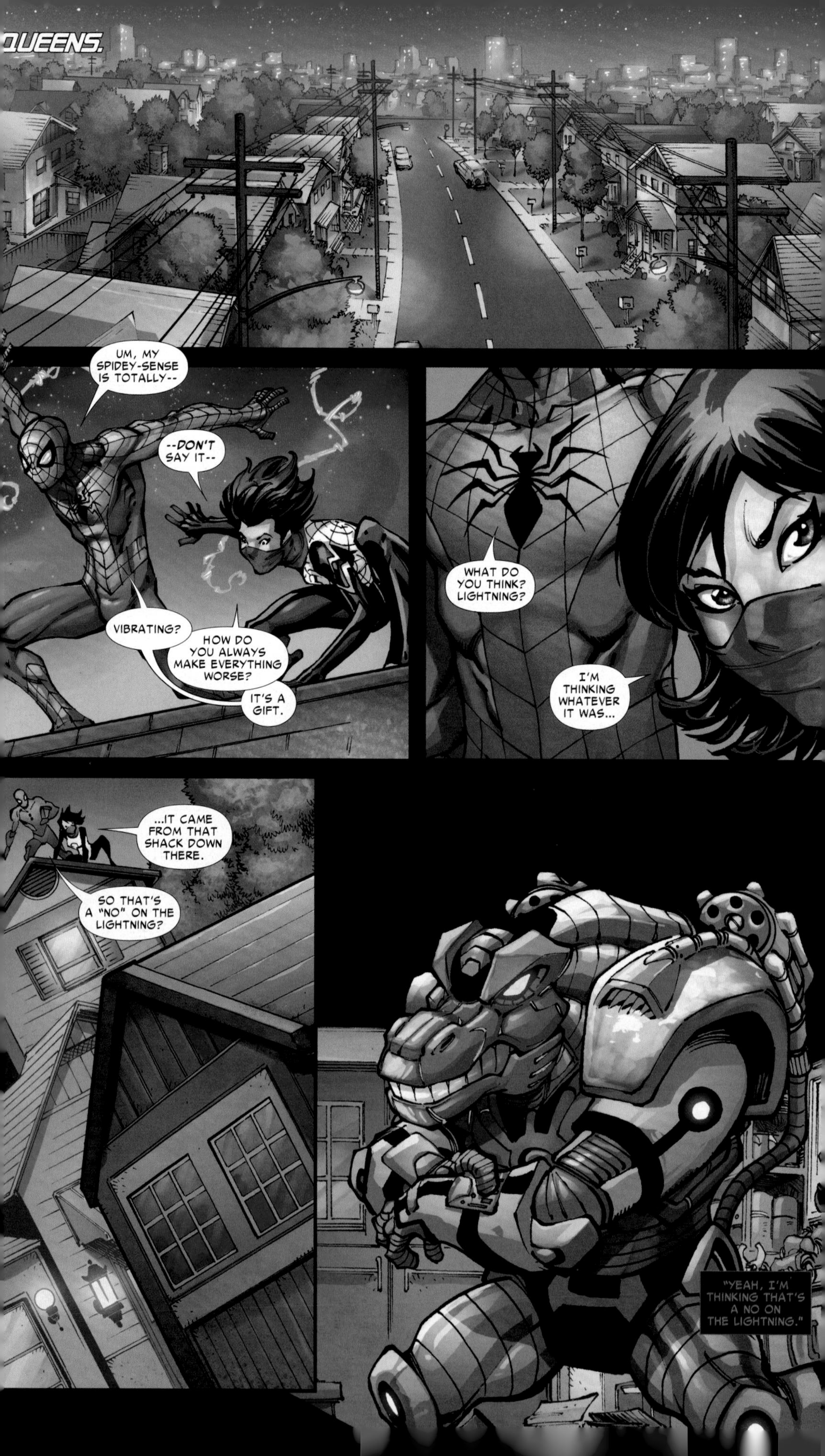
QUEENS.
UM, MY SPIDEY-SENSE IS TOTALLY--
--DON'T SAY IT--
VIBRATING?
HOW DO YOU ALWAYS MAKE EVERYTHING WORSE?
IT'S A GIFT.
WHAT DO YOU THINK? LIGHTNING?
I'M THINKING WHATEVER IT WAS...
...IT CAME FROM THAT SHACK DOWN THERE.
SO THAT'S A "NO" ON THE LIGHTNING?
"YEAH, I'M THINKING THAT'S A NO ON THE LIGHTNING."

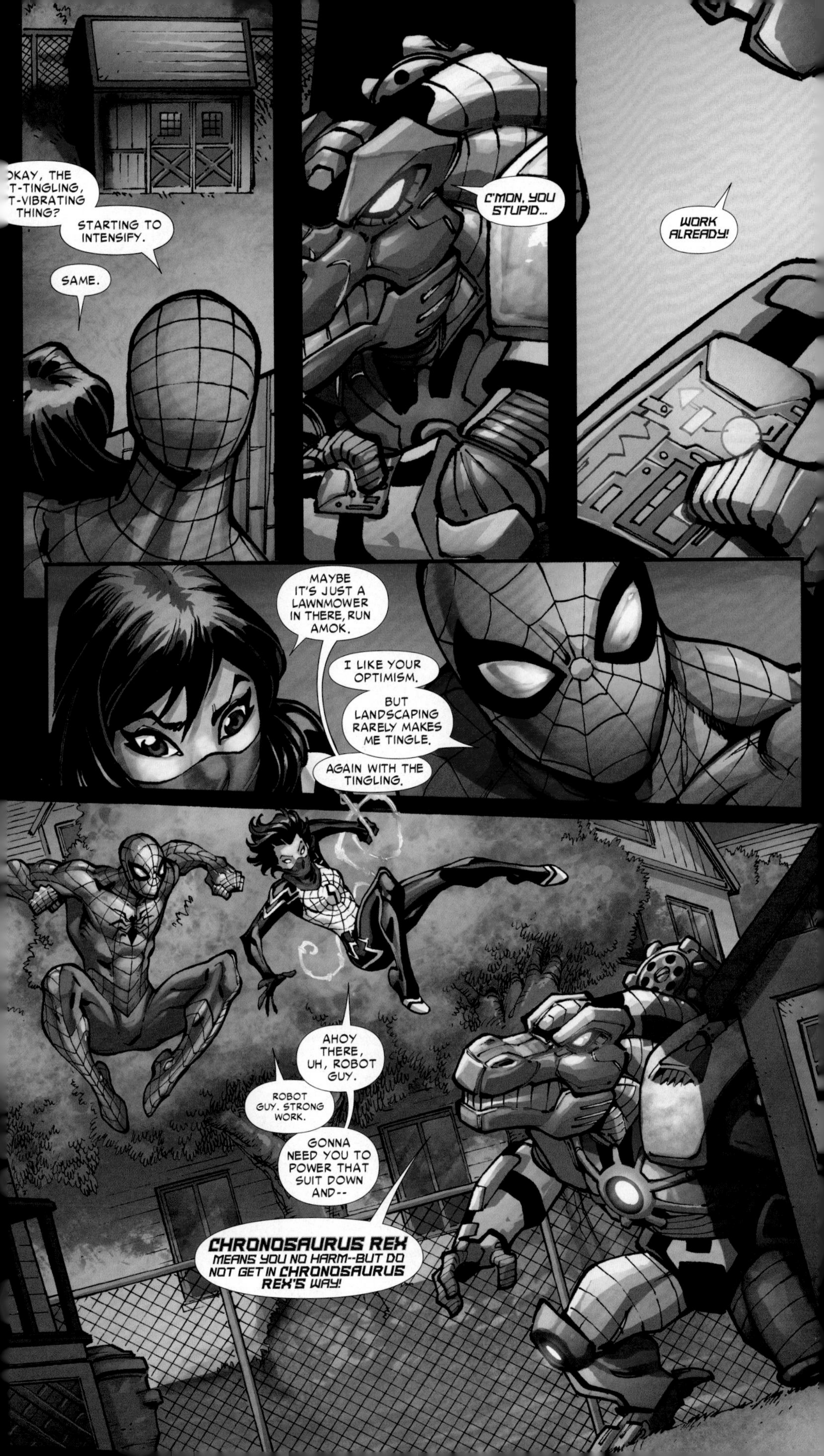
OKAY, THE T-TINGLING, T-VIBRATING THING?
STARTING TO INTENSIFY.
SAME.
C'MON, YOU STUPID...
WORK ALREADY!
MAYBE IT'S JUST A LAWNMOWER IN THERE, RUN AMOK.
I LIKE YOUR OPTIMISM.
BUT LANDSCAPING RARELY MAKES ME TINGLE.
AGAIN WITH THE TINGLING.
AHOY THERE, UH, ROBOT GUY.
ROBOT GUY. STRONG WORK.
GONNA NEED YOU TO POWER THAT SUIT DOWN AND--
CHRONOSAURUS REX MEANS YOU NO HARM--BUT DO NOT GET IN CHRONOSAURUS REX'S WAY!

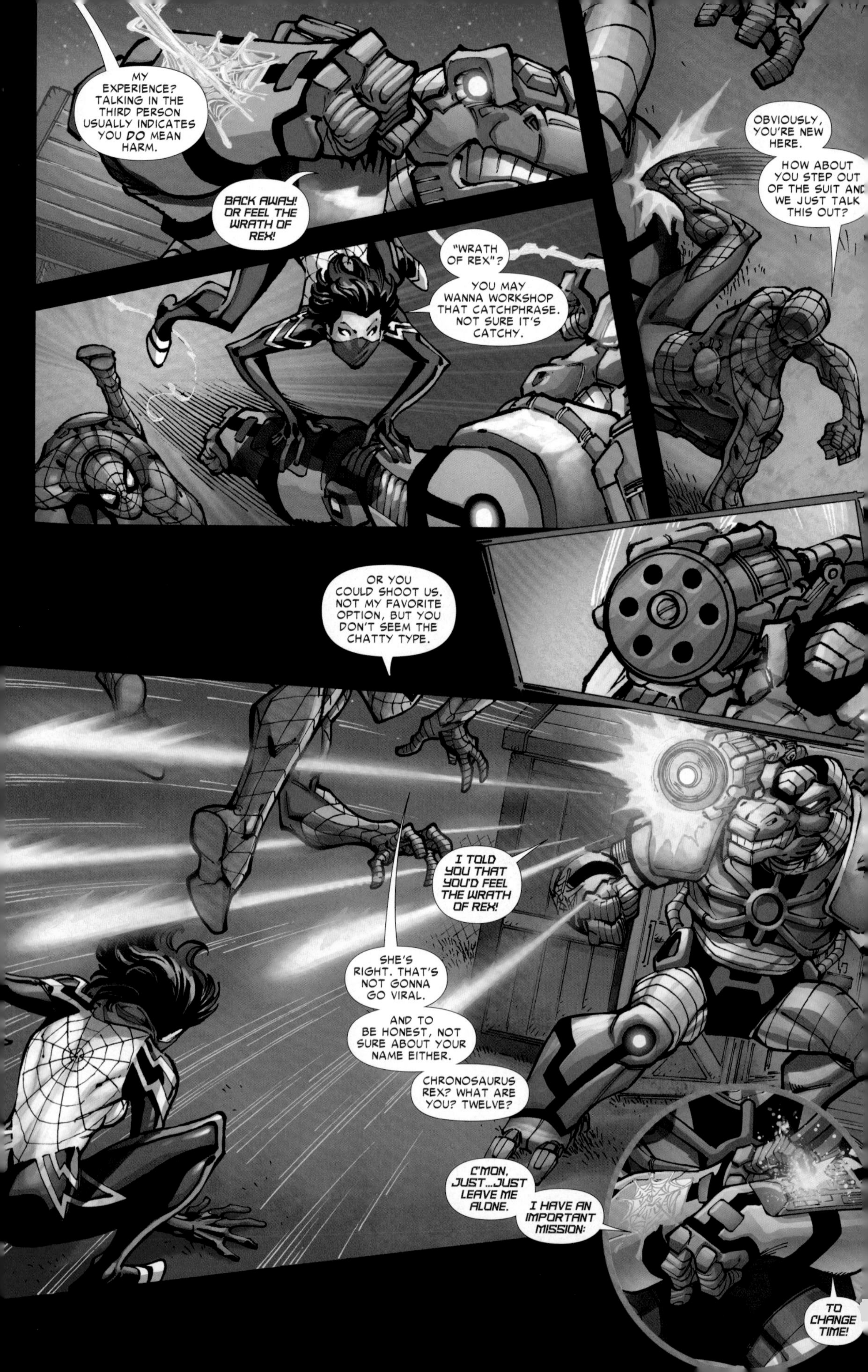
MY EXPERIENCE? TALKING IN THE THIRD PERSON USUALLY INDICATES YOU DO MEAN HARM.
BACK AWAY! OR FEEL THE WRATH OF REX!
"WRATH OF REX"?
YOU MAY WANNA WORKSHOP THAT CATCHPHRASE. NOT SURE IT'S CATCHY.
OBVIOUSLY, YOU'RE NEW HERE.
HOW ABOUT YOU STEP OUT OF THE SUIT AND WE JUST TALK THIS OUT?
OR YOU COULD SHOOT US. NOT MY FAVORITE OPTION, BUT YOU DON'T SEEM THE CHATTY TYPE.
I TOLD YOU THAT YOU'D FEEL THE WRATH OF REX!
SHE'S RIGHT. THAT'S NOT GONNA GO VIRAL.
AND TO BE HONEST, NOT SURE ABOUT YOUR NAME EITHER.
CHRONOSAURUS REX? WHAT ARE YOU? TWELVE?
C'MON, JUST...JUST LEAVE ME ALONE.
I HAVE AN IMPORTANT MISSION:
TO CHANGE TIME!

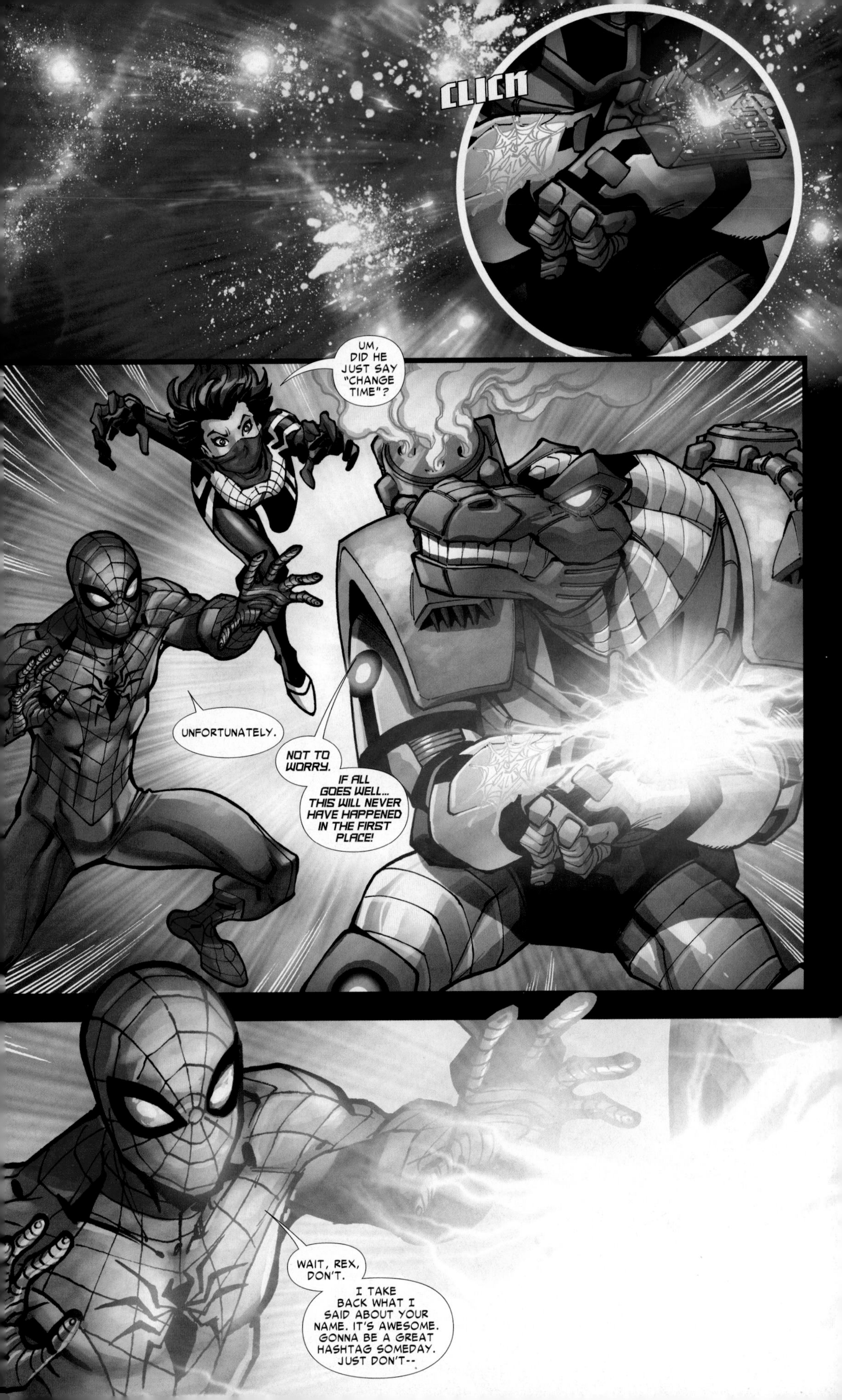
CLICK
UM, DID HE JUST SAY "CHANGE TIME"?
UNFORTUNATELY.
NOT TO WORRY.
IF ALL GOES WELL... THIS WILL NEVER HAVE HAPPENED IN THE FIRST PLACE!
WAIT, REX, DON'T.
I TAKE BACK WHAT I SAID ABOUT YOUR NAME. IT'S AWESOME. GONNA BE A GREAT HASHTAG SOMEDAY. JUST DON'T--

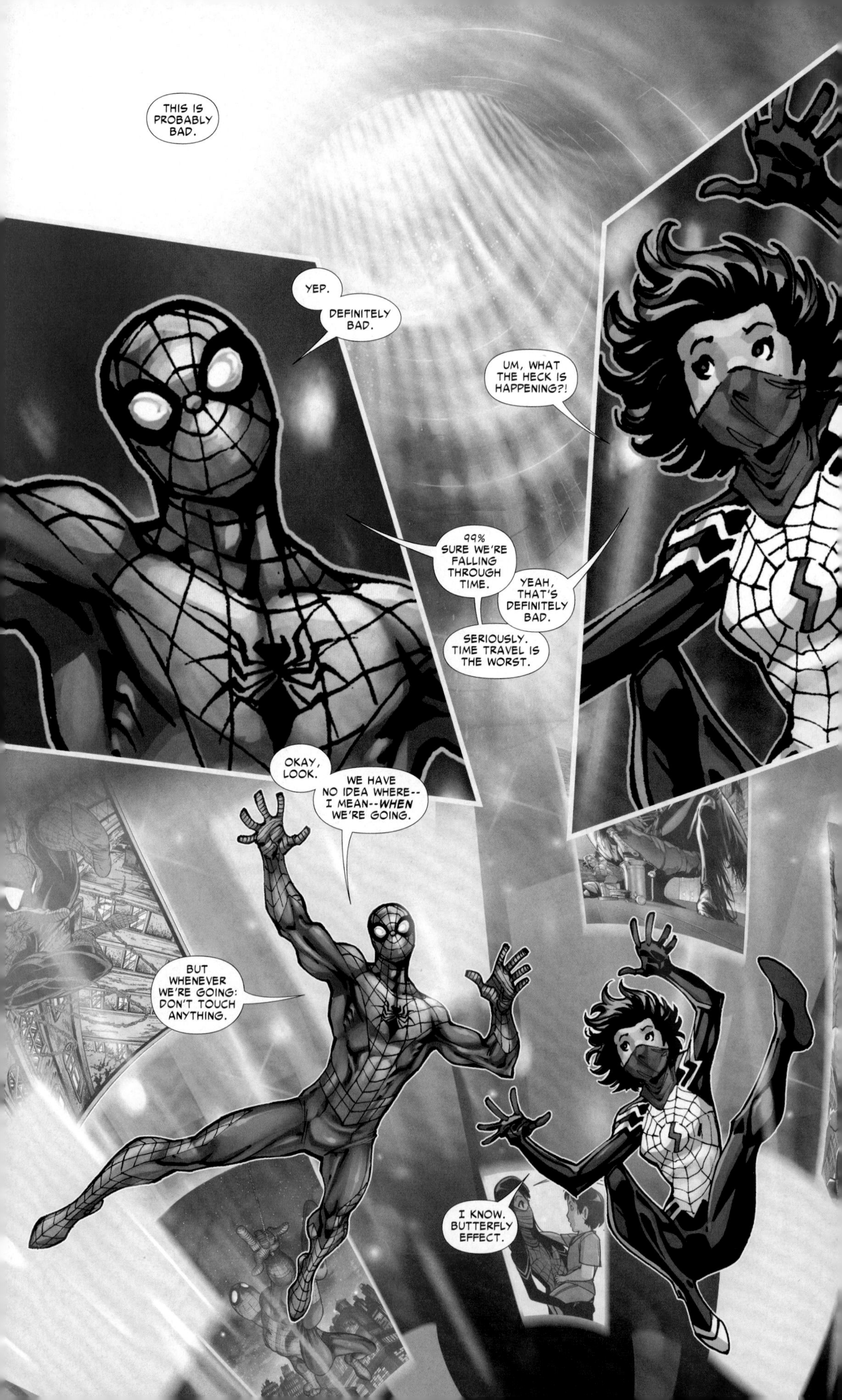
THIS IS PROBABLY BAD.
YEP.
DEFINITELY BAD.
UM, WHAT THE HECK IS HAPPENING?!
99% SURE WE'RE FALLING THROUGH TIME.
YEAH, THAT'S DEFINITELY BAD.
SERIOUSLY. TIME TRAVEL IS THE WORST.
OKAY, LOOK.
WE HAVE NO IDEA WHERE-- I MEAN--WHEN WE'RE GOING.
BUT WHENEVER WE'RE GOING: DON'T TOUCH ANYTHING.
I KNOW. BUTTERFLY EFFECT.

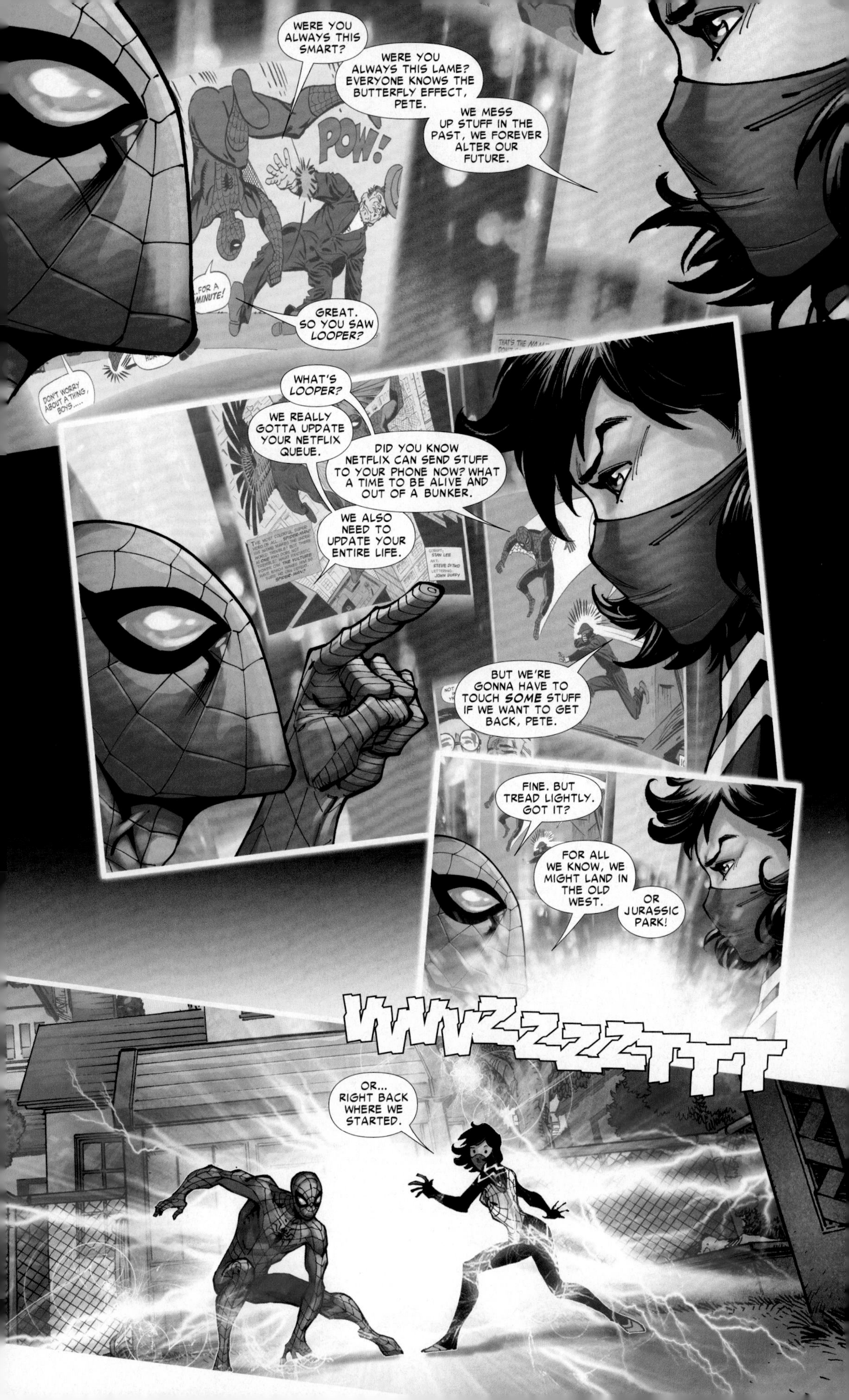
WERE YOU ALWAYS THIS SMART?
WERE YOU ALWAYS THIS LAME? EVERYONE KNOWS THE BUTTERFLY EFFECT, PETE.
WE MESS UP STUFF IN THE PAST, WE FOREVER ALTER OUR FUTURE.
POW!
...FOR A MINUTE!
GREAT. SO YOU SAW LOOPER?
DON'T WORRY ABOUT A THING, BOYS.....
WHAT'S LOOPER?
WE REALLY GOTTA UPDATE YOUR NETFLIX QUEUE.
DID YOU KNOW NETFLIX CAN SEND STUFF TO YOUR PHONE NOW? WHAT A TIME TO BE ALIVE AND OUT OF A BUNKER.
WE ALSO NEED TO UPDATE YOUR ENTIRE LIFE.
BUT WE'RE GONNA HAVE TO TOUCH SOME STUFF IF WE WANT TO GET BACK, PETE.
FINE. BUT TREAD LIGHTLY. GOT IT?
FOR ALL WE KNOW, WE MIGHT LAND IN THE OLD WEST.
OR JURASSIC PARK!
VVVVZZZZTTTT
OR... RIGHT BACK WHERE WE STARTED.

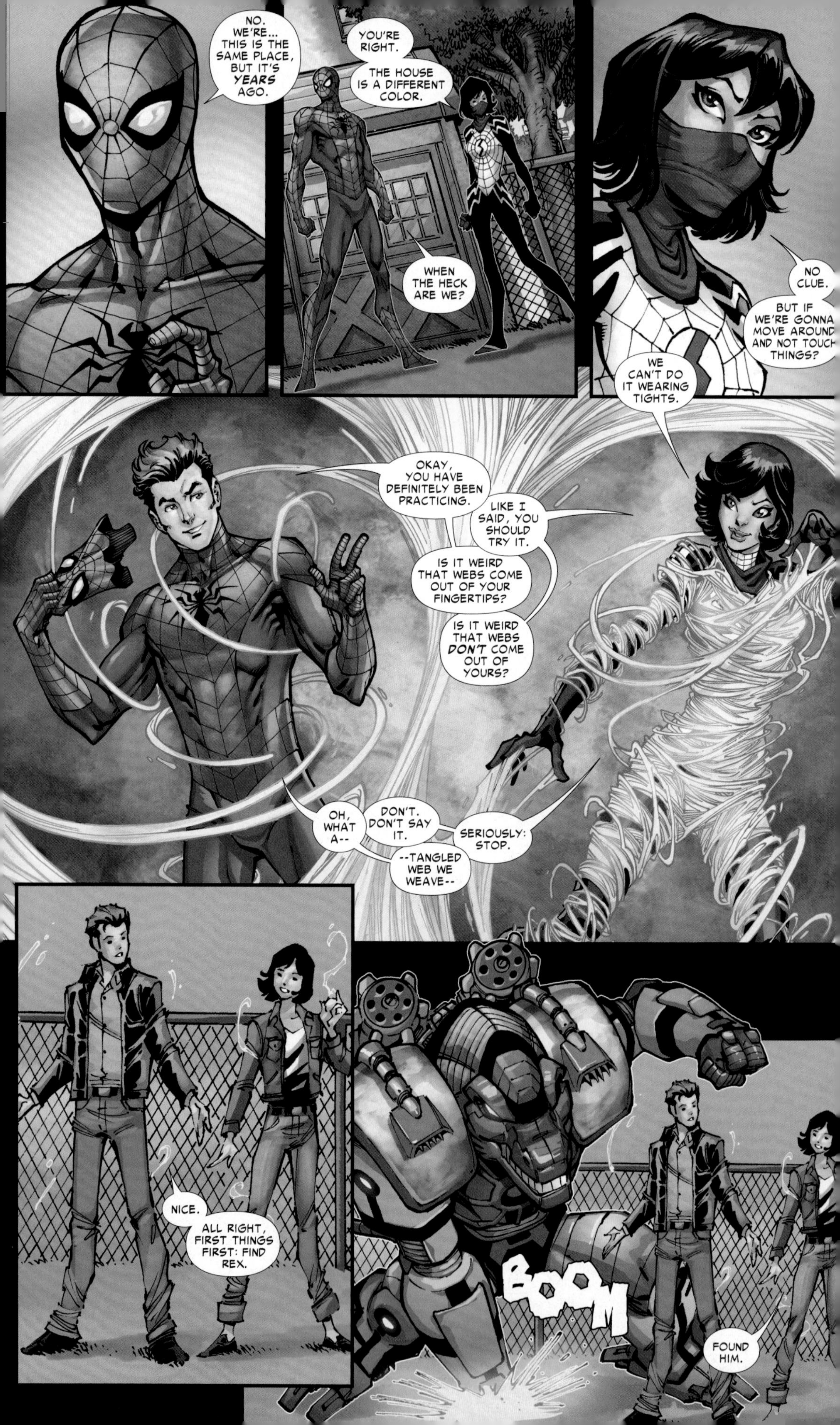
NO. WE'RE... THIS IS THE SAME PLACE, BUT IT'S *YEARS* AGO.
YOU'RE RIGHT.
THE HOUSE IS A DIFFERENT COLOR.
WHEN THE HECK ARE WE?
NO CLUE.
BUT IF WE'RE GONNA MOVE AROUND AND NOT TOUCH THINGS?
WE CAN'T DO IT WEARING TIGHTS.
OKAY, YOU HAVE DEFINITELY BEEN PRACTICING.
LIKE I SAID, YOU SHOULD TRY IT.
IS IT WEIRD THAT WEBS COME OUT OF YOUR FINGERTIPS?
IS IT WEIRD THAT WEBS *DON'T* COME OUT OF YOURS?
OH, WHAT A--
DON'T. DON'T SAY IT.
--TANGLED WEB WE WEAVE--
SERIOUSLY: STOP.
NICE.
ALL RIGHT, FIRST THINGS FIRST: FIND REX.
BOOM
FOUND HIM.

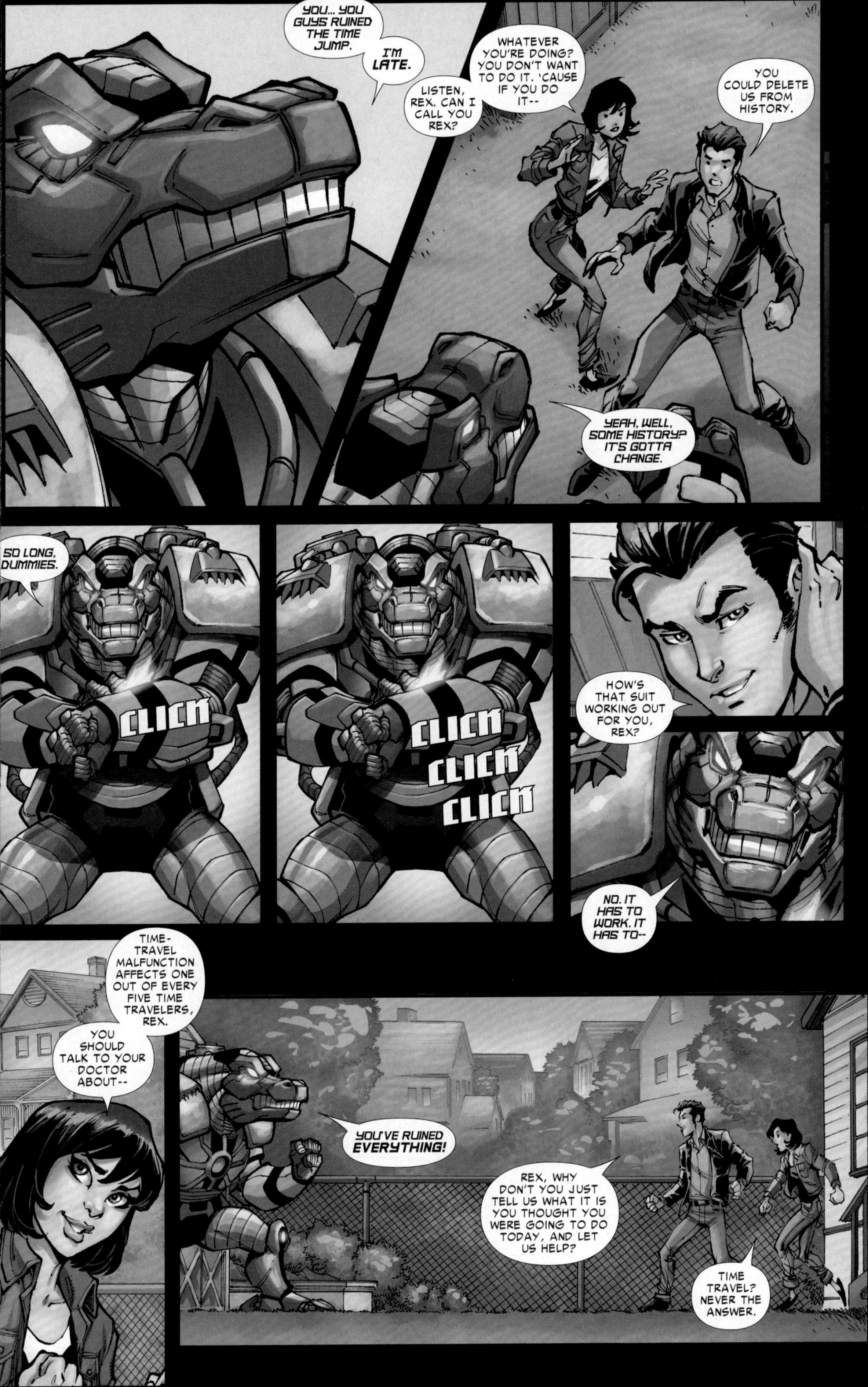
YOU... YOU GUYS RUINED THE TIME JUMP.
I'M LATE.
WHATEVER YOU'RE DOING? YOU DON'T WANT TO DO IT. 'CAUSE IF YOU DO IT--
LISTEN, REX. CAN I CALL YOU REX?
YOU COULD DELETE US FROM HISTORY.
YEAH, WELL, SOME HISTORY? IT'S GOTTA CHANGE.
SO LONG, DUMMIES.
CLICK
CLICK CLICK CLICK
HOW'S THAT SUIT WORKING OUT FOR YOU, REX?
NO. IT HAS TO WORK. IT HAS TO--
TIME-TRAVEL MALFUNCTION AFFECTS ONE OUT OF EVERY FIVE TIME TRAVELERS, REX.
YOU SHOULD TALK TO YOUR DOCTOR ABOUT--
YOU'VE RUINED EVERYTHING!
REX, WHY DON'T YOU JUST TELL US WHAT IT IS YOU THOUGHT YOU WERE GOING TO DO TODAY, AND LET US HELP?
TIME TRAVEL? NEVER THE ANSWER.

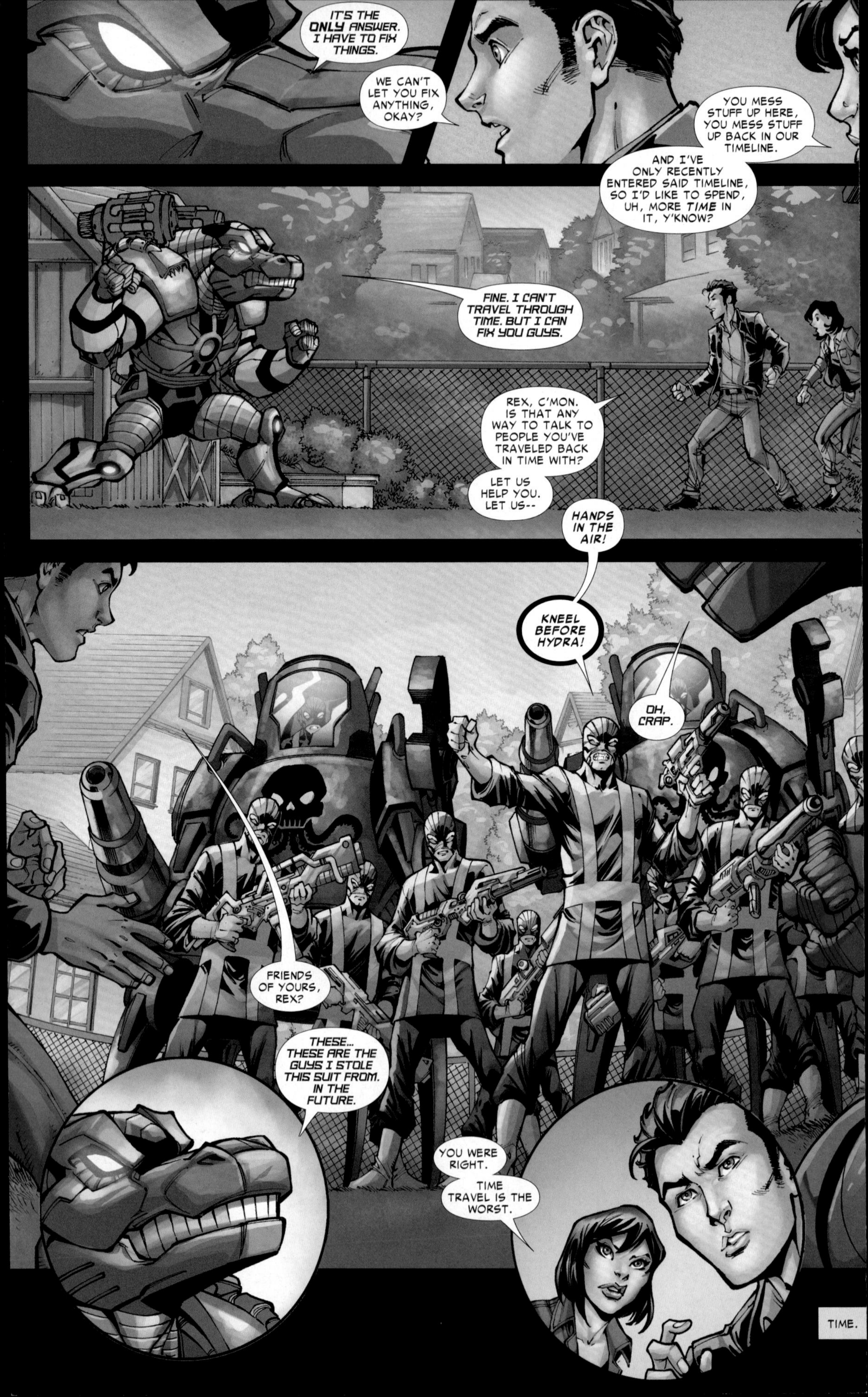
IT'S THE ONLY ANSWER. I HAVE TO FIX THINGS.
WE CAN'T LET YOU FIX ANYTHING, OKAY?
YOU MESS STUFF UP HERE, YOU MESS STUFF UP BACK IN OUR TIMELINE.
AND I'VE ONLY RECENTLY ENTERED SAID TIMELINE, SO I'D LIKE TO SPEND, UH, MORE TIME IN IT, Y'KNOW?
FINE. I CAN'T TRAVEL THROUGH TIME. BUT I CAN FIX YOU GUYS.
REX, C'MON. IS THAT ANY WAY TO TALK TO PEOPLE YOU'VE TRAVELED BACK IN TIME WITH?
LET US HELP YOU. LET US--
HANDS IN THE AIR!
KNEEL BEFORE HYDRA!
OH, CRAP.
FRIENDS OF YOURS, REX?
THESE... THESE ARE THE GUYS I STOLE THIS SUIT FROM. IN THE FUTURE.
YOU WERE RIGHT.
TIME TRAVEL IS THE WORST.
TIME.

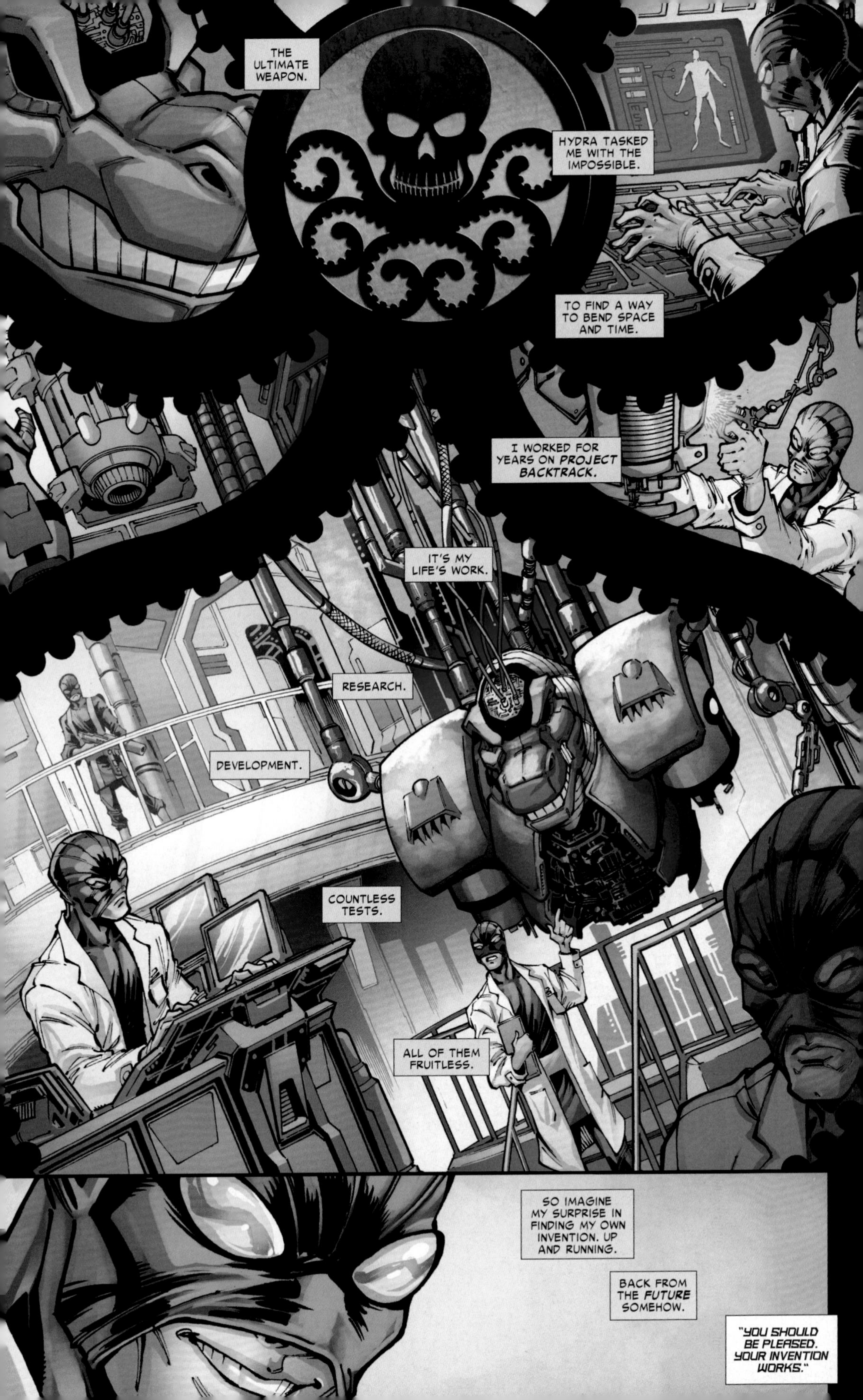
THE ULTIMATE WEAPON.
HYDRA TASKED ME WITH THE IMPOSSIBLE.
TO FIND A WAY TO BEND SPACE AND TIME.
I WORKED FOR YEARS ON *PROJECT BACKTRACK.*
IT'S MY LIFE'S WORK.
RESEARCH.
DEVELOPMENT.
COUNTLESS TESTS.
ALL OF THEM FRUITLESS.
SO IMAGINE MY SURPRISE IN FINDING MY OWN INVENTION. UP AND RUNNING.
BACK FROM THE *FUTURE* SOMEHOW.
"YOU SHOULD BE PLEASED. YOUR INVENTION WORKS."

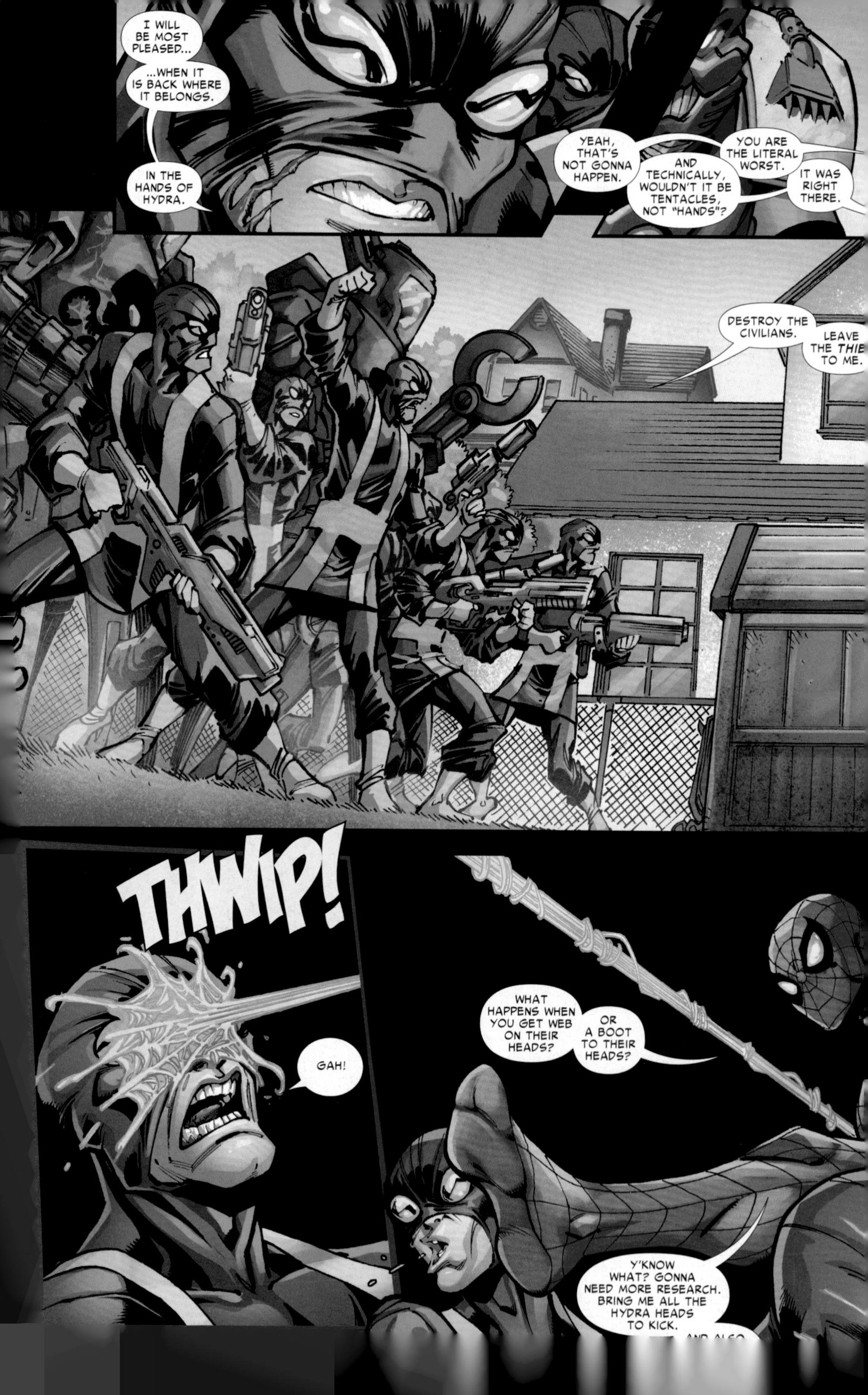
I WILL BE MOST PLEASED...
...WHEN IT IS BACK WHERE IT BELONGS.
IN THE HANDS OF HYDRA.
YEAH, THAT'S NOT GONNA HAPPEN.
AND TECHNICALLY, WOULDN'T IT BE TENTACLES, NOT "HANDS"?
YOU ARE THE LITERAL WORST.
IT WAS RIGHT THERE.
DESTROY THE CIVILIANS.
LEAVE THE *THIE* TO ME.
THWIP!
GAH!
WHAT HAPPENS WHEN YOU GET WEB ON THEIR HEADS?
OR A BOOT TO THEIR HEADS?
Y'KNOW WHAT? GONNA NEED MORE RESEARCH. BRING ME ALL THE HYDRA HEADS TO KICK.

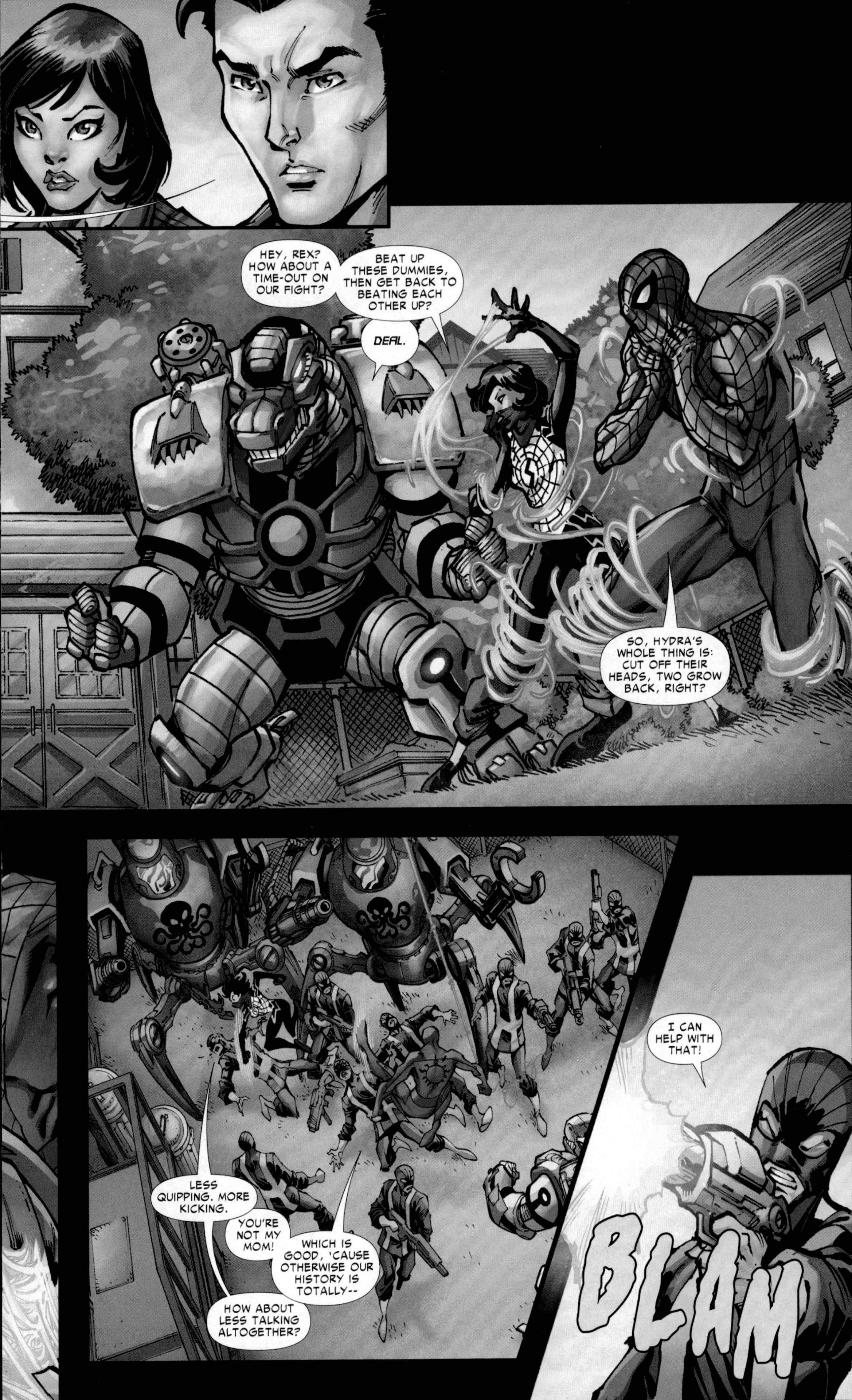
HEY, REX? HOW ABOUT A TIME-OUT ON OUR FIGHT?
BEAT UP THESE DUMMIES, THEN GET BACK TO BEATING EACH OTHER UP?
DEAL.
SO, HYDRA'S WHOLE THING IS: CUT OFF THEIR HEADS, TWO GROW BACK, RIGHT?
I CAN HELP WITH THAT!
LESS QUIPPING. MORE KICKING.
YOU'RE NOT MY MOM!
WHICH IS GOOD, 'CAUSE OTHERWISE OUR HISTORY IS TOTALLY--
HOW ABOUT LESS TALKING ALTOGETHER?
BLAM

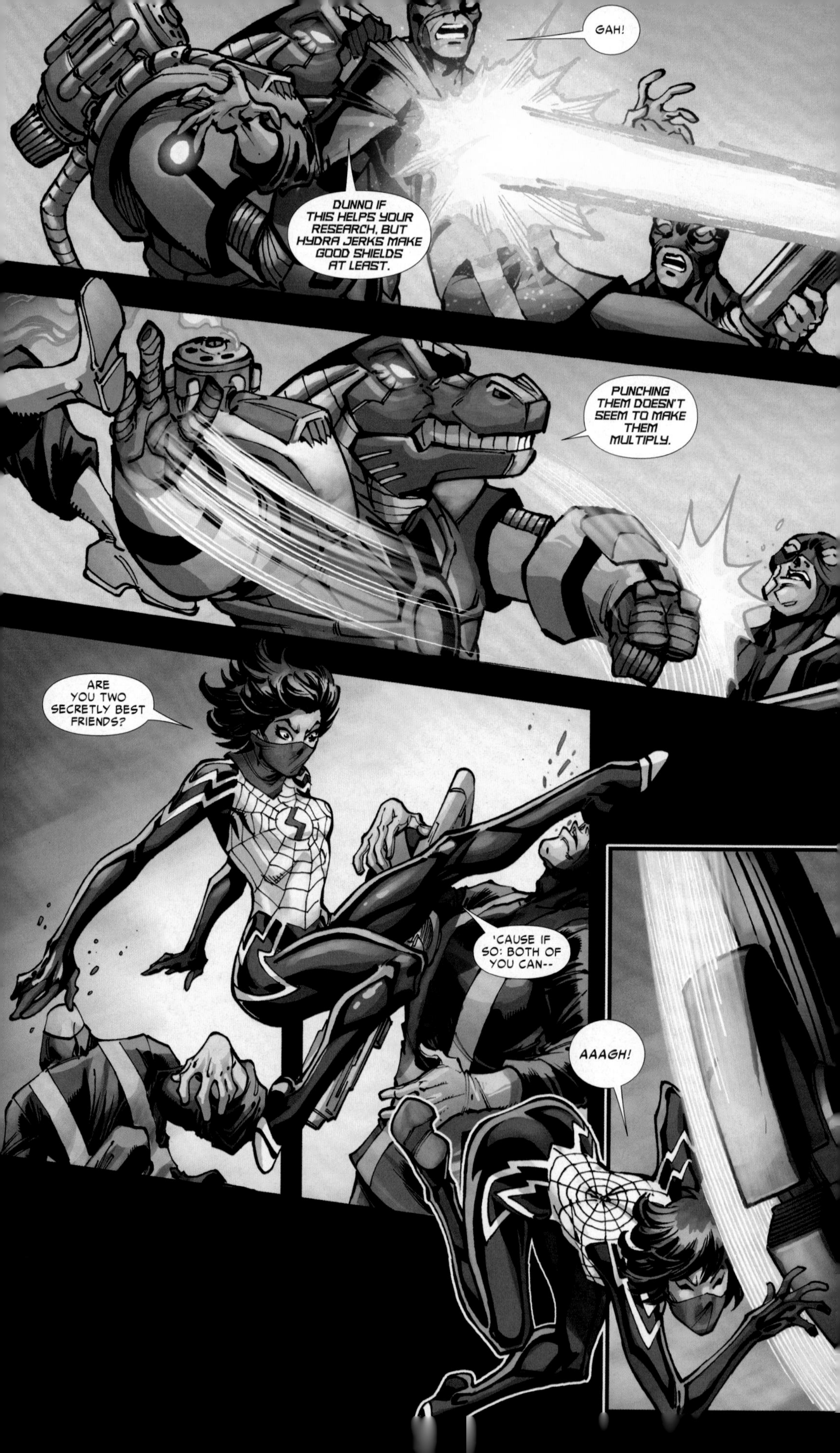
GAH!
DUNNO IF THIS HELPS YOUR RESEARCH, BUT HYDRA JERKS MAKE GOOD SHIELDS AT LEAST.
PUNCHING THEM DOESN'T SEEM TO MAKE THEM MULTIPLY.
ARE YOU TWO SECRETLY BEST FRIENDS?
'CAUSE IF SO: BOTH OF YOU CAN--
AAAGH!

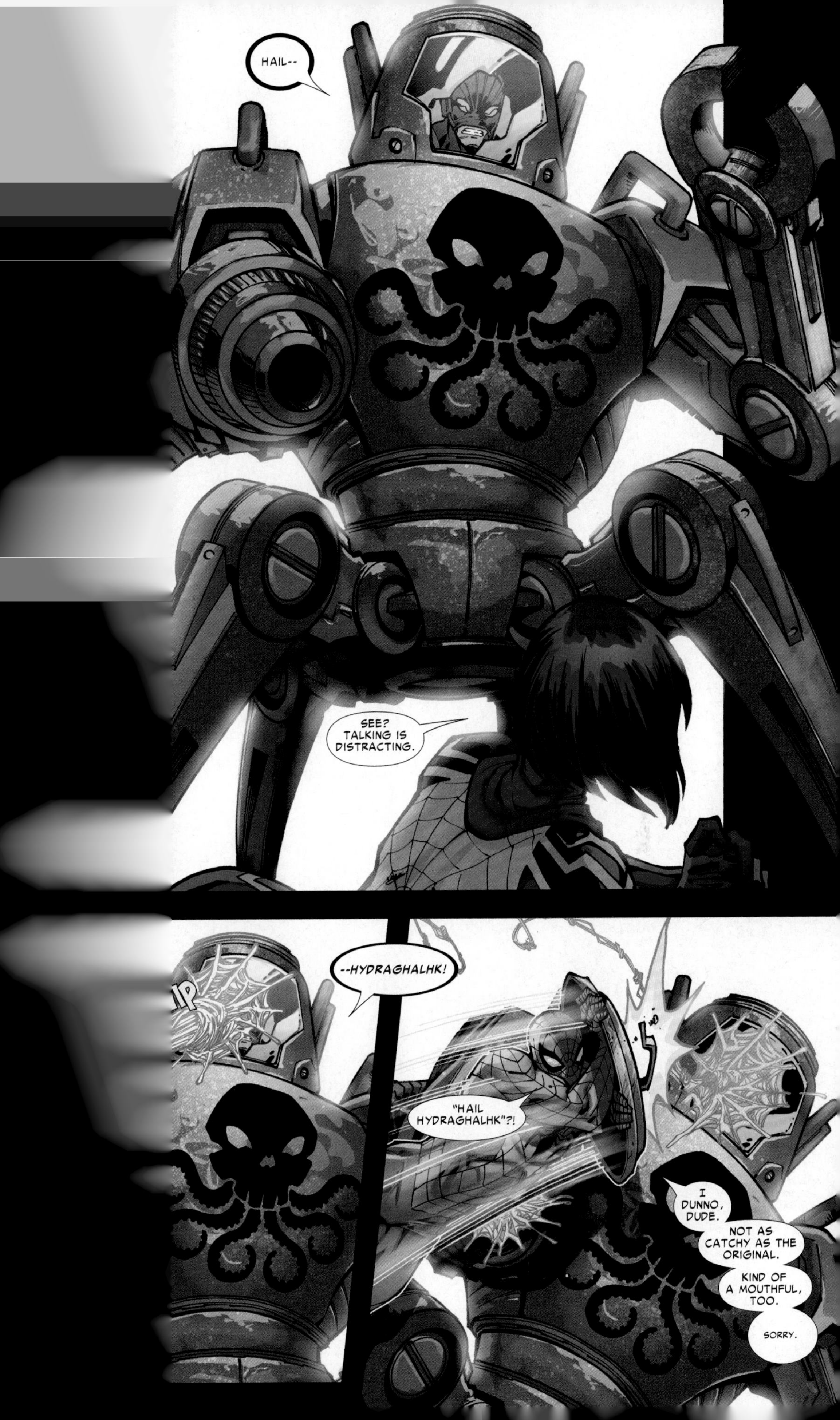
HAIL--
SEE? TALKING IS DISTRACTING.
--HYDRAGHALHK!
"HAIL HYDRAGHALHK"?!
I DUNNO, DUDE.
NOT AS CATCHY AS THE ORIGINAL.
KIND OF A MOUTHFUL, TOO.
SORRY.

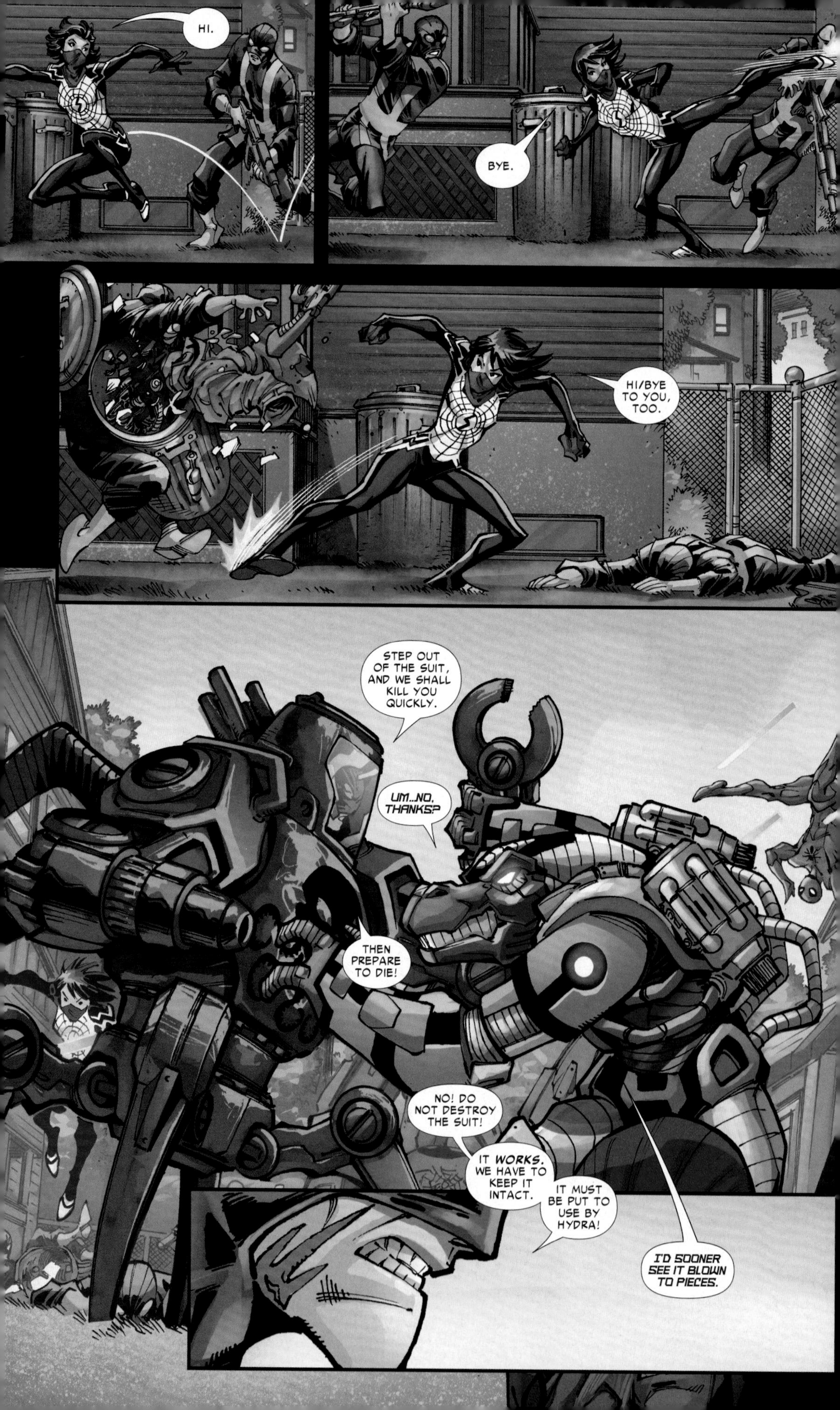

HI.
BYE.
HI/BYE TO YOU, TOO.
STEP OUT OF THE SUIT, AND WE SHALL KILL YOU QUICKLY.
UM...NO, THANKS?
THEN PREPARE TO DIE!
NO! DO NOT DESTROY THE SUIT!
IT WORKS. WE HAVE TO KEEP IT INTACT.
IT MUST BE PUT TO USE BY HYDRA!
I'D SOONER SEE IT BLOWN TO PIECES.

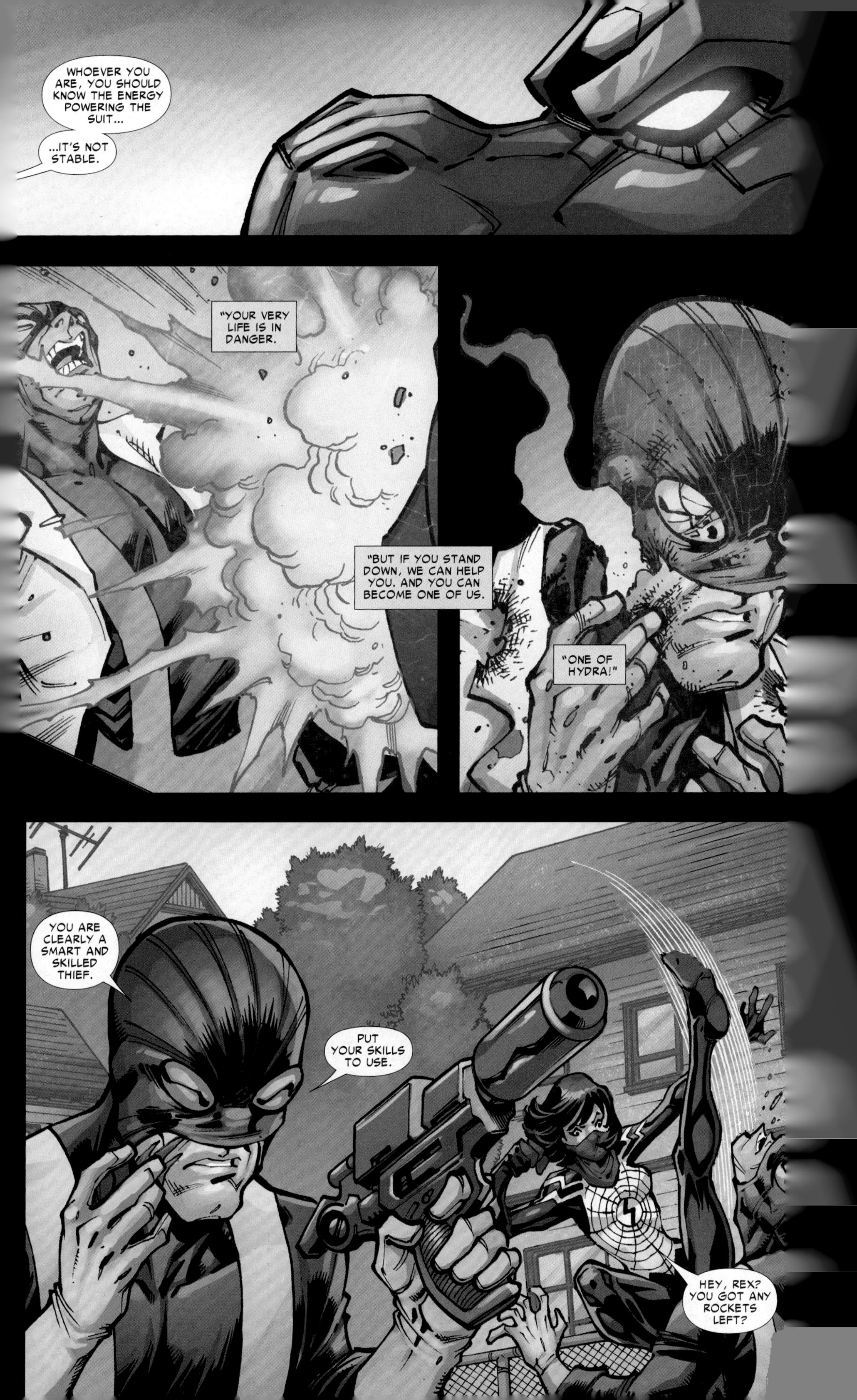
WHOEVER YOU ARE, YOU SHOULD KNOW THE ENERGY POWERING THE SUIT...
...IT'S NOT STABLE.
"YOUR VERY LIFE IS IN DANGER.
"BUT IF YOU STAND DOWN, WE CAN HELP YOU. AND YOU CAN BECOME ONE OF US.
"ONE OF HYDRA!"
YOU ARE CLEARLY A SMART AND SKILLED THIEF.
PUT YOUR SKILLS TO USE.
HEY, REX? YOU GOT ANY ROCKETS LEFT?

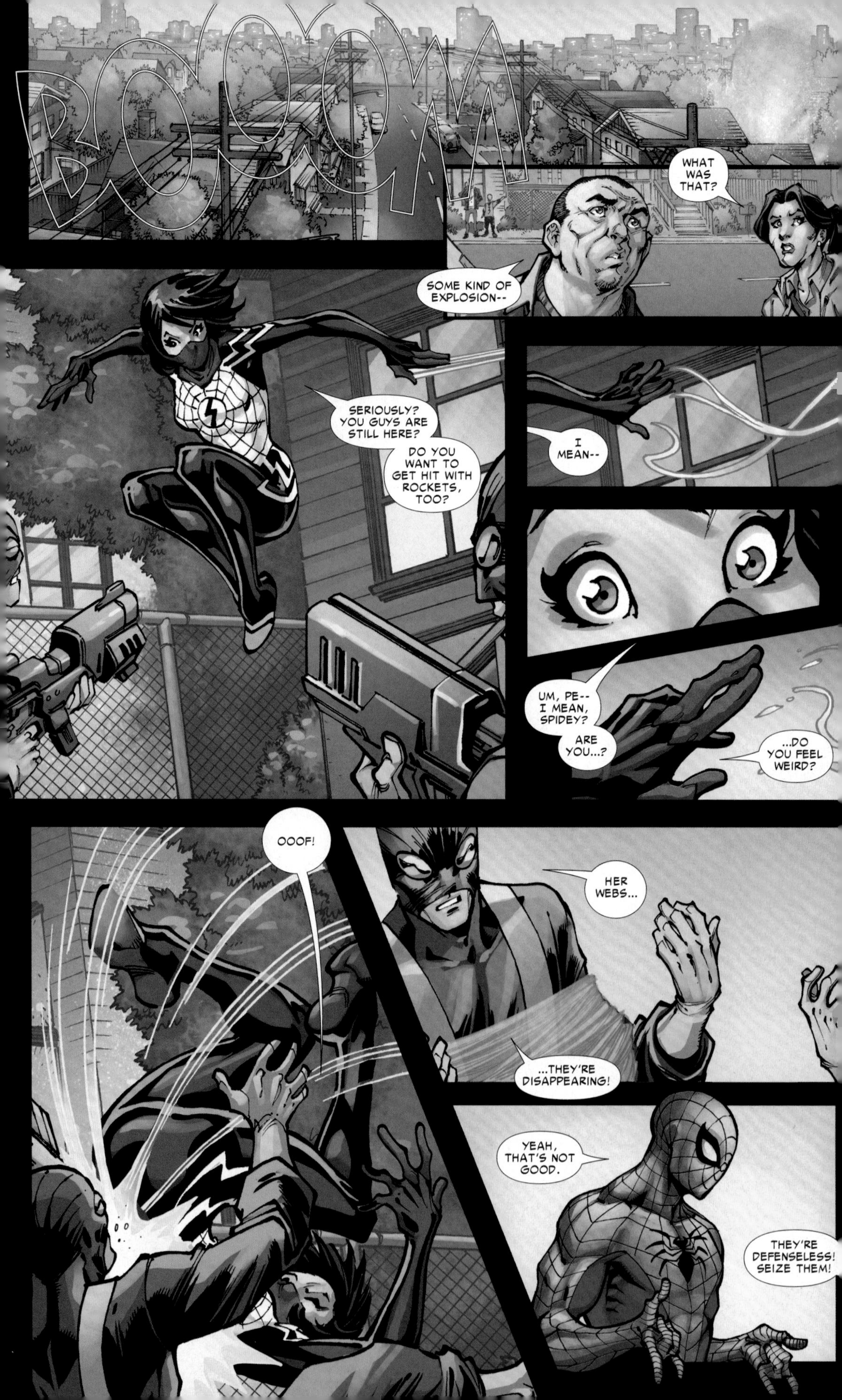
BOOOOOM
WHAT WAS THAT?
SOME KIND OF EXPLOSION--
SERIOUSLY? YOU GUYS ARE STILL HERE?
DO YOU WANT TO GET HIT WITH ROCKETS, TOO?
I MEAN--
UM, PE-- I MEAN, SPIDEY?
ARE YOU...?
...DO YOU FEEL WEIRD?
OOOF!
HER WEBS...
...THEY'RE DISAPPEARING!
YEAH, THAT'S NOT GOOD.
THEY'RE DEFENSELESS! SEIZE THEM!

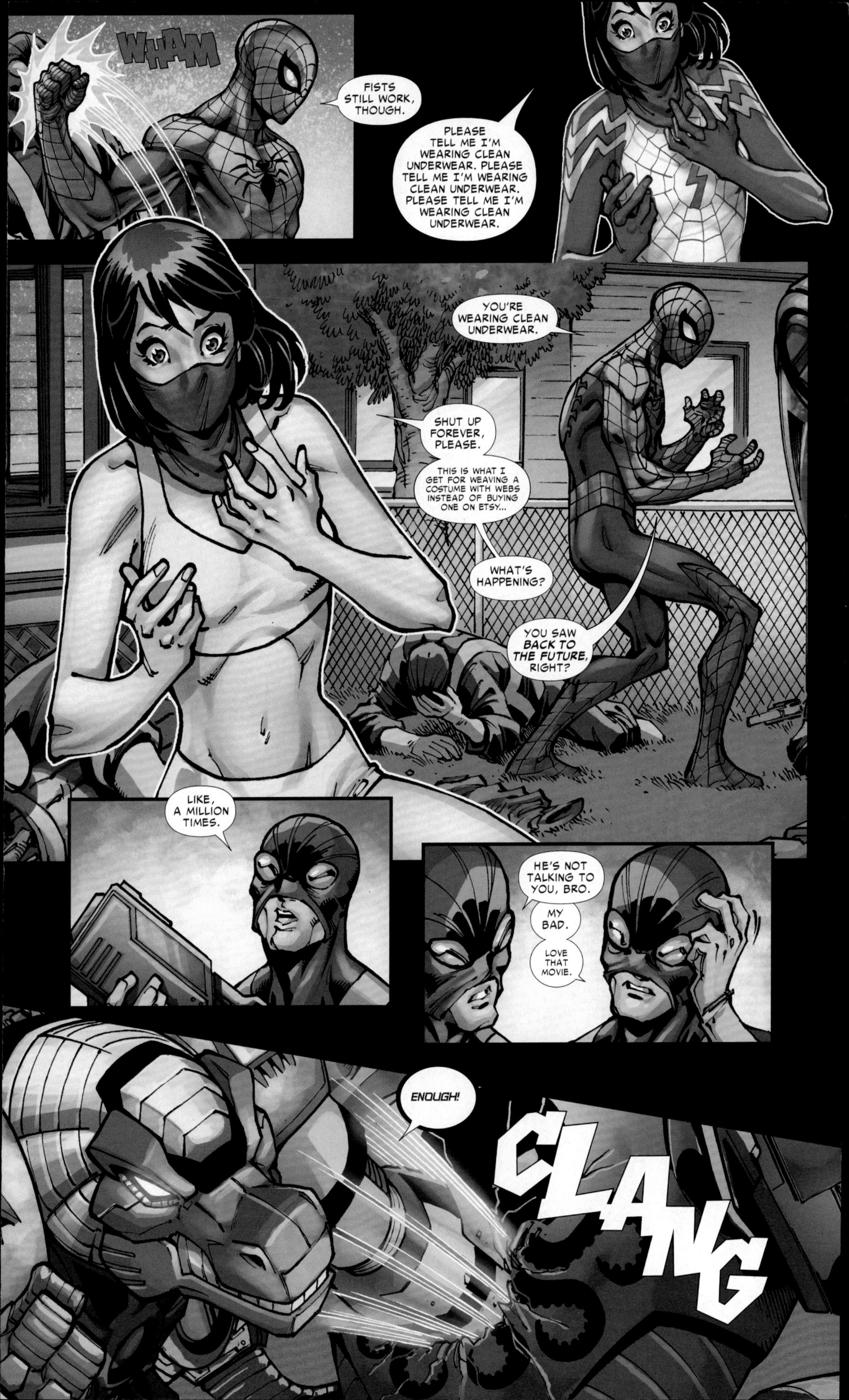
WHAM
FISTS STILL WORK, THOUGH.
PLEASE TELL ME I'M WEARING CLEAN UNDERWEAR. PLEASE TELL ME I'M WEARING CLEAN UNDERWEAR. PLEASE TELL ME I'M WEARING CLEAN UNDERWEAR.
YOU'RE WEARING CLEAN UNDERWEAR.
SHUT UP FOREVER, PLEASE.
THIS IS WHAT I GET FOR WEAVING A COSTUME WITH WEBS INSTEAD OF BUYING ONE ON ETSY...
WHAT'S HAPPENING?
YOU SAW *BACK TO THE FUTURE*, RIGHT?
LIKE, A MILLION TIMES.
HE'S NOT TALKING TO YOU, BRO.
MY BAD.
LOVE THAT MOVIE.
ENOUGH!
CLANG

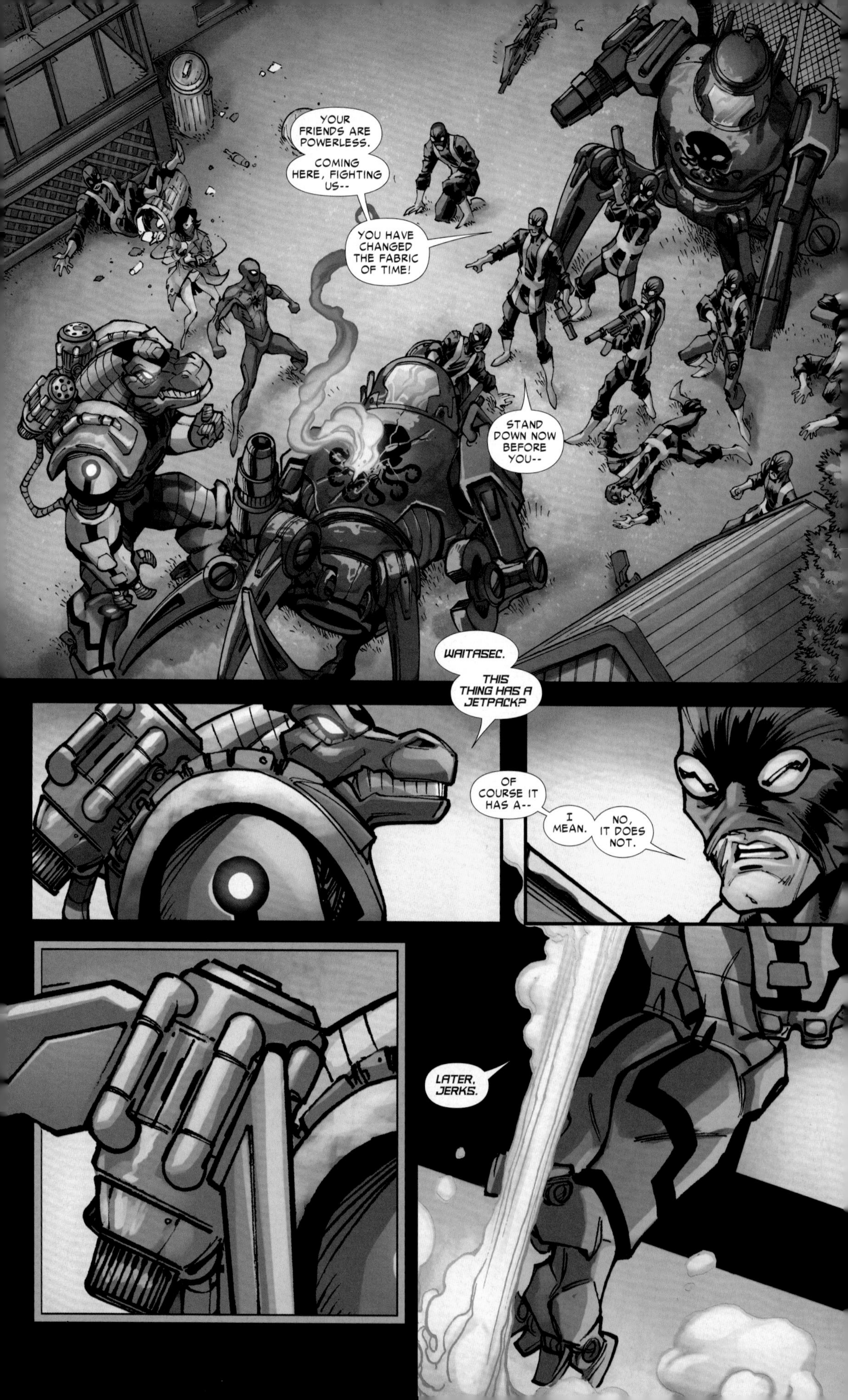
YOUR FRIENDS ARE POWERLESS.
COMING HERE, FIGHTING US--
YOU HAVE CHANGED THE FABRIC OF TIME!
STAND DOWN NOW BEFORE YOU--
WAITASEC.
THIS THING HAS A JETPACK?
OF COURSE IT HAS A--
I MEAN.
NO, IT DOES NOT.
LATER, JERKS.

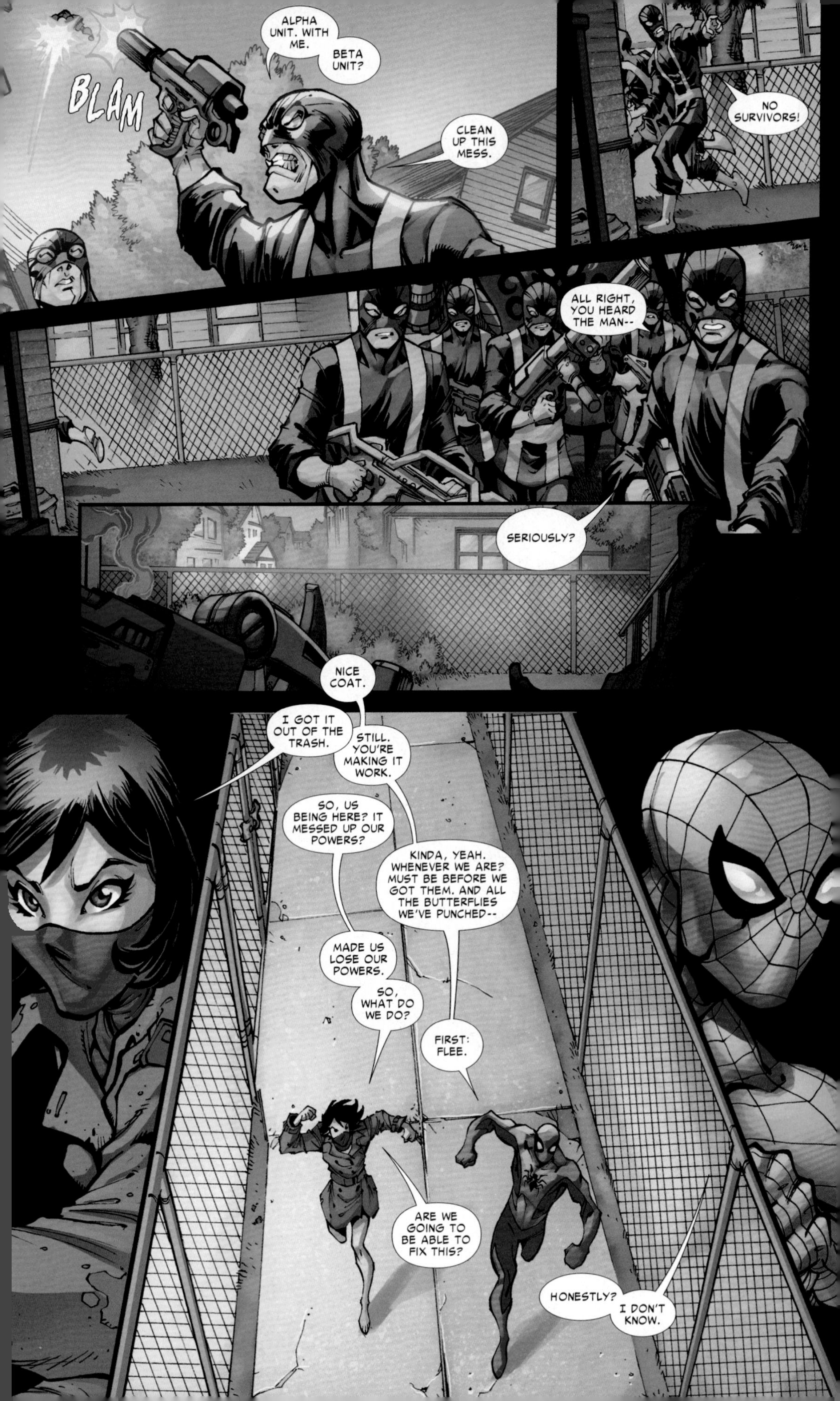

BLAM
ALPHA UNIT. WITH ME.
BETA UNIT?
CLEAN UP THIS MESS.
NO SURVIVORS!
ALL RIGHT, YOU HEARD THE MAN--
SERIOUSLY?
NICE COAT.
I GOT IT OUT OF THE TRASH.
STILL. YOU'RE MAKING IT WORK.
SO, US BEING HERE? IT MESSED UP OUR POWERS?
KINDA, YEAH. WHENEVER WE ARE? MUST BE BEFORE WE GOT THEM. AND ALL THE BUTTERFLIES WE'VE PUNCHED--
MADE US LOSE OUR POWERS.
SO, WHAT DO WE DO?
FIRST: FLEE.
ARE WE GOING TO BE ABLE TO FIX THIS?
HONESTLY?
I DON'T KNOW.

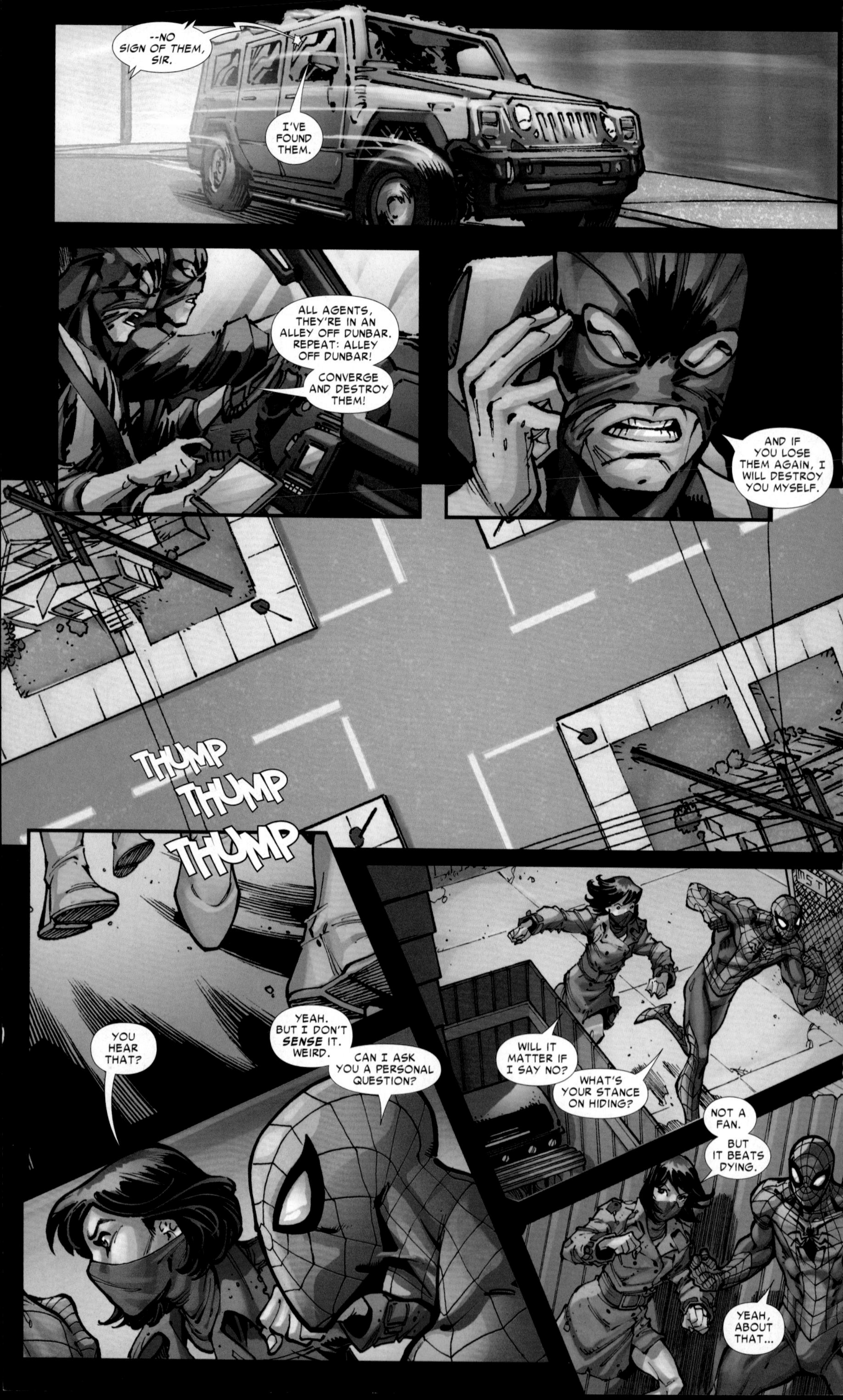
--NO SIGN OF THEM, SIR.
I'VE FOUND THEM.
ALL AGENTS, THEY'RE IN AN ALLEY OFF DUNBAR. REPEAT: ALLEY OFF DUNBAR!
CONVERGE AND DESTROY THEM!
AND IF YOU LOSE THEM AGAIN, I WILL DESTROY YOU MYSELF.
THUMP
THUMP
THUMP
YOU HEAR THAT?
YEAH. BUT I DON'T SENSE IT. WEIRD.
CAN I ASK YOU A PERSONAL QUESTION?
WILL IT MATTER IF I SAY NO?
WHAT'S YOUR STANCE ON HIDING?
NOT A FAN.
BUT IT BEATS DYING.
YEAH, ABOUT THAT...

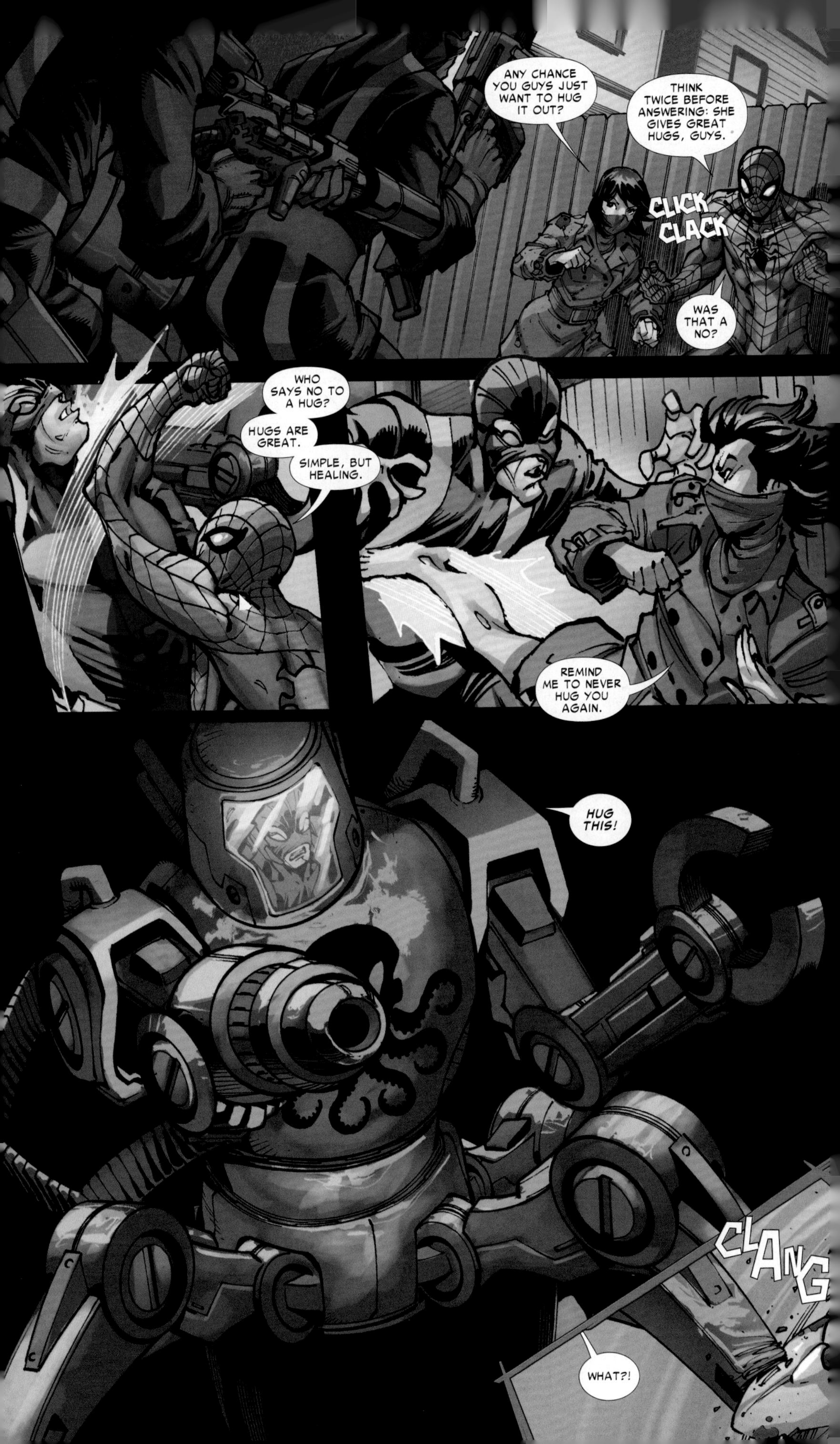
ANY CHANCE YOU GUYS JUST WANT TO HUG IT OUT?
THINK TWICE BEFORE ANSWERING: SHE GIVES GREAT HUGS, GUYS.
CLICK CLACK
WAS THAT A NO?
WHO SAYS NO TO A HUG?
HUGS ARE GREAT.
SIMPLE, BUT HEALING.
REMIND ME TO NEVER HUG YOU AGAIN.
HUG THIS!
CLANG
WHAT?!

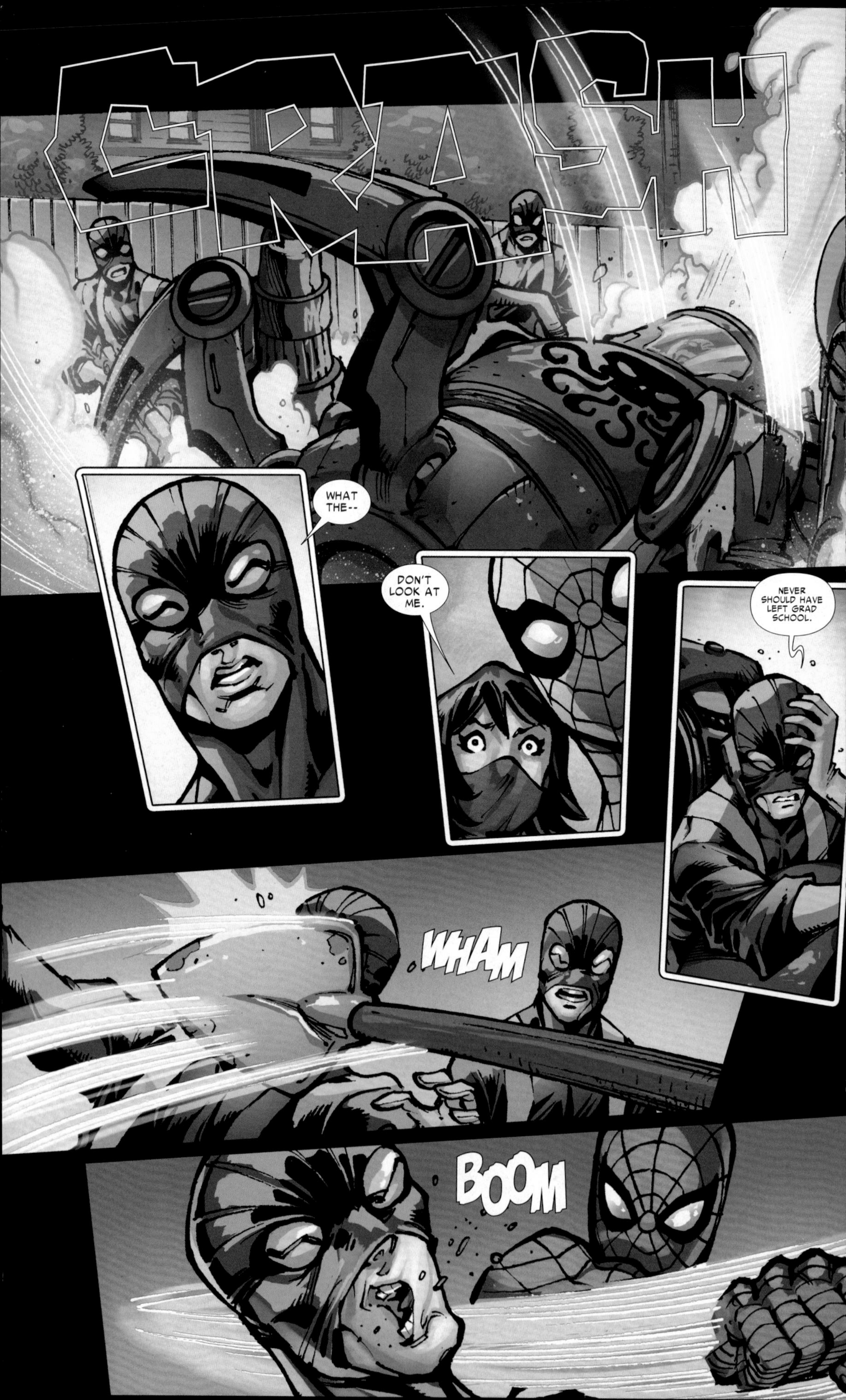
CRASH
WHAT THE--
DON'T LOOK AT ME.
NEVER SHOULD HAVE LEFT GRAD SCHOOL.
WHAM
BOOM

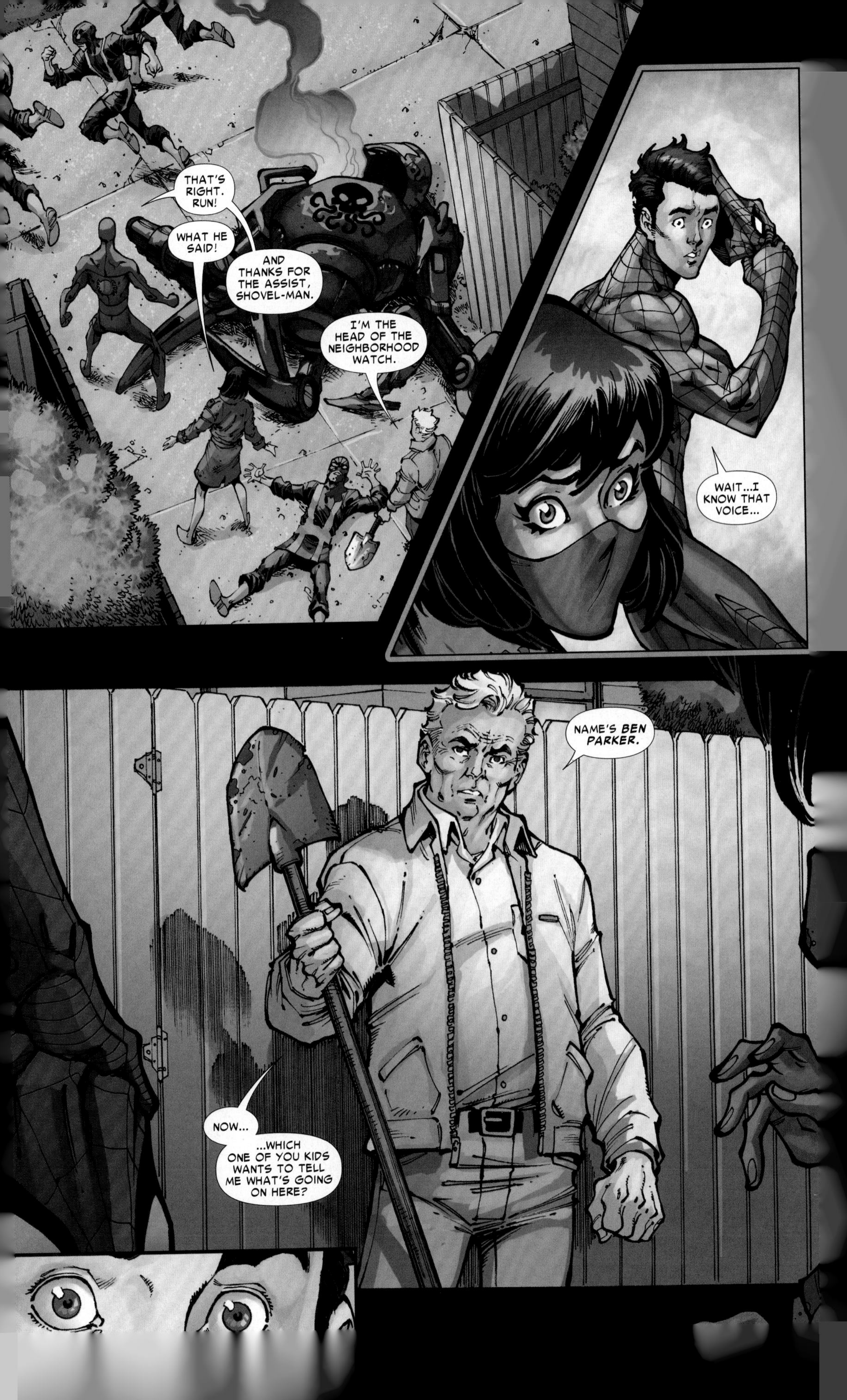
THAT'S RIGHT. RUN!
WHAT HE SAID!
AND THANKS FOR THE ASSIST, SHOVEL-MAN.
I'M THE HEAD OF THE NEIGHBORHOOD WATCH.
WAIT...I KNOW THAT VOICE...
NAME'S BEN PARKER.
NOW...
...WHICH ONE OF YOU KIDS WANTS TO TELL ME WHAT'S GOING ON HERE?

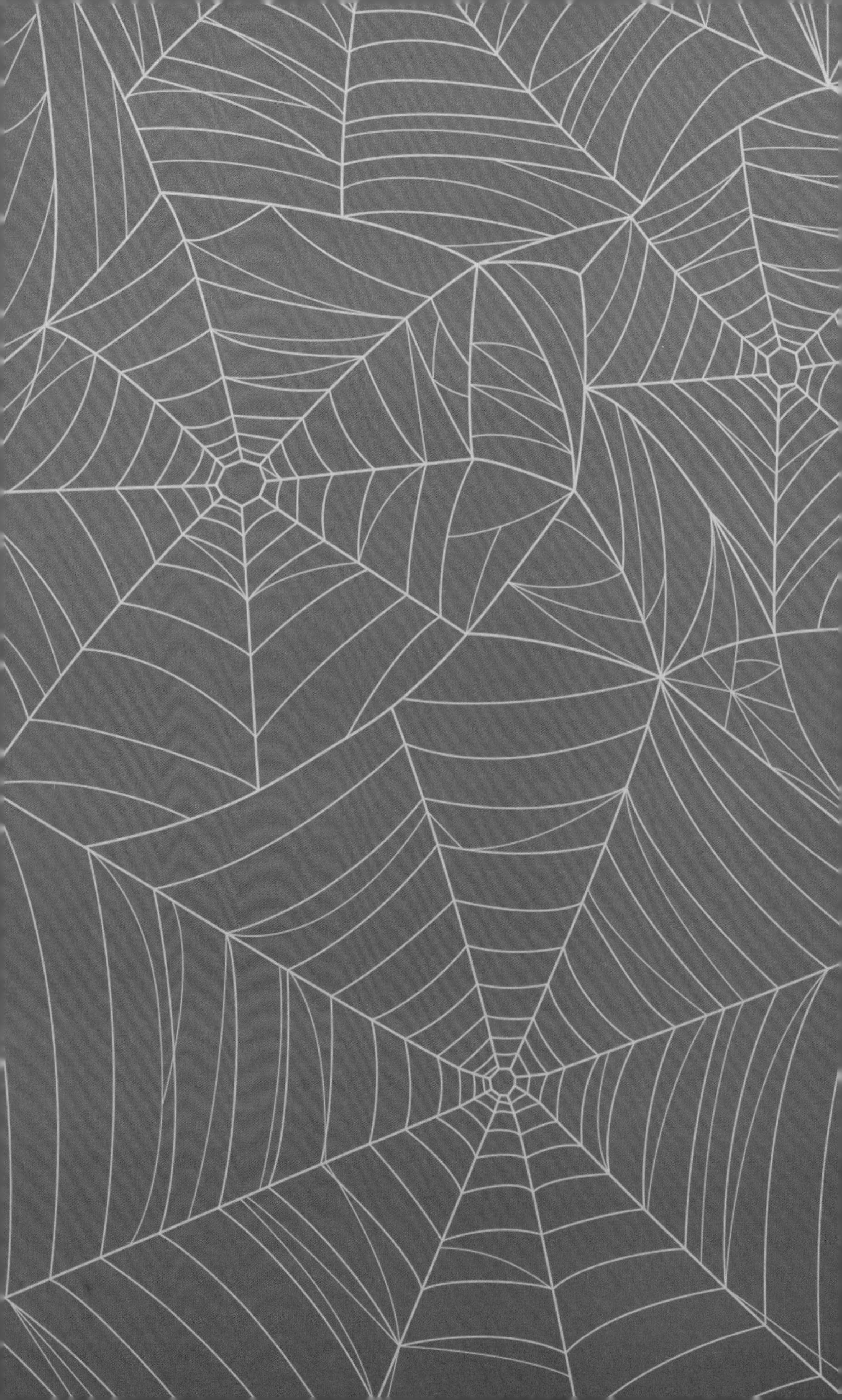

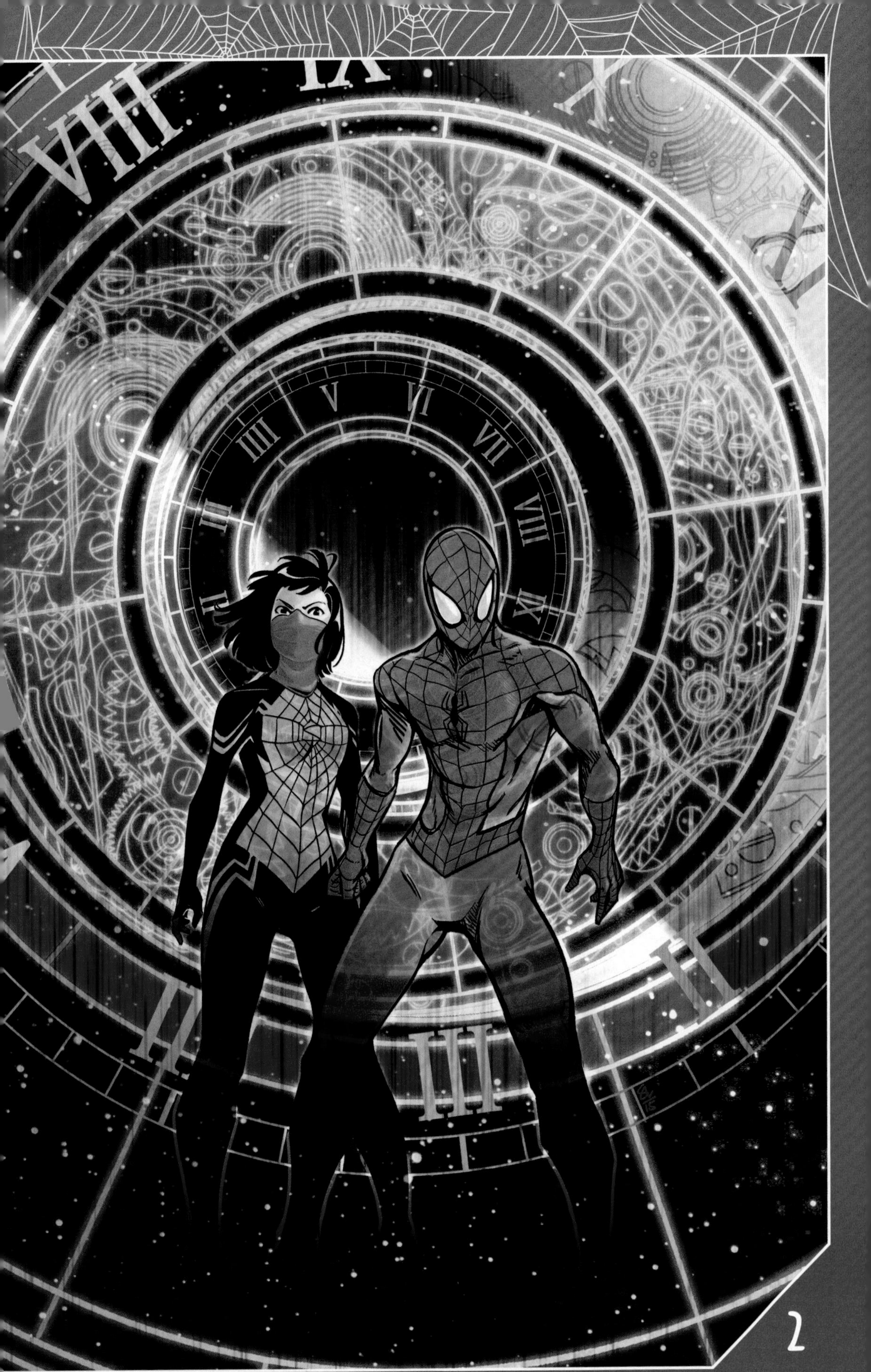

2

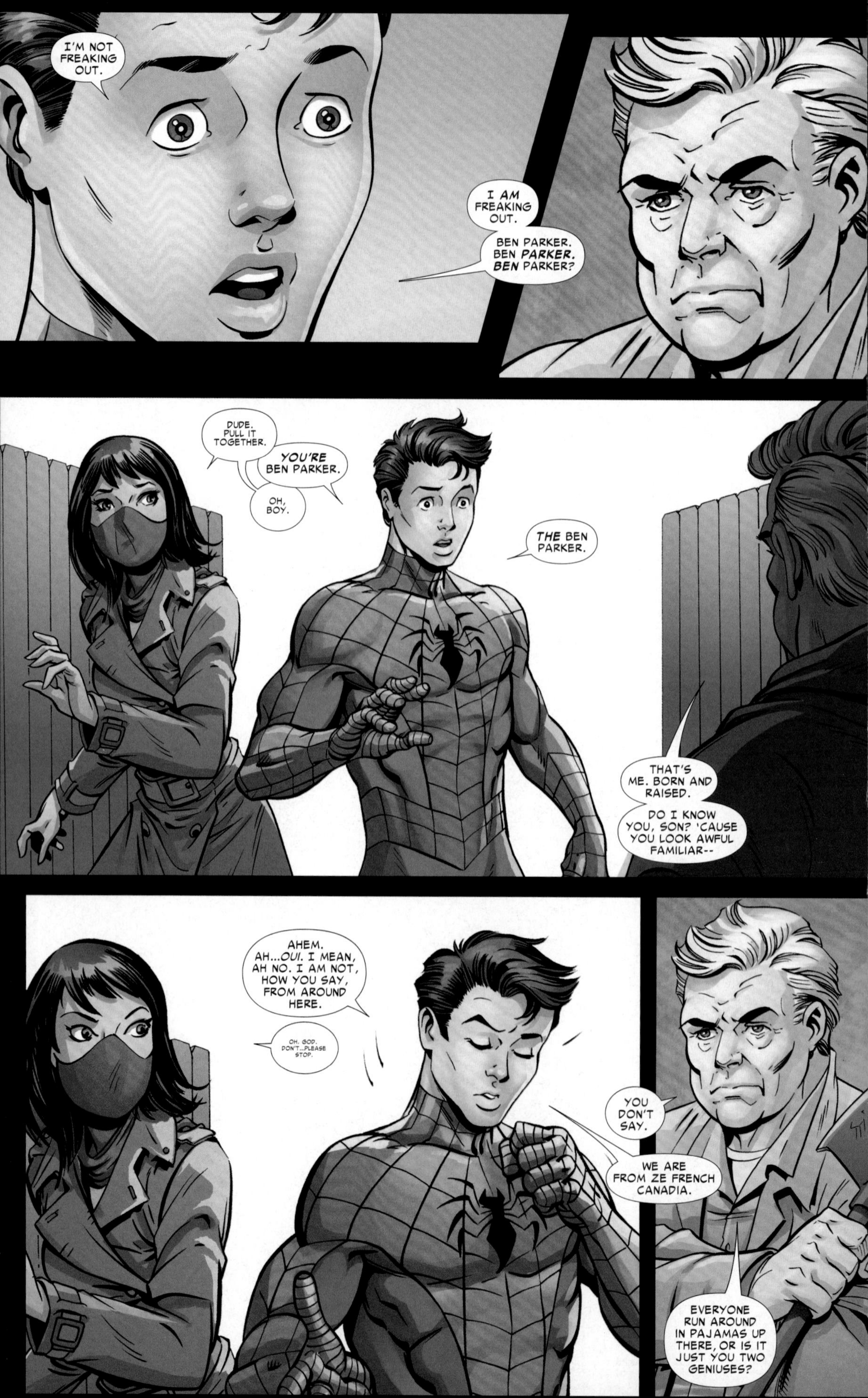
I'M NOT FREAKING OUT.
I AM FREAKING OUT.
BEN PARKER. BEN PARKER. BEN PARKER?
DUDE. PULL IT TOGETHER.
YOU'RE BEN PARKER.
OH, BOY.
THE BEN PARKER.
THAT'S ME. BORN AND RAISED.
DO I KNOW YOU, SON? 'CAUSE YOU LOOK AWFUL FAMILIAR--
AHEM. AH...OUI. I MEAN, AH NO. I AM NOT, HOW YOU SAY, FROM AROUND HERE.
OH, GOD. DON'T...PLEASE STOP.
YOU DON'T SAY.
WE ARE FROM ZE FRENCH CANADIA.
EVERYONE RUN AROUND IN PAJAMAS UP THERE, OR IS IT JUST YOU TWO GENIUSES?

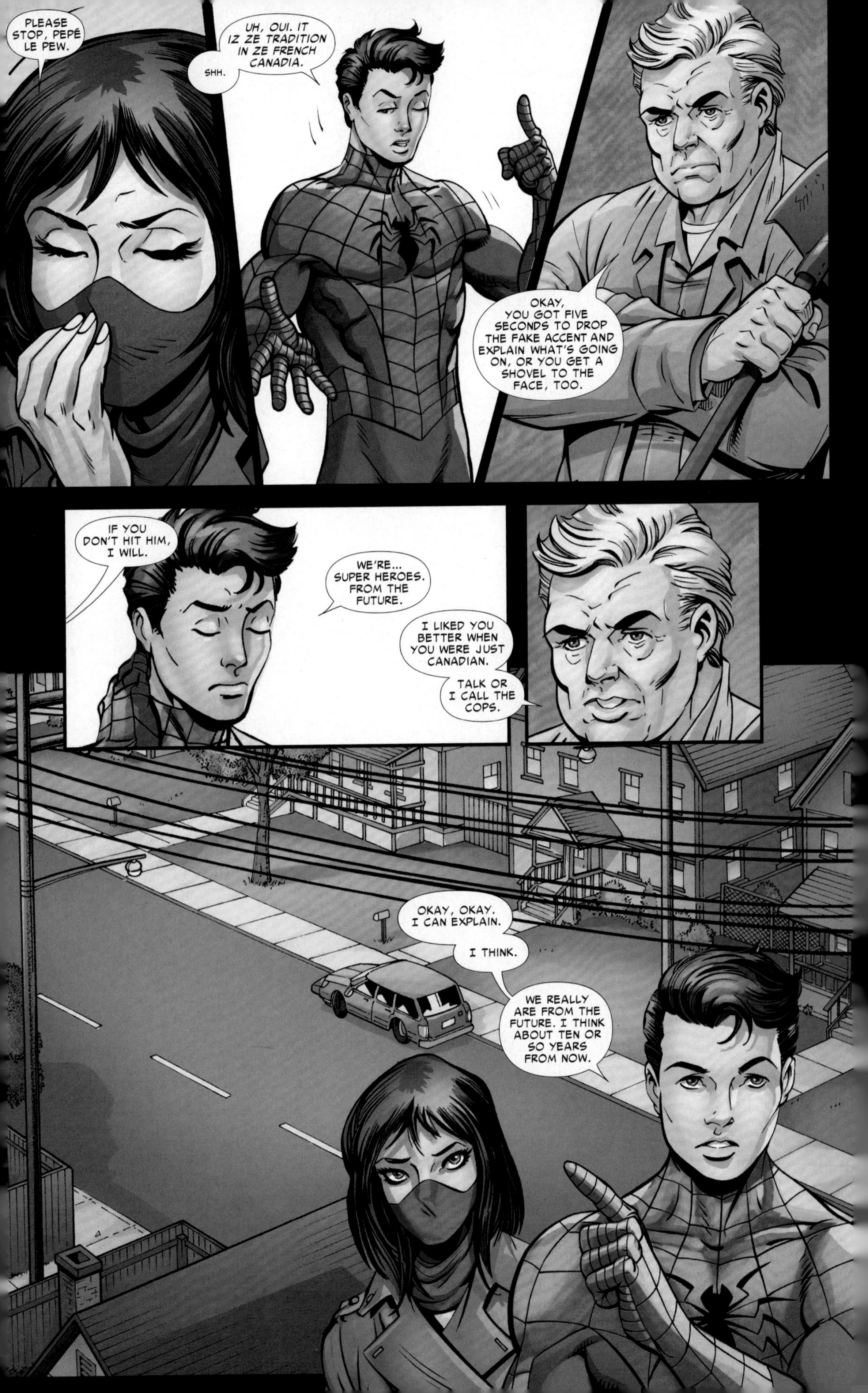
PLEASE STOP, PEPÉ LE PEW.
UH, OUI. IT IZ ZE TRADITION IN ZE FRENCH CANADIA.
SHH.
OKAY, YOU GOT FIVE SECONDS TO DROP THE FAKE ACCENT AND EXPLAIN WHAT'S GOING ON, OR YOU GET A SHOVEL TO THE FACE, TOO.
IF YOU DON'T HIT HIM, I WILL.
WE'RE... SUPER HEROES. FROM THE FUTURE.
I LIKED YOU BETTER WHEN YOU WERE JUST CANADIAN.
TALK OR I CALL THE COPS.
OKAY, OKAY. I CAN EXPLAIN.
I THINK.
WE REALLY ARE FROM THE FUTURE. I THINK ABOUT TEN OR SO YEARS FROM NOW.

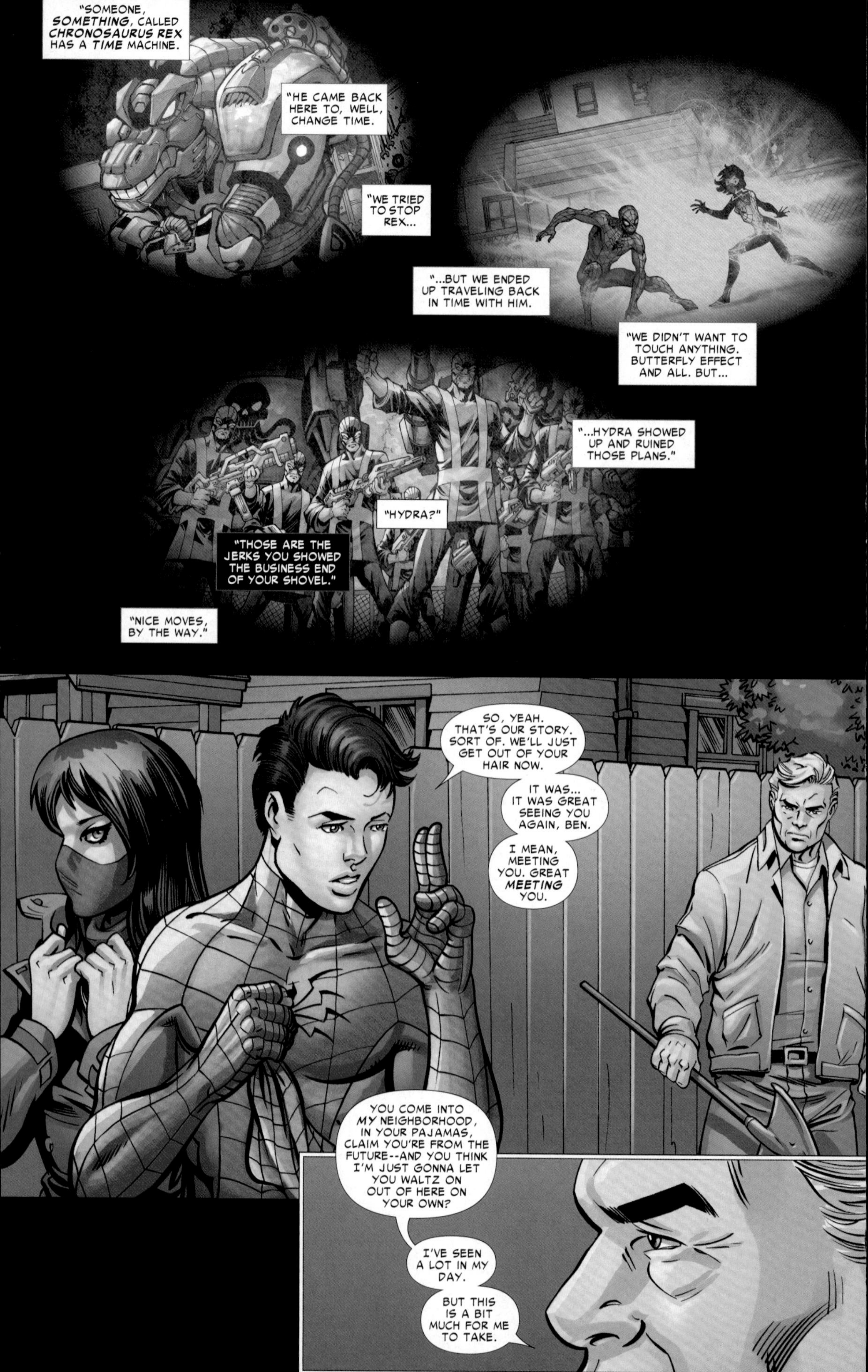
"SOMEONE, SOMETHING, CALLED CHRONOSAURUS REX HAS A TIME MACHINE.
"HE CAME BACK HERE TO, WELL, CHANGE TIME.
"WE TRIED TO STOP REX...
"...BUT WE ENDED UP TRAVELING BACK IN TIME WITH HIM.
"WE DIDN'T WANT TO TOUCH ANYTHING. BUTTERFLY EFFECT AND ALL. BUT...
"...HYDRA SHOWED UP AND RUINED THOSE PLANS."
"HYDRA?"
"THOSE ARE THE JERKS YOU SHOWED THE BUSINESS END OF YOUR SHOVEL."
"NICE MOVES, BY THE WAY."
SO, YEAH. THAT'S OUR STORY. SORT OF. WE'LL JUST GET OUT OF YOUR HAIR NOW.
IT WAS... IT WAS GREAT SEEING YOU AGAIN, BEN.
I MEAN, MEETING YOU. GREAT MEETING YOU.
YOU COME INTO MY NEIGHBORHOOD, IN YOUR PAJAMAS, CLAIM YOU'RE FROM THE FUTURE--AND YOU THINK I'M JUST GONNA LET YOU WALTZ ON OUT OF HERE ON YOUR OWN?
I'VE SEEN A LOT IN MY DAY.
BUT THIS IS A BIT MUCH FOR ME TO TAKE.

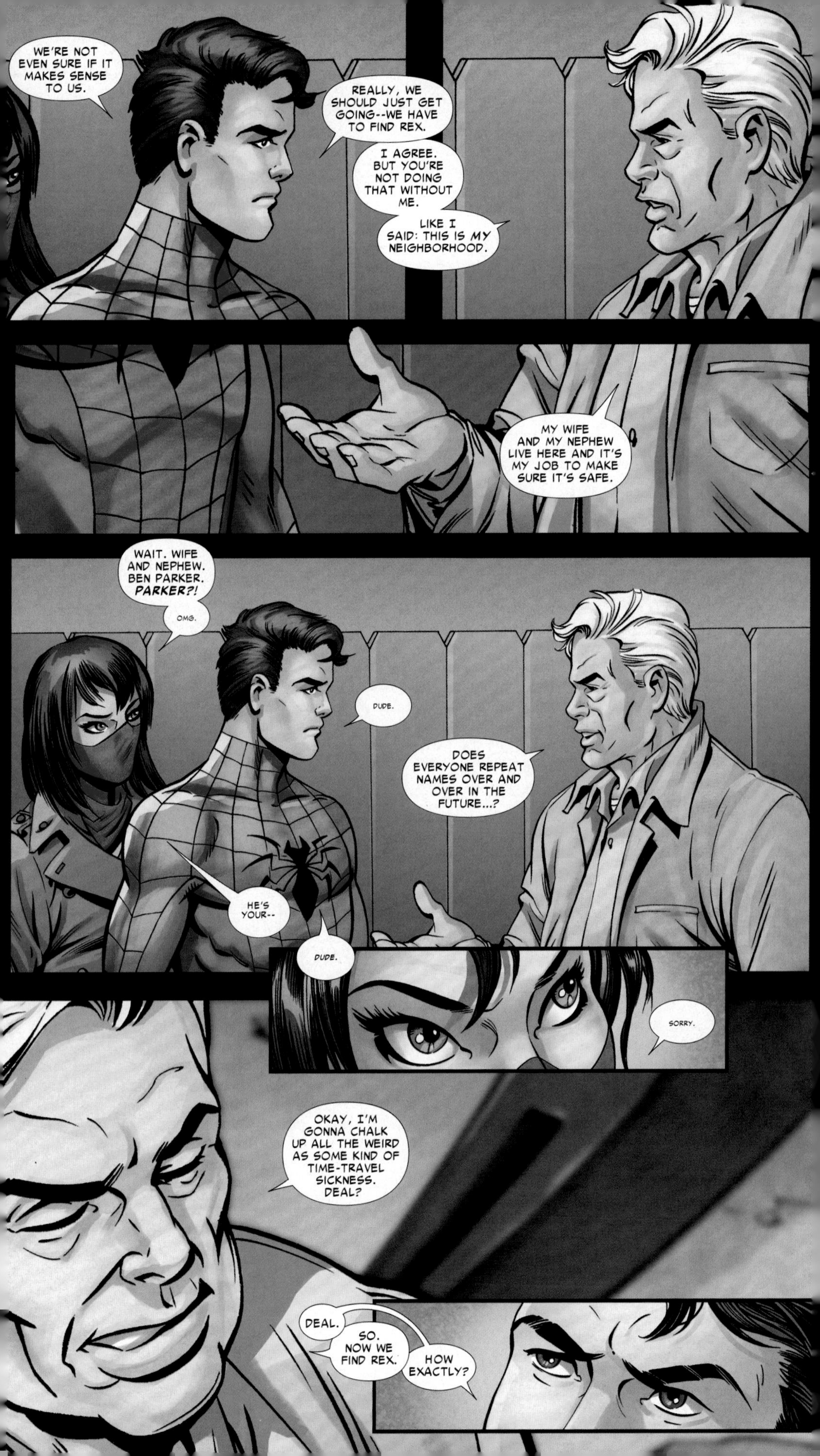
WE'RE NOT EVEN SURE IF IT MAKES SENSE TO US.
REALLY, WE SHOULD JUST GET GOING--WE HAVE TO FIND REX.
I AGREE. BUT YOU'RE NOT DOING THAT WITHOUT ME.
LIKE I SAID: THIS IS *MY* NEIGHBORHOOD.
MY WIFE AND MY NEPHEW LIVE HERE AND IT'S MY JOB TO MAKE SURE IT'S SAFE.
WAIT. WIFE AND NEPHEW. BEN PARKER. ***PARKER?!***
OMG.
DUDE.
DOES EVERYONE REPEAT NAMES OVER AND OVER IN THE FUTURE...?
HE'S YOUR--
DUDE.
SORRY.
OKAY, I'M GONNA CHALK UP ALL THE WEIRD AS SOME KIND OF TIME-TRAVEL SICKNESS. DEAL?
DEAL.
SO. NOW WE FIND REX.
HOW EXACTLY?

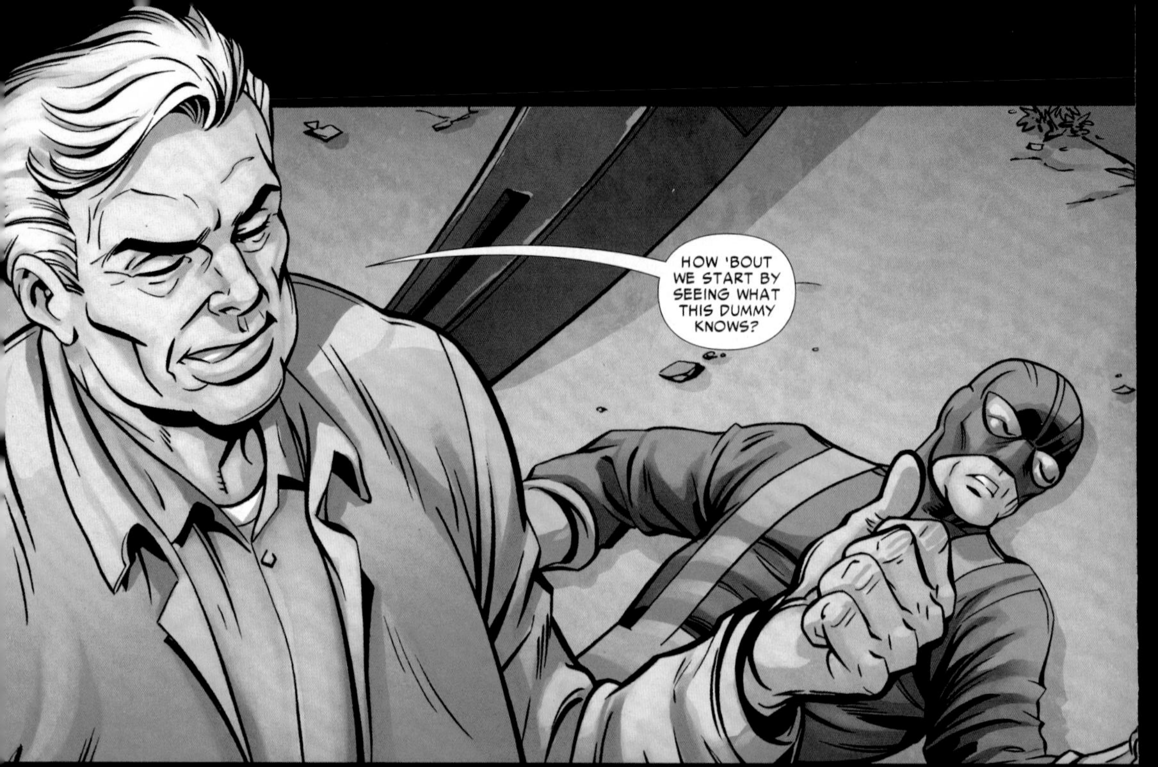
HOW 'BOUT WE START BY SEEING WHAT THIS DUMMY KNOWS?

THE SPIDER(FLY) EFFECT

CHAPTERS THREE & FOUR

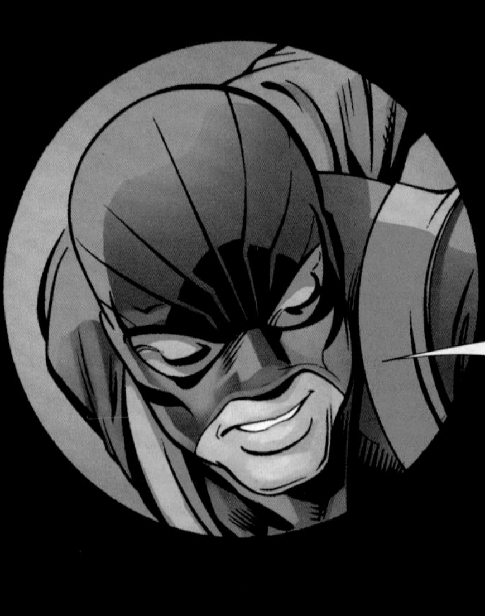
I'LL NEVER TALK! I'M A TRAINED AGENT OF HYDRA. I CAN WITHSTAND ANY--

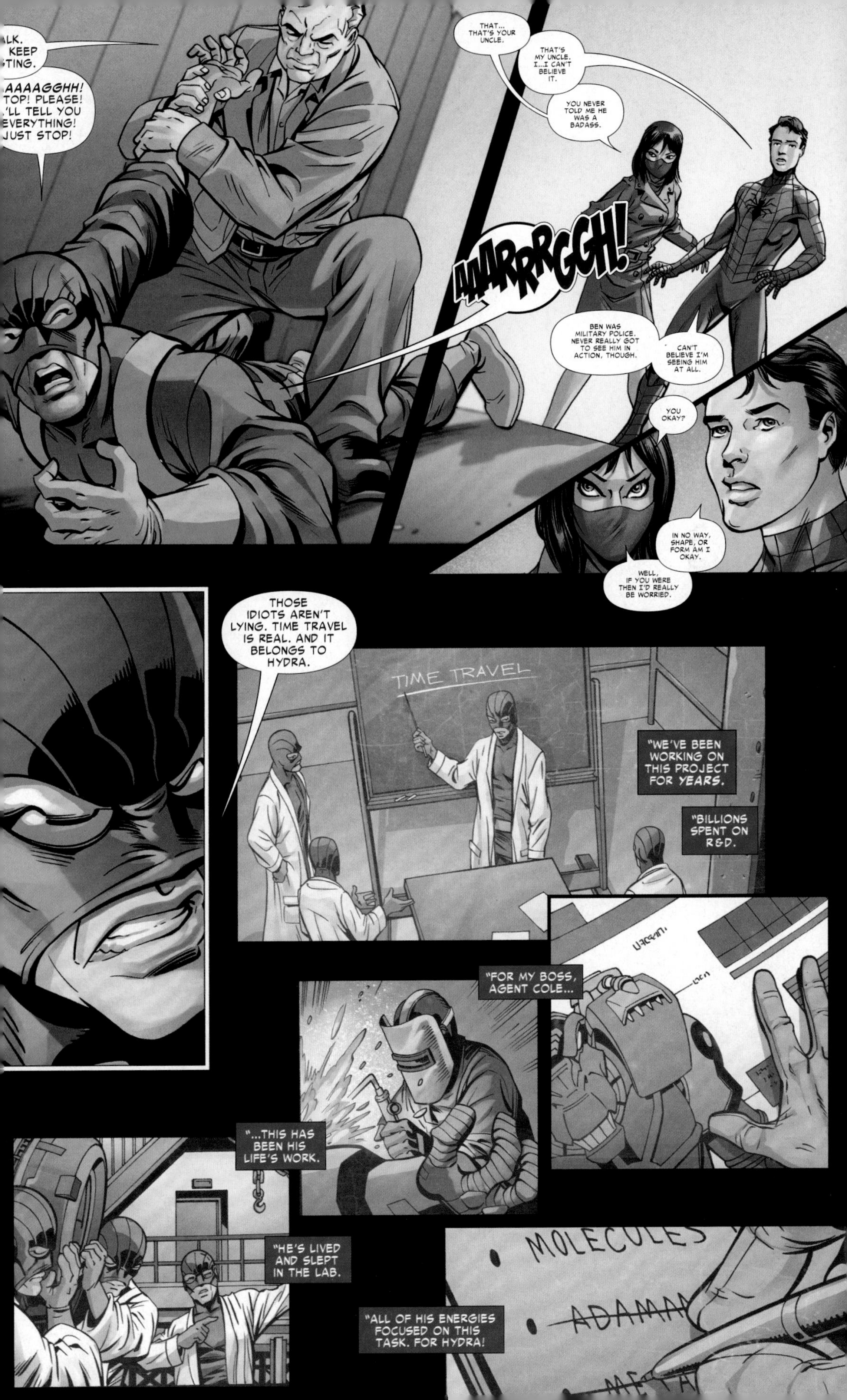

ALK. KEEP TING.
AAAAAGGHH! TOP! PLEASE! 'LL TELL YOU EVERYTHING! JUST STOP!
AAARRRGGH!
THAT... THAT'S YOUR UNCLE.
THAT'S MY UNCLE. I...I CAN'T BELIEVE IT.
YOU NEVER TOLD ME HE WAS A BADASS.
BEN WAS MILITARY POLICE. NEVER REALLY GOT TO SEE HIM IN ACTION, THOUGH.
CAN'T BELIEVE I'M SEEING HIM AT ALL.
YOU OKAY?
IN NO WAY, SHAPE, OR FORM AM I OKAY.
WELL, IF YOU WERE THEN I'D REALLY BE WORRIED.
THOSE IDIOTS AREN'T LYING. TIME TRAVEL IS REAL. AND IT BELONGS TO HYDRA.
TIME TRAVEL
"WE'VE BEEN WORKING ON THIS PROJECT FOR YEARS.
"BILLIONS SPENT ON R&D.
"FOR MY BOSS, AGENT COLE...
"...THIS HAS BEEN HIS LIFE'S WORK.
"HE'S LIVED AND SLEPT IN THE LAB.
"ALL OF HIS ENERGIES FOCUSED ON THIS TASK. FOR HYDRA!
MOLECULES
ADAMA

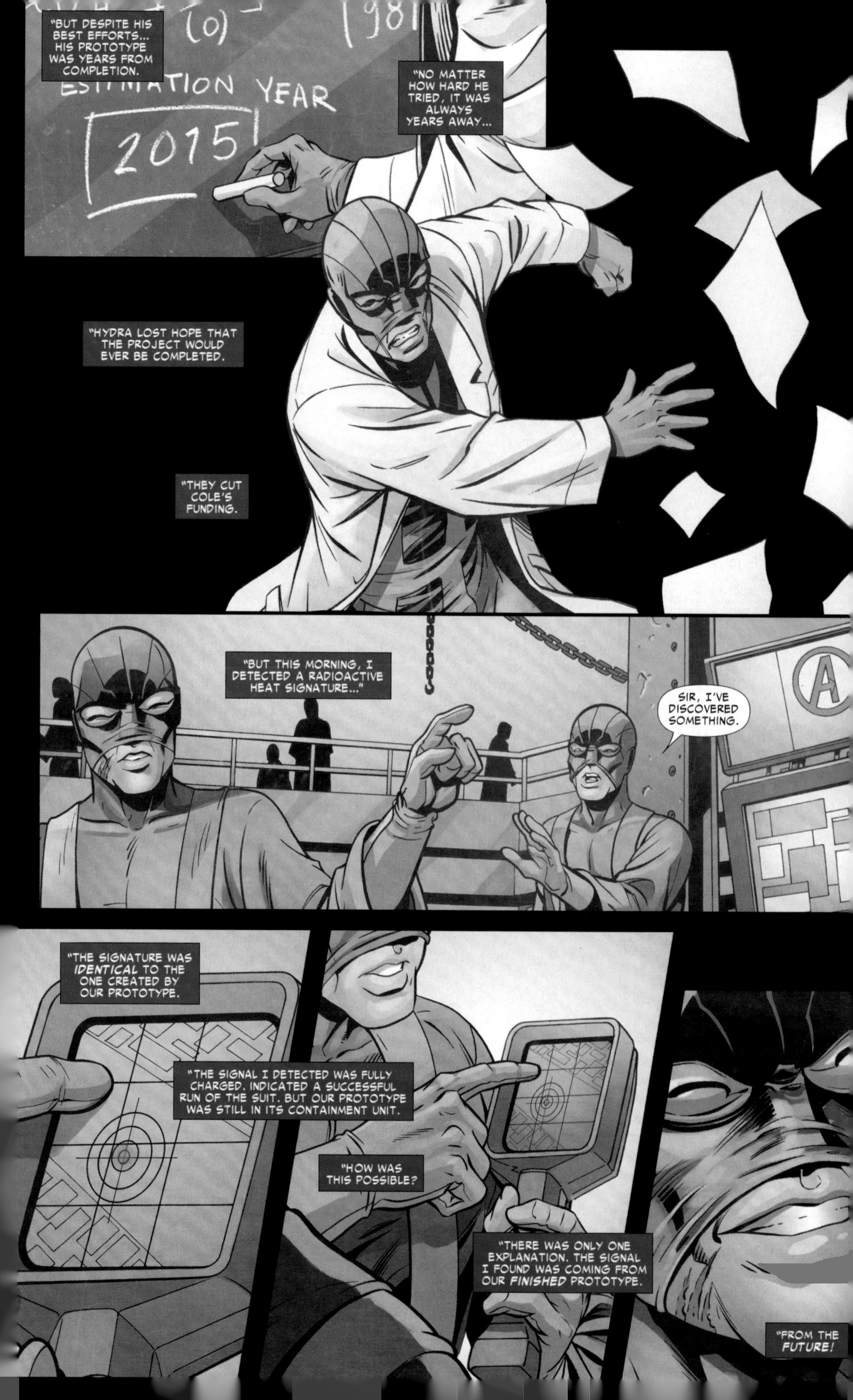
"BUT DESPITE HIS BEST EFFORTS... HIS PROTOTYPE WAS YEARS FROM COMPLETION.
ESTIMATION YEAR
2015
"NO MATTER HOW HARD HE TRIED, IT WAS ALWAYS YEARS AWAY...
"HYDRA LOST HOPE THAT THE PROJECT WOULD EVER BE COMPLETED.
"THEY CUT COLE'S FUNDING.
"BUT THIS MORNING, I DETECTED A RADIOACTIVE HEAT SIGNATURE..."
SIR, I'VE DISCOVERED SOMETHING.
"THE SIGNATURE WAS *IDENTICAL* TO THE ONE CREATED BY OUR PROTOTYPE.
"THE SIGNAL I DETECTED WAS FULLY CHARGED. INDICATED A SUCCESSFUL RUN OF THE SUIT. BUT OUR PROTOTYPE WAS STILL IN ITS CONTAINMENT UNIT.
"HOW WAS THIS POSSIBLE?
"THERE WAS ONLY ONE EXPLANATION. THE SIGNAL I FOUND WAS COMING FROM OUR *FINISHED* PROTOTYPE.
"FROM THE *FUTURE!*

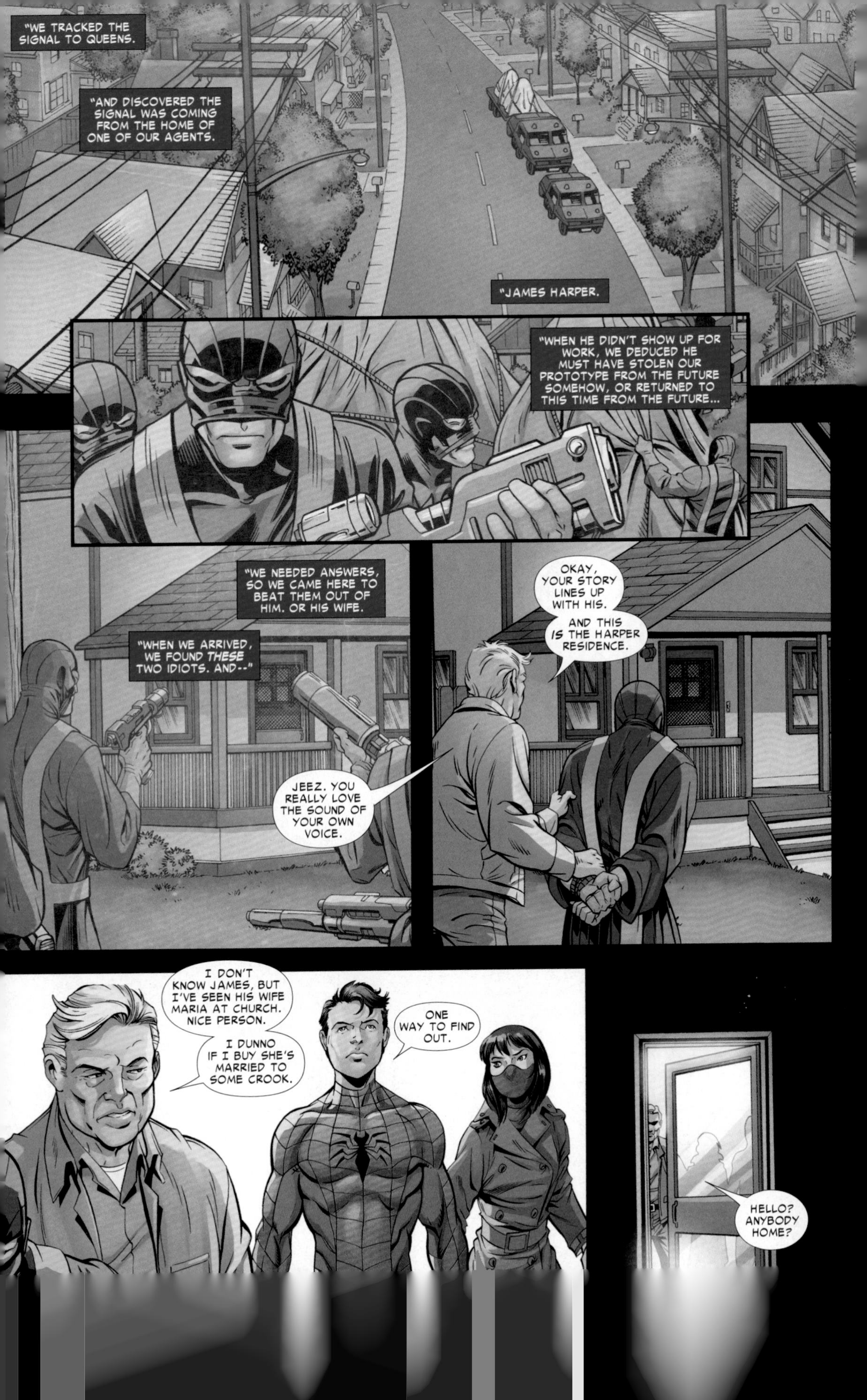
"WE TRACKED THE SIGNAL TO QUEENS.
"AND DISCOVERED THE SIGNAL WAS COMING FROM THE HOME OF ONE OF OUR AGENTS.
"JAMES HARPER.
"WHEN HE DIDN'T SHOW UP FOR WORK, WE DEDUCED HE MUST HAVE STOLEN OUR PROTOTYPE FROM THE FUTURE SOMEHOW, OR RETURNED TO THIS TIME FROM THE FUTURE...
"WE NEEDED ANSWERS, SO WE CAME HERE TO BEAT THEM OUT OF HIM. OR HIS WIFE.
"WHEN WE ARRIVED, WE FOUND THESE TWO IDIOTS. AND--"
JEEZ. YOU REALLY LOVE THE SOUND OF YOUR OWN VOICE.
OKAY, YOUR STORY LINES UP WITH HIS.
AND THIS IS THE HARPER RESIDENCE.
I DON'T KNOW JAMES, BUT I'VE SEEN HIS WIFE MARIA AT CHURCH. NICE PERSON.
I DUNNO IF I BUY SHE'S MARRIED TO SOME CROOK.
ONE WAY TO FIND OUT.
HELLO? ANYBODY HOME?

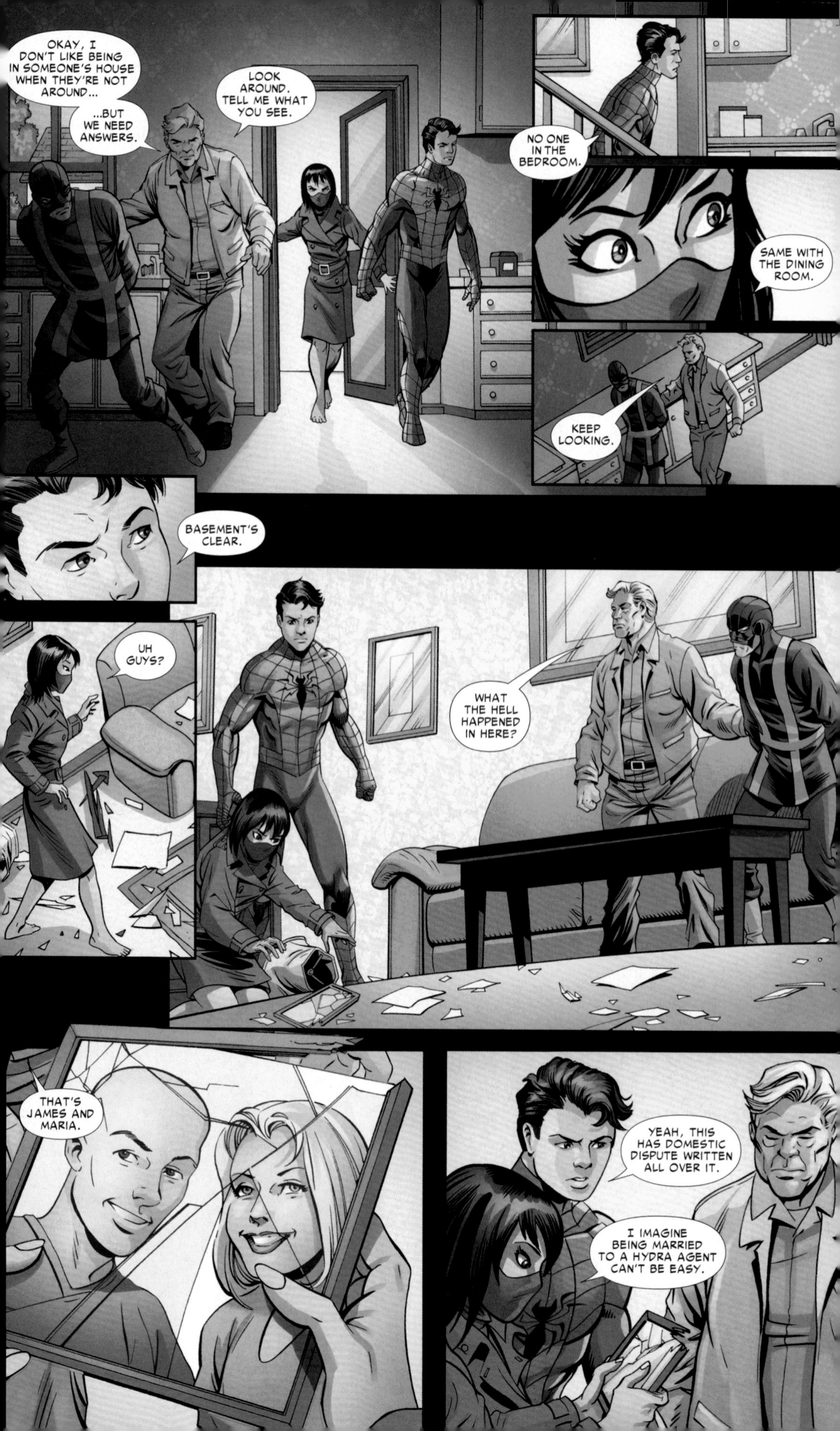
OKAY, I DON'T LIKE BEING IN SOMEONE'S HOUSE WHEN THEY'RE NOT AROUND...
...BUT WE NEED ANSWERS.
LOOK AROUND. TELL ME WHAT YOU SEE.
NO ONE IN THE BEDROOM.
SAME WITH THE DINING ROOM.
KEEP LOOKING.
BASEMENT'S CLEAR.
UH GUYS?
WHAT THE HELL HAPPENED IN HERE?
THAT'S JAMES AND MARIA.
YEAH, THIS HAS DOMESTIC DISPUTE WRITTEN ALL OVER IT.
I IMAGINE BEING MARRIED TO A HYDRA AGENT CAN'T BE EASY.

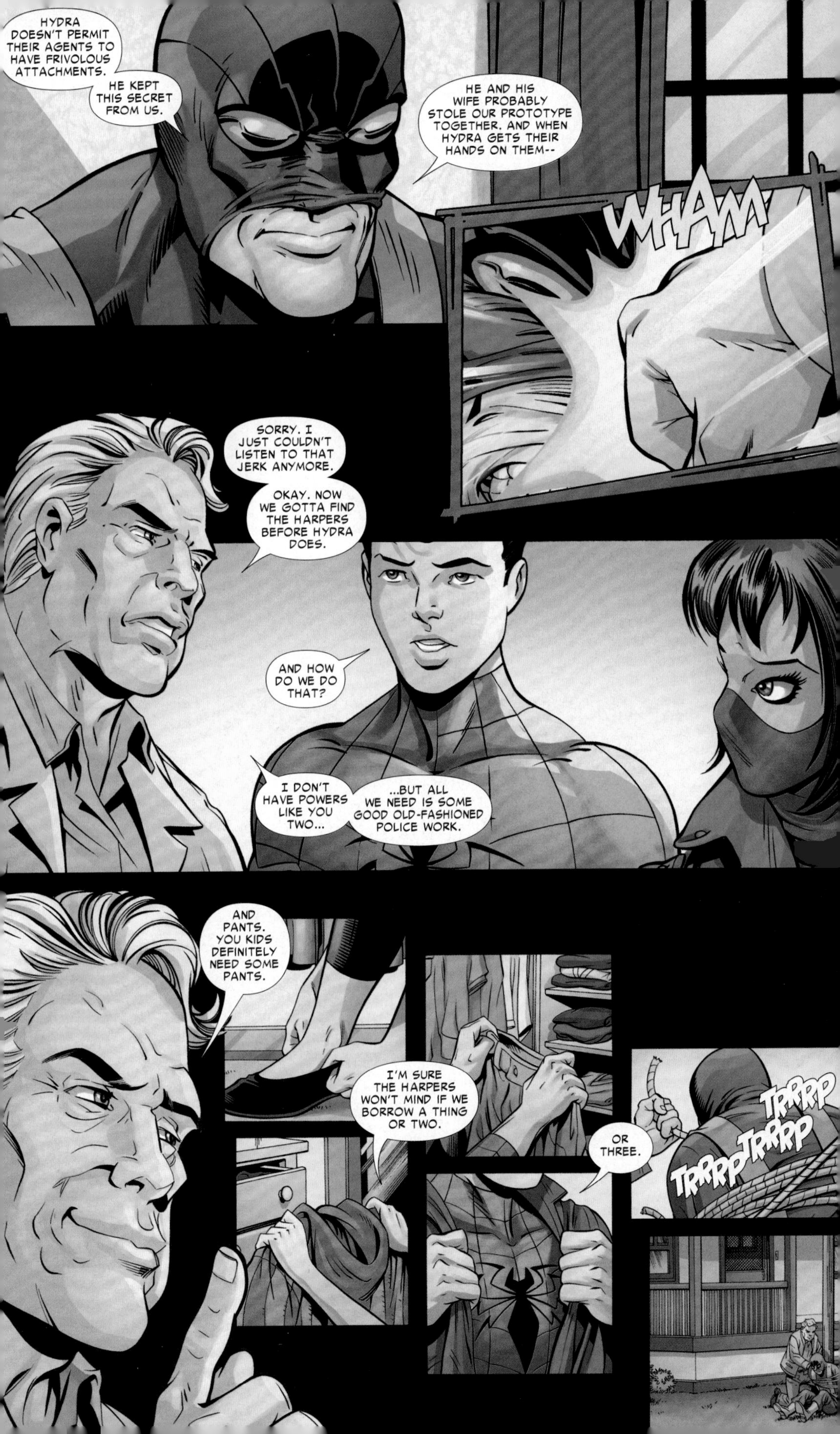
HYDRA DOESN'T PERMIT THEIR AGENTS TO HAVE FRIVOLOUS ATTACHMENTS.
HE KEPT THIS SECRET FROM US.
HE AND HIS WIFE PROBABLY STOLE OUR PROTOTYPE TOGETHER. AND WHEN HYDRA GETS THEIR HANDS ON THEM--
WHAM
SORRY. I JUST COULDN'T LISTEN TO THAT JERK ANYMORE.
OKAY. NOW WE GOTTA FIND THE HARPERS BEFORE HYDRA DOES.
AND HOW DO WE DO THAT?
I DON'T HAVE POWERS LIKE YOU TWO...
...BUT ALL WE NEED IS SOME GOOD OLD-FASHIONED POLICE WORK.
AND PANTS. YOU KIDS DEFINITELY NEED SOME PANTS.
I'M SURE THE HARPERS WON'T MIND IF WE BORROW A THING OR TWO.
OR THREE.
TRRRP TRRRP TRRRP

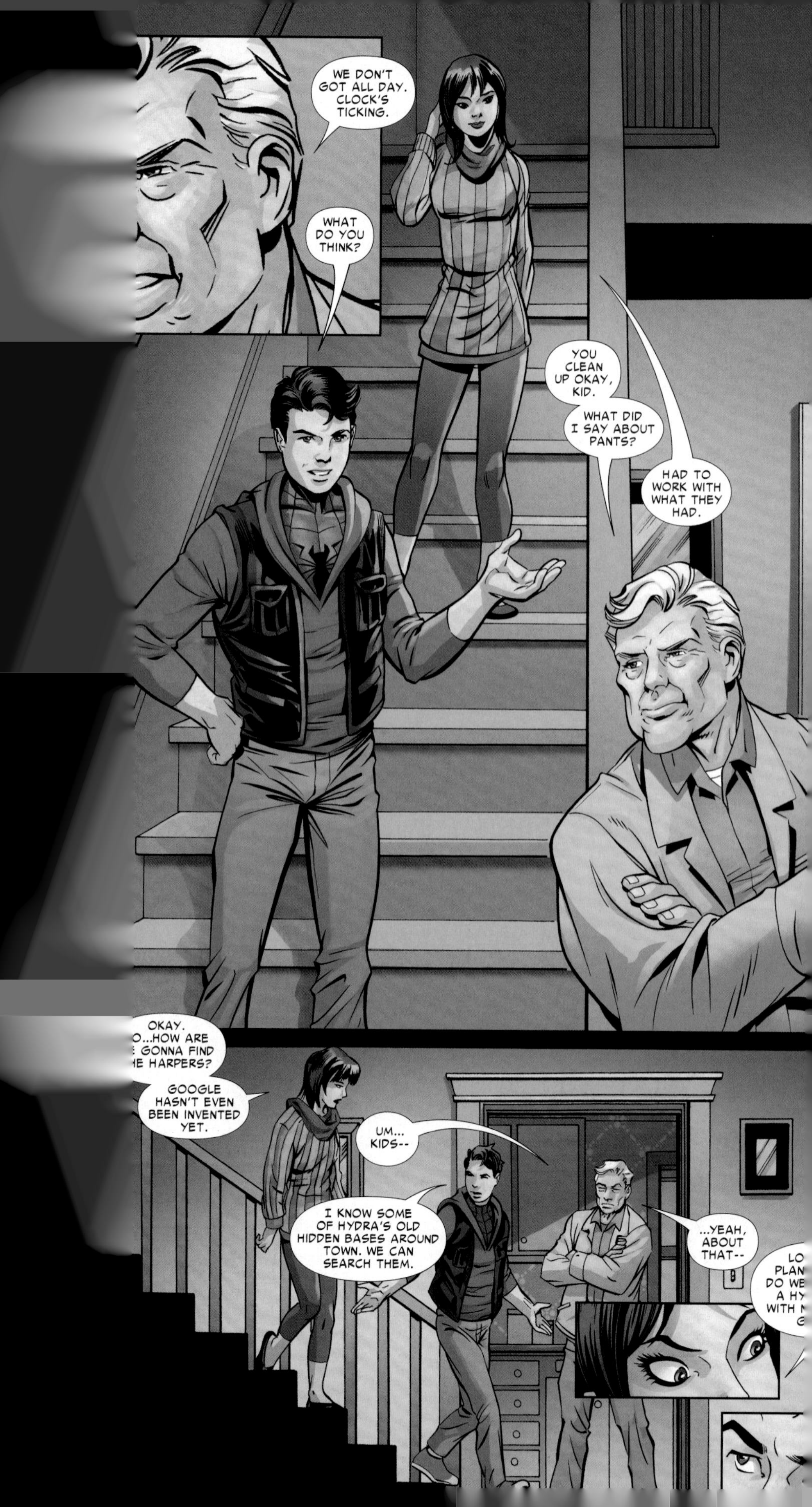
WE DON'T GOT ALL DAY. CLOCK'S TICKING.
WHAT DO YOU THINK?
YOU CLEAN UP OKAY, KID.
WHAT DID I SAY ABOUT PANTS?
HAD TO WORK WITH WHAT THEY HAD.
OKAY. O...HOW ARE E GONNA FIND HE HARPERS?
GOOGLE HASN'T EVEN BEEN INVENTED YET.
UM... KIDS--
I KNOW SOME OF HYDRA'S OLD HIDDEN BASES AROUND TOWN. WE CAN SEARCH THEM.
...YEAH, ABOUT THAT--

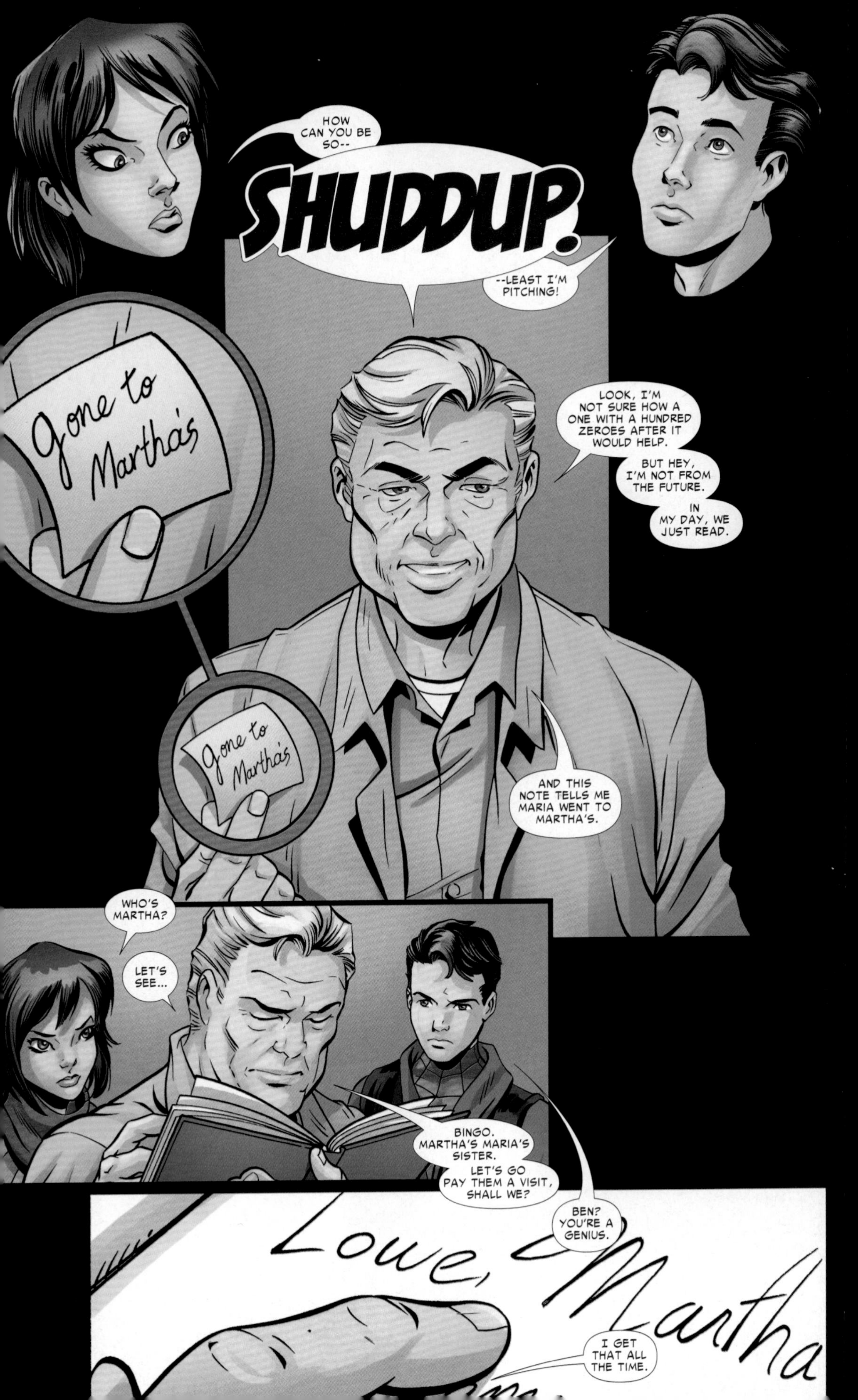
HOW CAN YOU BE SO--
SHUDDUP.
--LEAST I'M PITCHING!
Gone to Martha's
LOOK, I'M NOT SURE HOW A ONE WITH A HUNDRED ZEROES AFTER IT WOULD HELP.
BUT HEY, I'M NOT FROM THE FUTURE.
IN MY DAY, WE JUST READ.
Gone to Martha's
AND THIS NOTE TELLS ME MARIA WENT TO MARTHA'S.
WHO'S MARTHA?
LET'S SEE...
BINGO. MARTHA'S MARIA'S SISTER.
LET'S GO PAY THEM A VISIT, SHALL WE?
BEN? YOU'RE A GENIUS.
Love, Martha
I GET THAT ALL THE TIME.

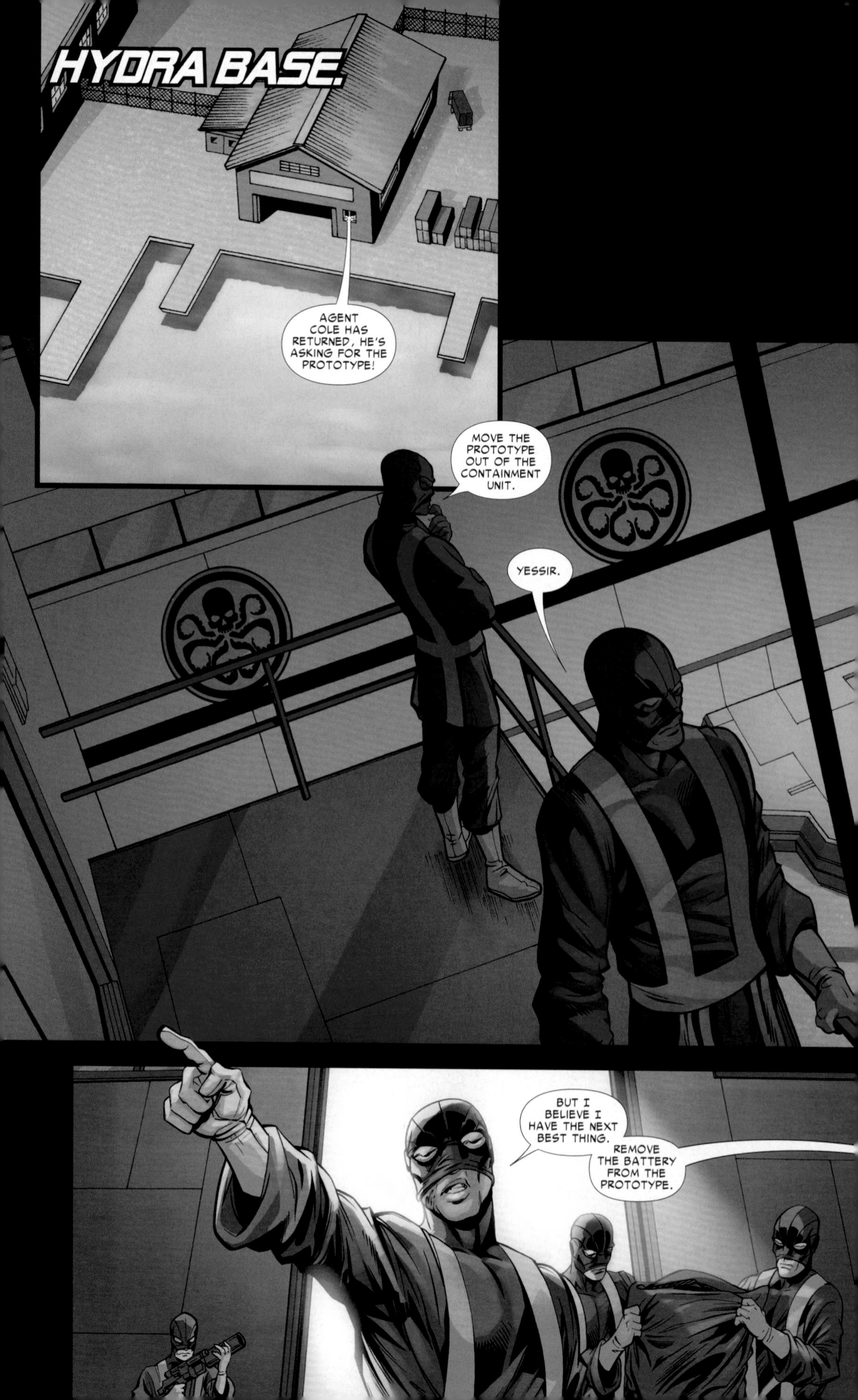
HYDRA BASE.
AGENT COLE HAS RETURNED, HE'S ASKING FOR THE PROTOTYPE!
MOVE THE PROTOTYPE OUT OF THE CONTAINMENT UNIT.
YESSIR.
BUT I BELIEVE I HAVE THE NEXT BEST THING.
REMOVE THE BATTERY FROM THE PROTOTYPE.

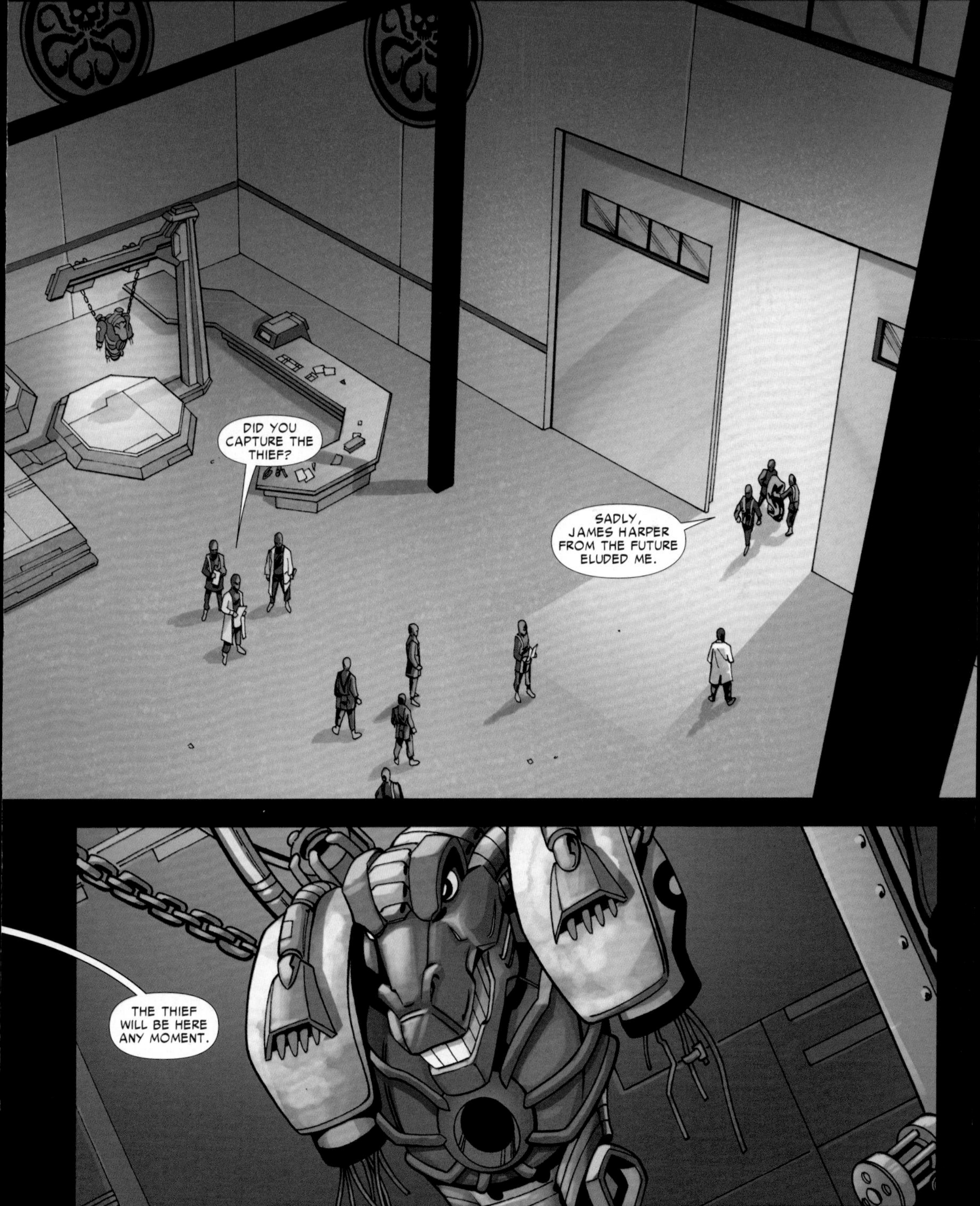
DID YOU CAPTURE THE THIEF?
SADLY, JAMES HARPER FROM THE FUTURE ELUDED ME.
THE THIEF WILL BE HERE ANY MOMENT.

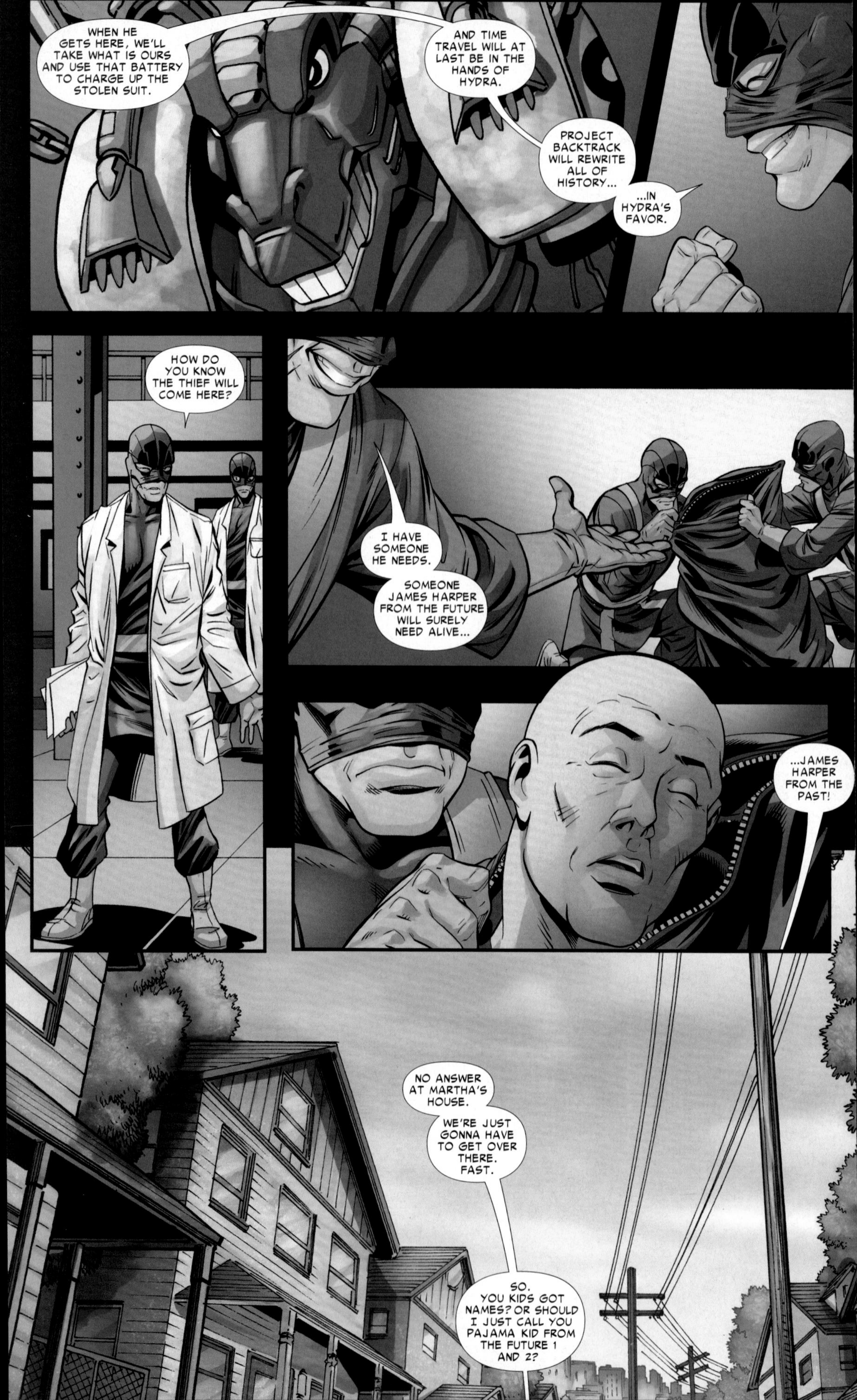
WHEN HE GETS HERE, WE'LL TAKE WHAT IS OURS AND USE THAT BATTERY TO CHARGE UP THE STOLEN SUIT.
AND TIME TRAVEL WILL AT LAST BE IN THE HANDS OF HYDRA.
PROJECT BACKTRACK WILL REWRITE ALL OF HISTORY...
...IN HYDRA'S FAVOR.
HOW DO YOU KNOW THE THIEF WILL COME HERE?
I HAVE SOMEONE HE NEEDS.
SOMEONE JAMES HARPER FROM THE FUTURE WILL SURELY NEED ALIVE...
...JAMES HARPER FROM THE PAST!
NO ANSWER AT MARTHA'S HOUSE.
WE'RE JUST GONNA HAVE TO GET OVER THERE. FAST.
SO. YOU KIDS GOT NAMES? OR SHOULD I JUST CALL YOU PAJAMA KID FROM THE FUTURE 1 AND 2?

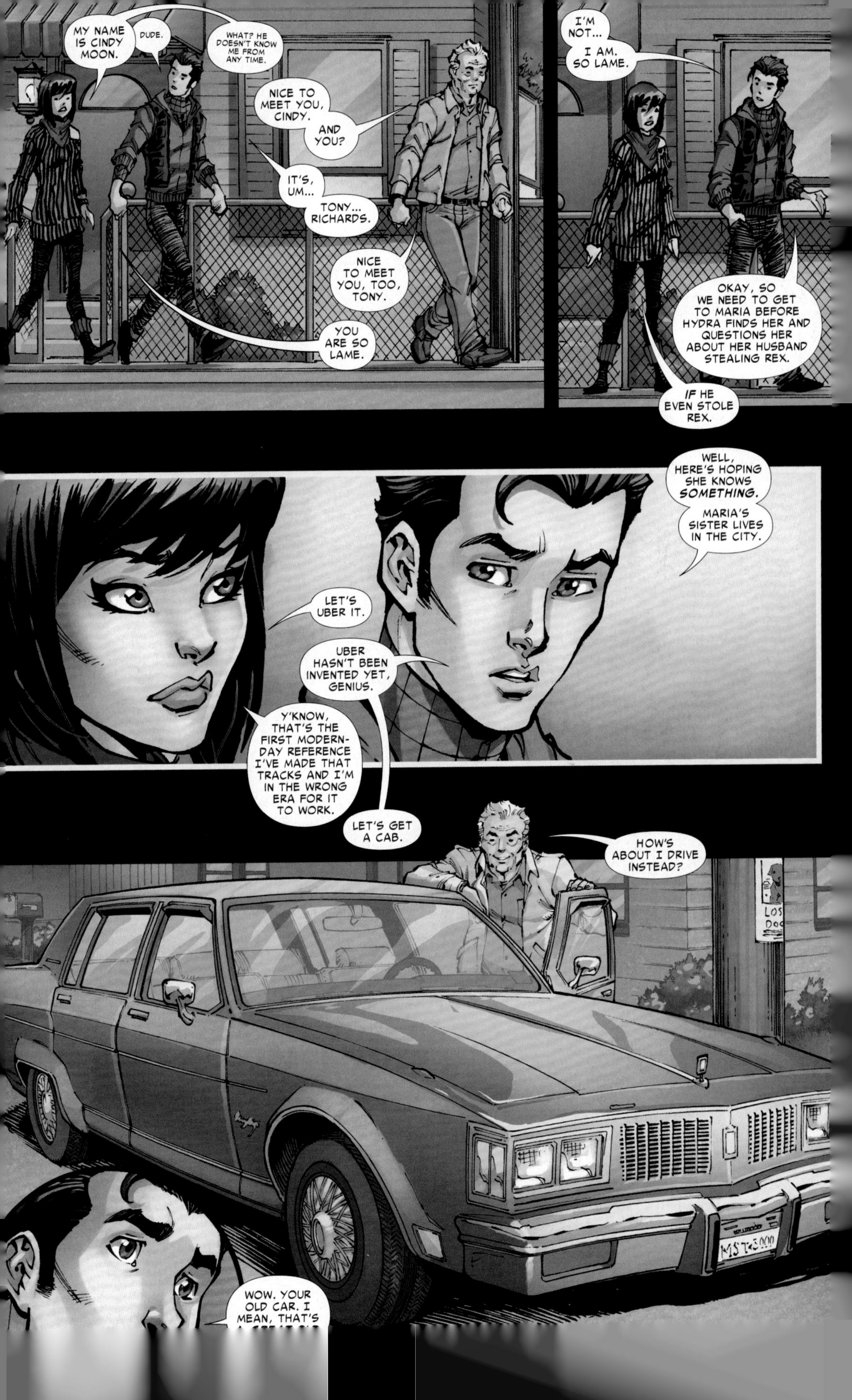
MY NAME IS CINDY MOON.
DUDE.
WHAT? HE DOESN'T KNOW ME FROM ANY TIME.
NICE TO MEET YOU, CINDY.
AND YOU?
IT'S, UM...
TONY... RICHARDS.
NICE TO MEET YOU, TOO, TONY.
YOU ARE SO LAME.
I'M NOT...
I AM. SO LAME.
OKAY, SO WE NEED TO GET TO MARIA BEFORE HYDRA FINDS HER AND QUESTIONS HER ABOUT HER HUSBAND STEALING REX.
IF HE EVEN STOLE REX.
WELL, HERE'S HOPING SHE KNOWS ***SOMETHING.***
MARIA'S SISTER LIVES IN THE CITY.
LET'S UBER IT.
UBER HASN'T BEEN INVENTED YET, GENIUS.
Y'KNOW, THAT'S THE FIRST MODERN-DAY REFERENCE I'VE MADE THAT TRACKS AND I'M IN THE WRONG ERA FOR IT TO WORK.
LET'S GET A CAB.
HOW'S ABOUT I DRIVE INSTEAD?
WOW. YOUR OLD CAR. I MEAN, THAT'S

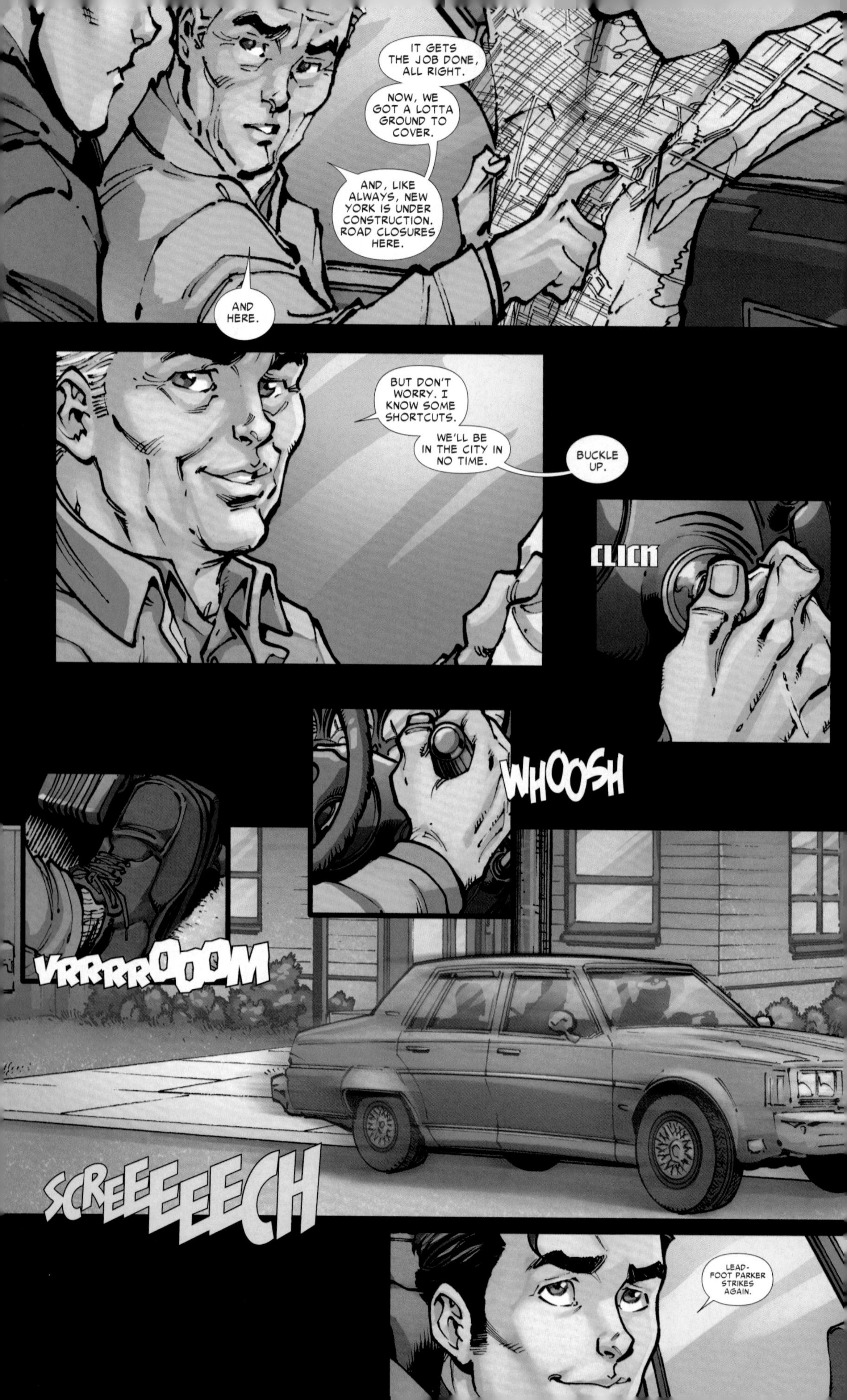
IT GETS THE JOB DONE, ALL RIGHT.
NOW, WE GOT A LOTTA GROUND TO COVER.
AND, LIKE ALWAYS, NEW YORK IS UNDER CONSTRUCTION. ROAD CLOSURES HERE.
AND HERE.
BUT DON'T WORRY. I KNOW SOME SHORTCUTS.
WE'LL BE IN THE CITY IN NO TIME.
BUCKLE UP.
CLICK
WHOOSH
VRRRRROOOOM
SCREEEEEECH
LEAD-FOOT PARKER STRIKES AGAIN.

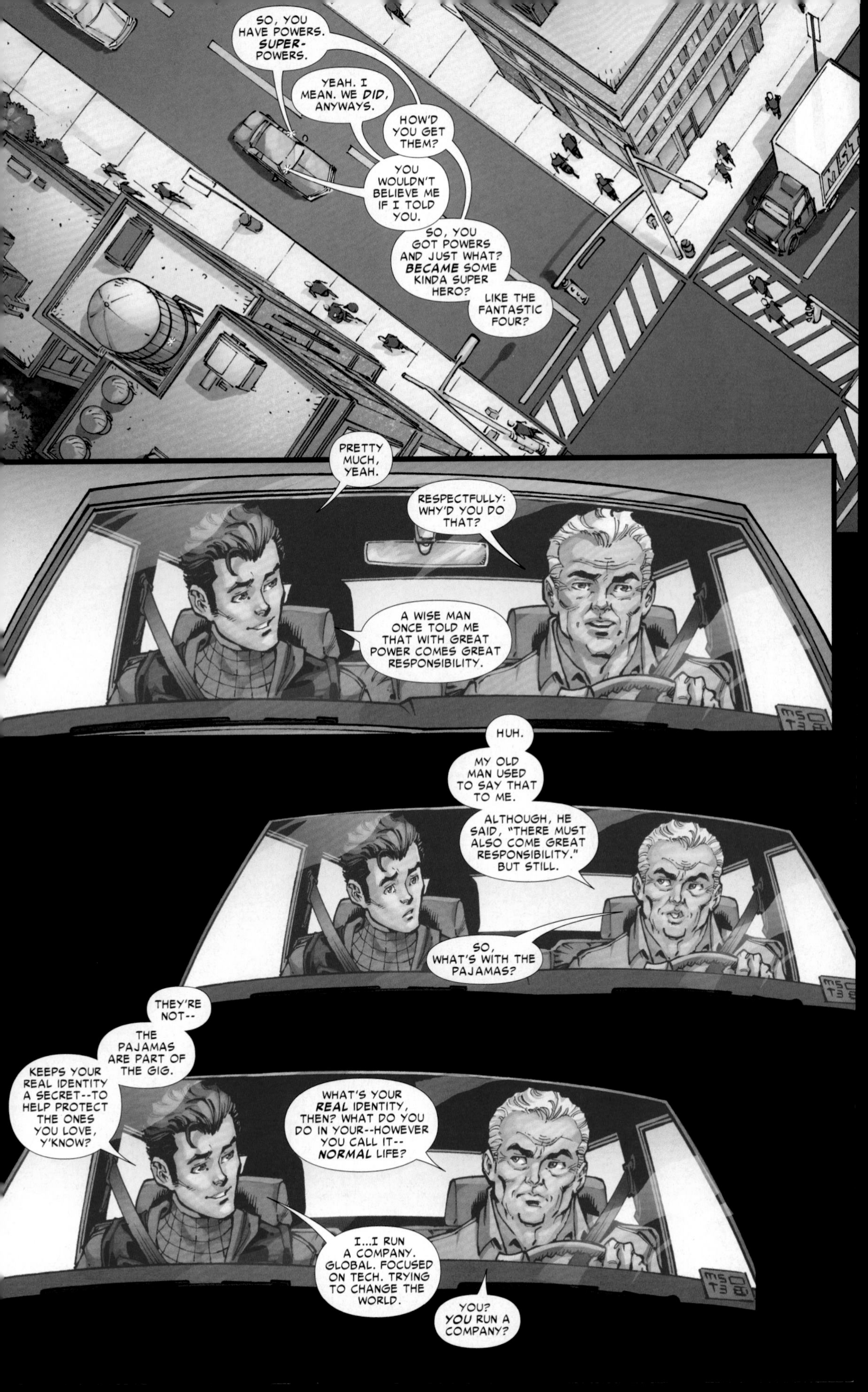
SO, YOU HAVE POWERS. SUPER-POWERS.
YEAH. I MEAN. WE DID, ANYWAYS.
HOW'D YOU GET THEM?
YOU WOULDN'T BELIEVE ME IF I TOLD YOU.
SO, YOU GOT POWERS AND JUST WHAT? BECAME SOME KINDA SUPER HERO?
LIKE THE FANTASTIC FOUR?
PRETTY MUCH, YEAH.
RESPECTFULLY: WHY'D YOU DO THAT?
A WISE MAN ONCE TOLD ME THAT WITH GREAT POWER COMES GREAT RESPONSIBILITY.
HUH.
MY OLD MAN USED TO SAY THAT TO ME.
ALTHOUGH, HE SAID, "THERE MUST ALSO COME GREAT RESPONSIBILITY." BUT STILL.
SO, WHAT'S WITH THE PAJAMAS?
THEY'RE NOT--
THE PAJAMAS ARE PART OF THE GIG.
KEEPS YOUR REAL IDENTITY A SECRET--TO HELP PROTECT THE ONES YOU LOVE, Y'KNOW?
WHAT'S YOUR REAL IDENTITY, THEN? WHAT DO YOU DO IN YOUR--HOWEVER YOU CALL IT--NORMAL LIFE?
I...I RUN A COMPANY. GLOBAL. FOCUSED ON TECH. TRYING TO CHANGE THE WORLD.
YOU? YOU RUN A COMPANY?

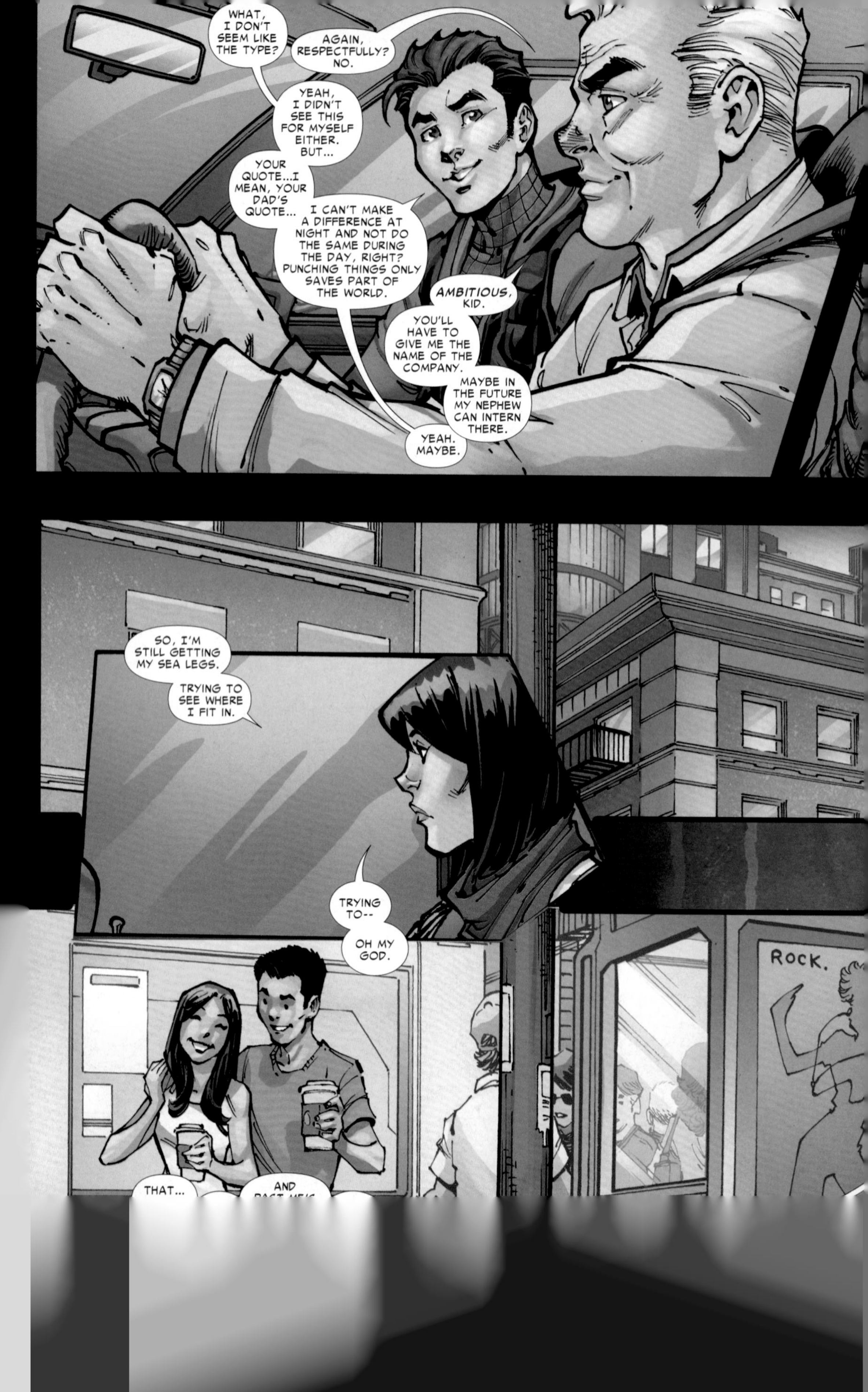
WHAT, I DON'T SEEM LIKE THE TYPE?
AGAIN, RESPECTFULLY? NO.
YEAH, I DIDN'T SEE THIS FOR MYSELF EITHER. BUT...
YOUR QUOTE...I MEAN, YOUR DAD'S QUOTE...
I CAN'T MAKE A DIFFERENCE AT NIGHT AND NOT DO THE SAME DURING THE DAY, RIGHT? PUNCHING THINGS ONLY SAVES PART OF THE WORLD.
AMBITIOUS, KID.
YOU'LL HAVE TO GIVE ME THE NAME OF THE COMPANY.
MAYBE IN THE FUTURE MY NEPHEW CAN INTERN THERE.
YEAH. MAYBE.
SO, I'M STILL GETTING MY SEA LEGS.
TRYING TO SEE WHERE I FIT IN.
TRYING TO--
OH MY GOD.
ROCK.
THAT...
AND

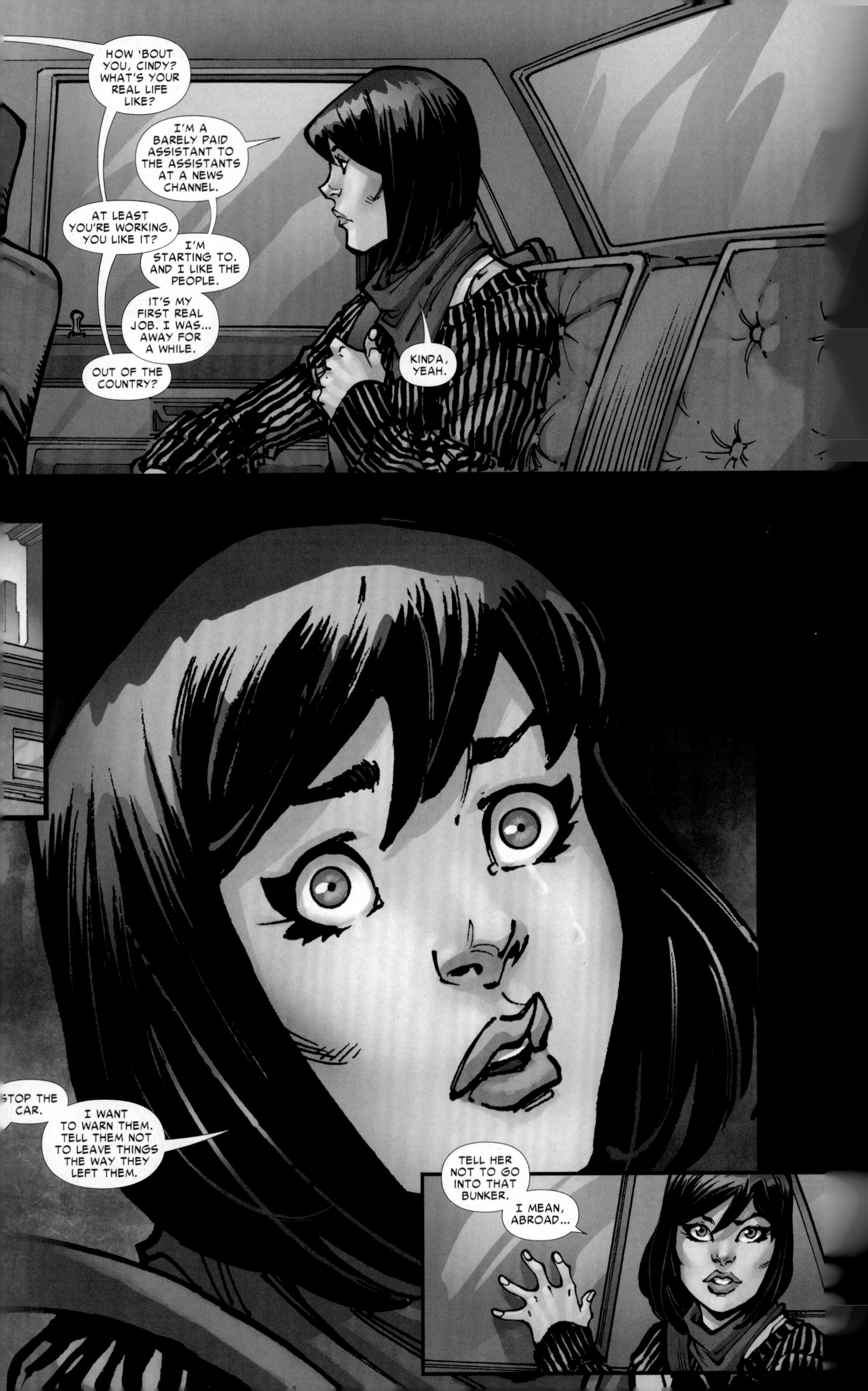
HOW 'BOUT YOU, CINDY? WHAT'S YOUR REAL LIFE LIKE?
I'M A BARELY PAID ASSISTANT TO THE ASSISTANTS AT A NEWS CHANNEL.
AT LEAST YOU'RE WORKING. YOU LIKE IT?
I'M STARTING TO. AND I LIKE THE PEOPLE.
IT'S MY FIRST REAL JOB. I WAS... AWAY FOR A WHILE.
OUT OF THE COUNTRY?
KINDA, YEAH.
STOP THE CAR.
I WANT TO WARN THEM. TELL THEM NOT TO LEAVE THINGS THE WAY THEY LEFT THEM.
TELL HER NOT TO GO INTO THAT BUNKER.
I MEAN, ABROAD...

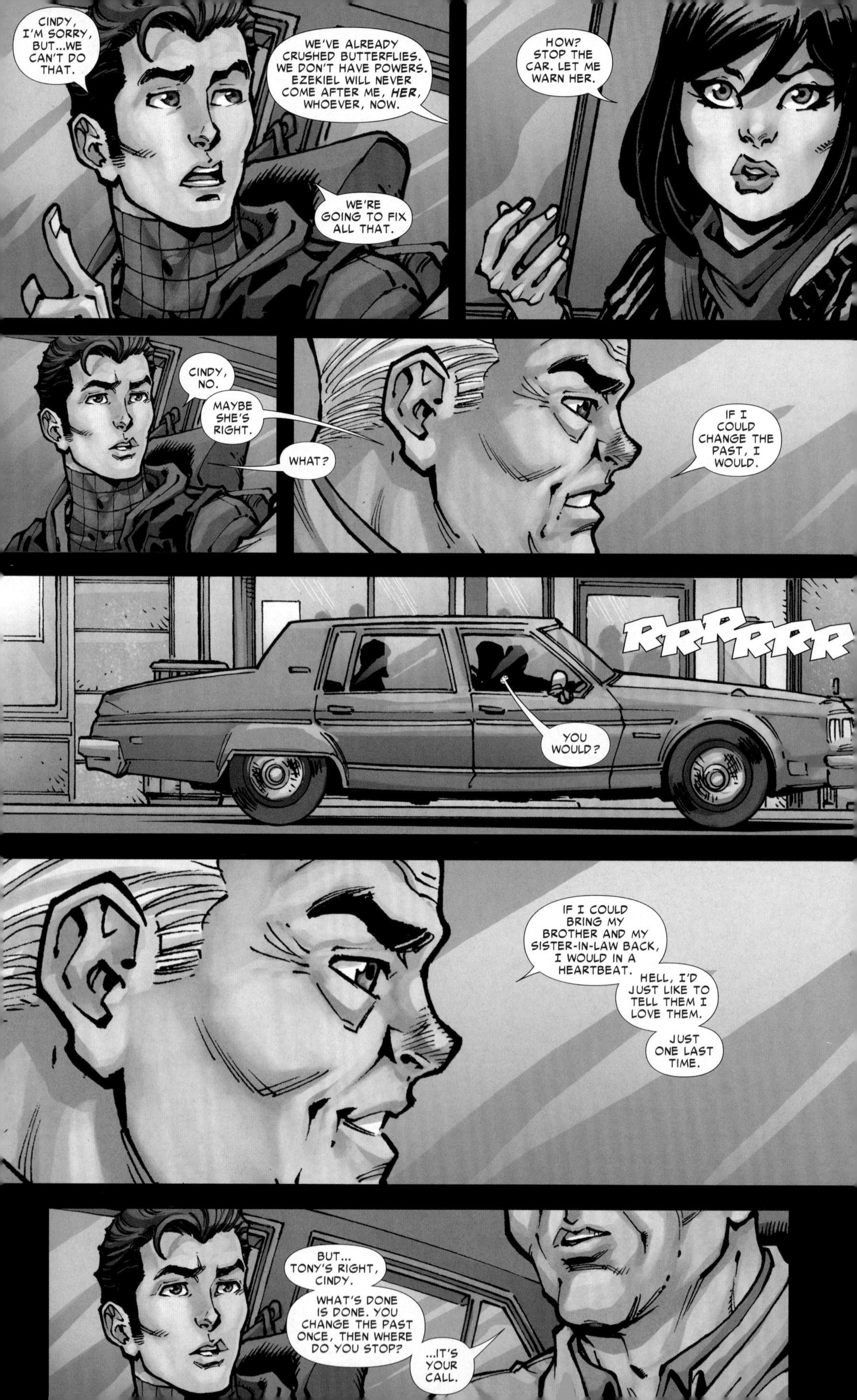
CINDY, I'M SORRY, BUT...WE CAN'T DO THAT.
WE'VE ALREADY CRUSHED BUTTERFLIES. WE DON'T HAVE POWERS. EZEKIEL WILL NEVER COME AFTER ME, HER, WHOEVER, NOW.
WE'RE GOING TO FIX ALL THAT.
HOW? STOP THE CAR. LET ME WARN HER.
CINDY, NO.
MAYBE SHE'S RIGHT.
WHAT?
IF I COULD CHANGE THE PAST, I WOULD.
RRRRRR
YOU WOULD?
IF I COULD BRING MY BROTHER AND MY SISTER-IN-LAW BACK, I WOULD IN A HEARTBEAT.
HELL, I'D JUST LIKE TO TELL THEM I LOVE THEM.
JUST ONE LAST TIME.
BUT... TONY'S RIGHT, CINDY.
WHAT'S DONE IS DONE. YOU CHANGE THE PAST ONCE, THEN WHERE DO YOU STOP?
...IT'S YOUR CALL.

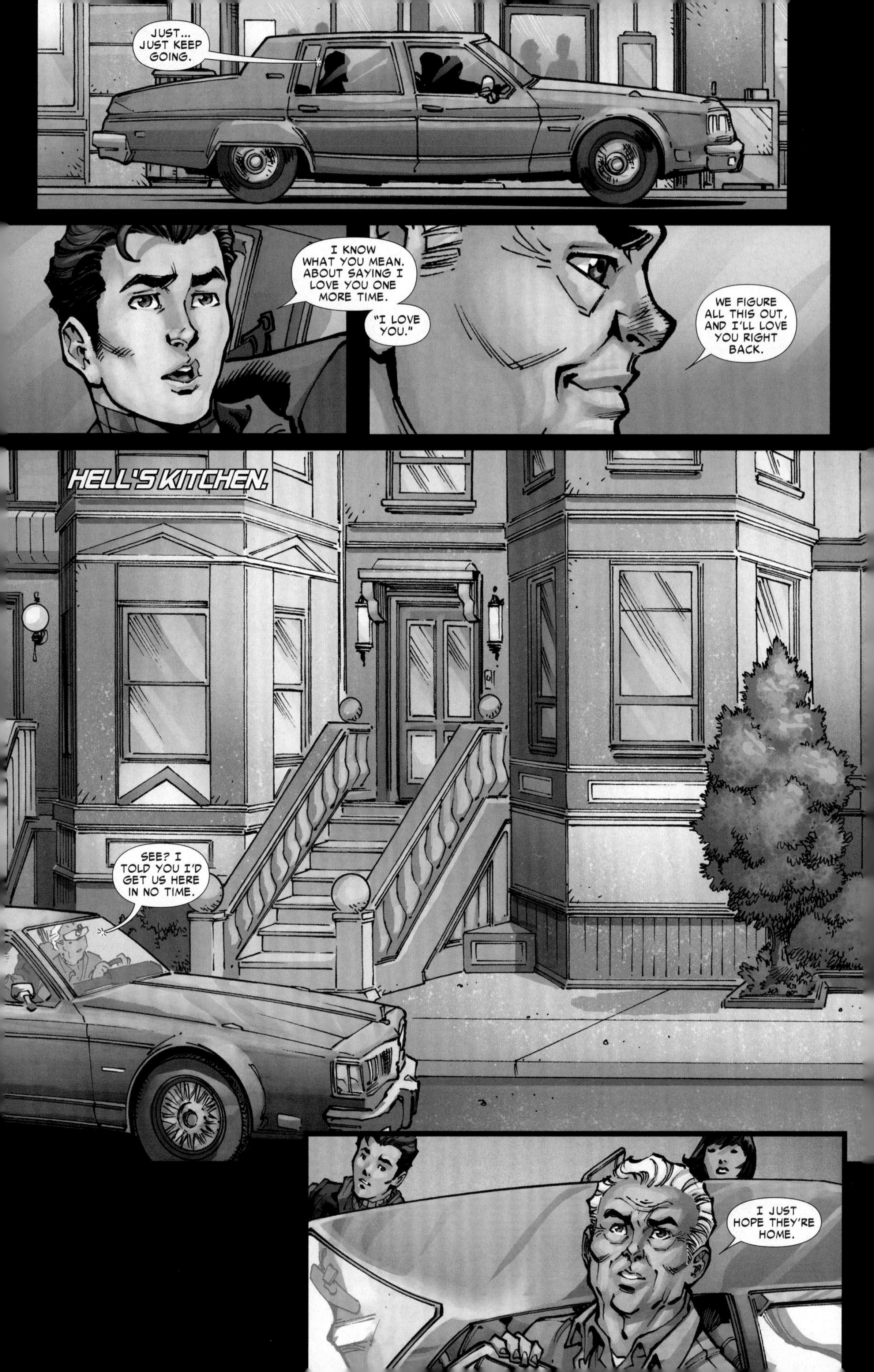
JUST... JUST KEEP GOING.
I KNOW WHAT YOU MEAN. ABOUT SAYING I LOVE YOU ONE MORE TIME.
"I LOVE YOU."
WE FIGURE ALL THIS OUT, AND I'LL LOVE YOU RIGHT BACK.
HELL'S KITCHEN.
SEE? I TOLD YOU I'D GET US HERE IN NO TIME.
I JUST HOPE THEY'RE HOME.

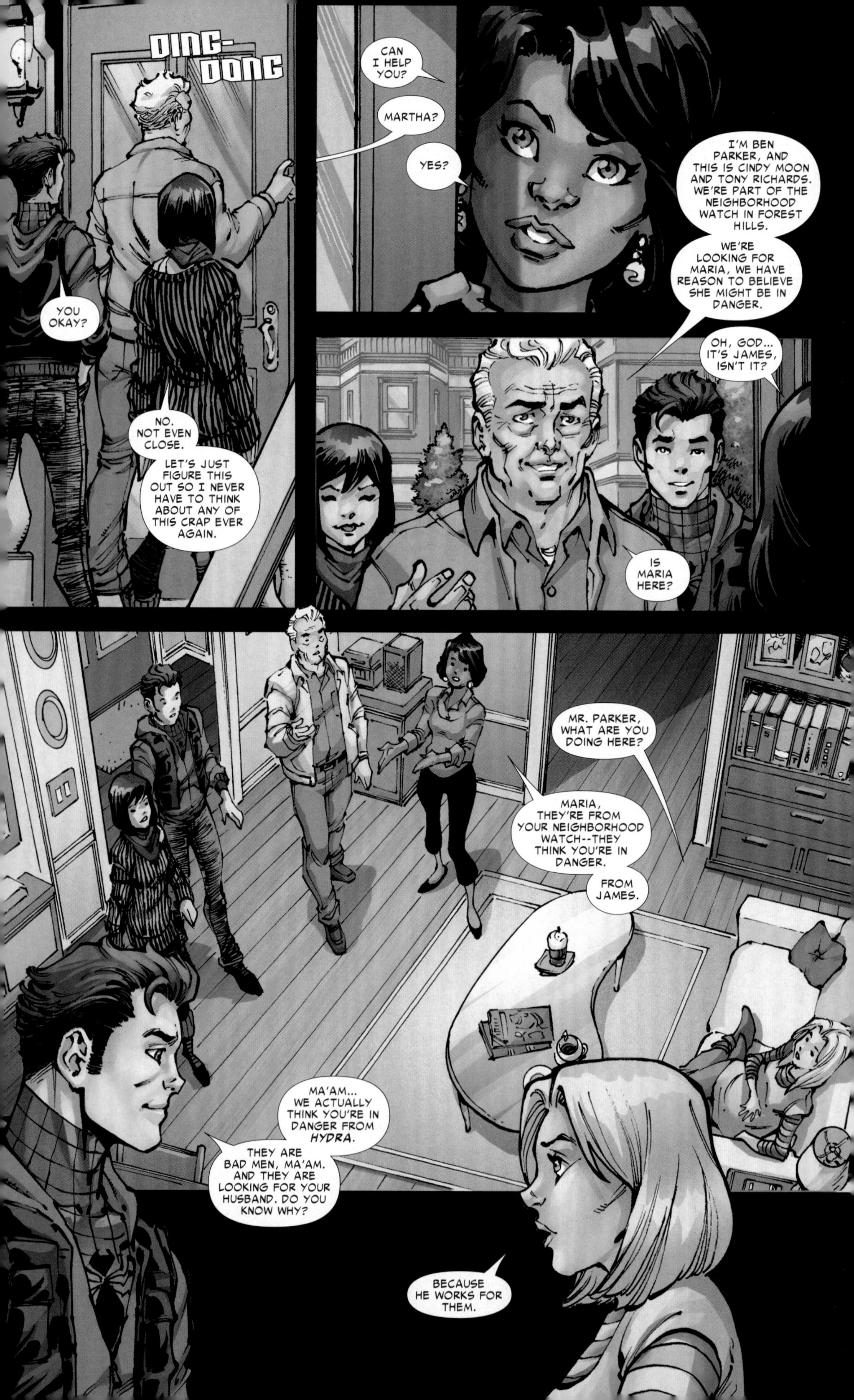
DING-DONG
YOU OKAY?
NO. NOT EVEN CLOSE.
LET'S JUST FIGURE THIS OUT SO I NEVER HAVE TO THINK ABOUT ANY OF THIS CRAP EVER AGAIN.
CAN I HELP YOU?
MARTHA?
YES?
I'M BEN PARKER, AND THIS IS CINDY MOON AND TONY RICHARDS. WE'RE PART OF THE NEIGHBORHOOD WATCH IN FOREST HILLS.
WE'RE LOOKING FOR MARIA, WE HAVE REASON TO BELIEVE SHE MIGHT BE IN DANGER.
OH, GOD... IT'S JAMES, ISN'T IT?
IS MARIA HERE?
MR. PARKER, WHAT ARE YOU DOING HERE?
MARIA, THEY'RE FROM YOUR NEIGHBORHOOD WATCH--THEY THINK YOU'RE IN DANGER.
FROM JAMES.
MA'AM... WE ACTUALLY THINK YOU'RE IN DANGER FROM HYDRA.
THEY ARE BAD MEN, MA'AM. AND THEY ARE LOOKING FOR YOUR HUSBAND. DO YOU KNOW WHY?
BECAUSE HE WORKS FOR THEM.

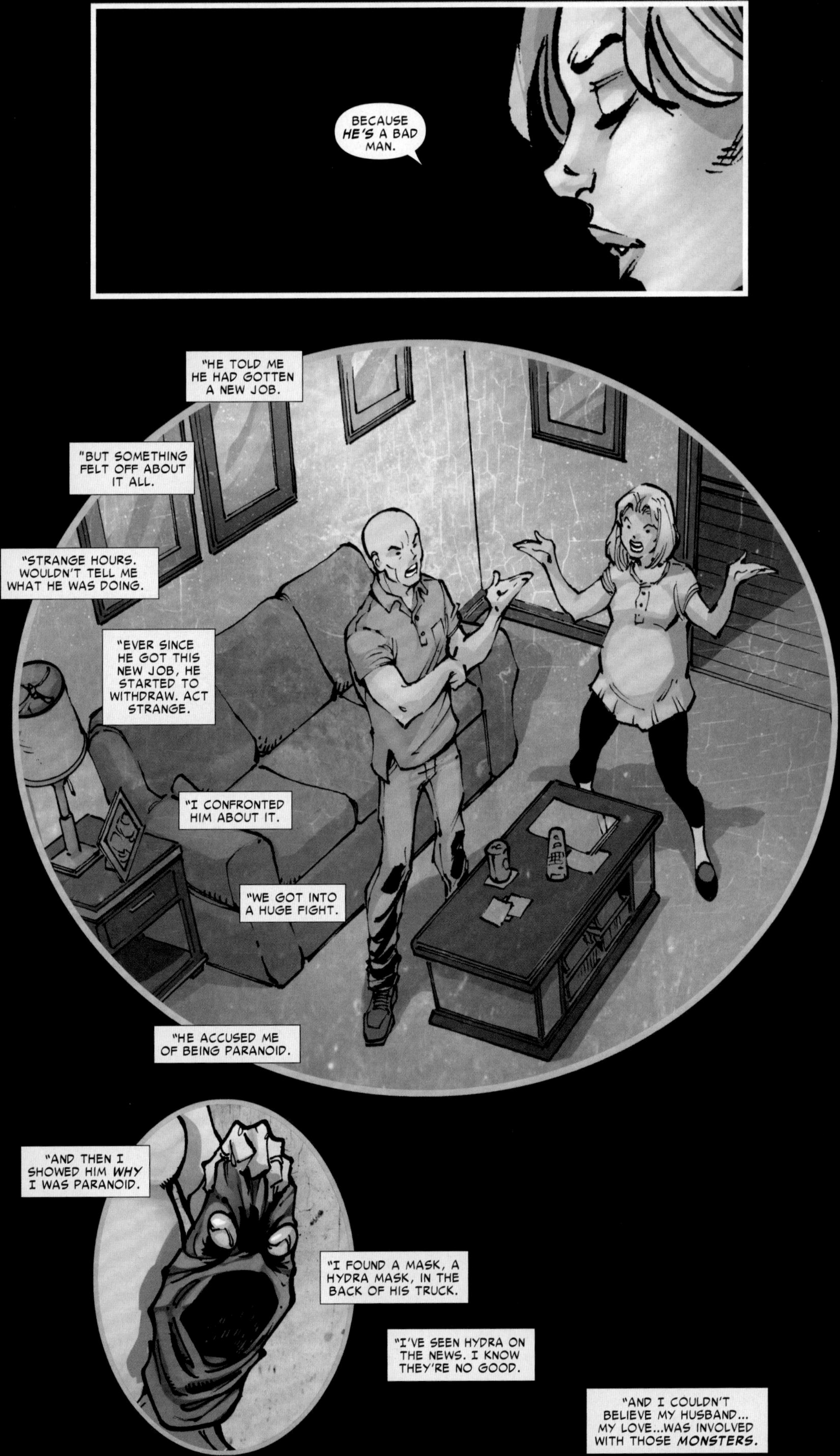
BECAUSE *HE'S* A BAD MAN.
"HE TOLD ME HE HAD GOTTEN A NEW JOB.
"BUT SOMETHING FELT OFF ABOUT IT ALL.
"STRANGE HOURS. WOULDN'T TELL ME WHAT HE WAS DOING.
"EVER SINCE HE GOT THIS NEW JOB, HE STARTED TO WITHDRAW. ACT STRANGE.
"I CONFRONTED HIM ABOUT IT.
"WE GOT INTO A HUGE FIGHT.
"HE ACCUSED ME OF BEING PARANOID.
"AND THEN I SHOWED HIM *WHY* I WAS PARANOID.
"I FOUND A MASK, A HYDRA MASK, IN THE BACK OF HIS TRUCK.
"I'VE SEEN HYDRA ON THE NEWS. I KNOW THEY'RE NO GOOD.
"AND I COULDN'T BELIEVE MY HUSBAND... MY LOVE...WAS INVOLVED WITH THOSE *MONSTERS*.

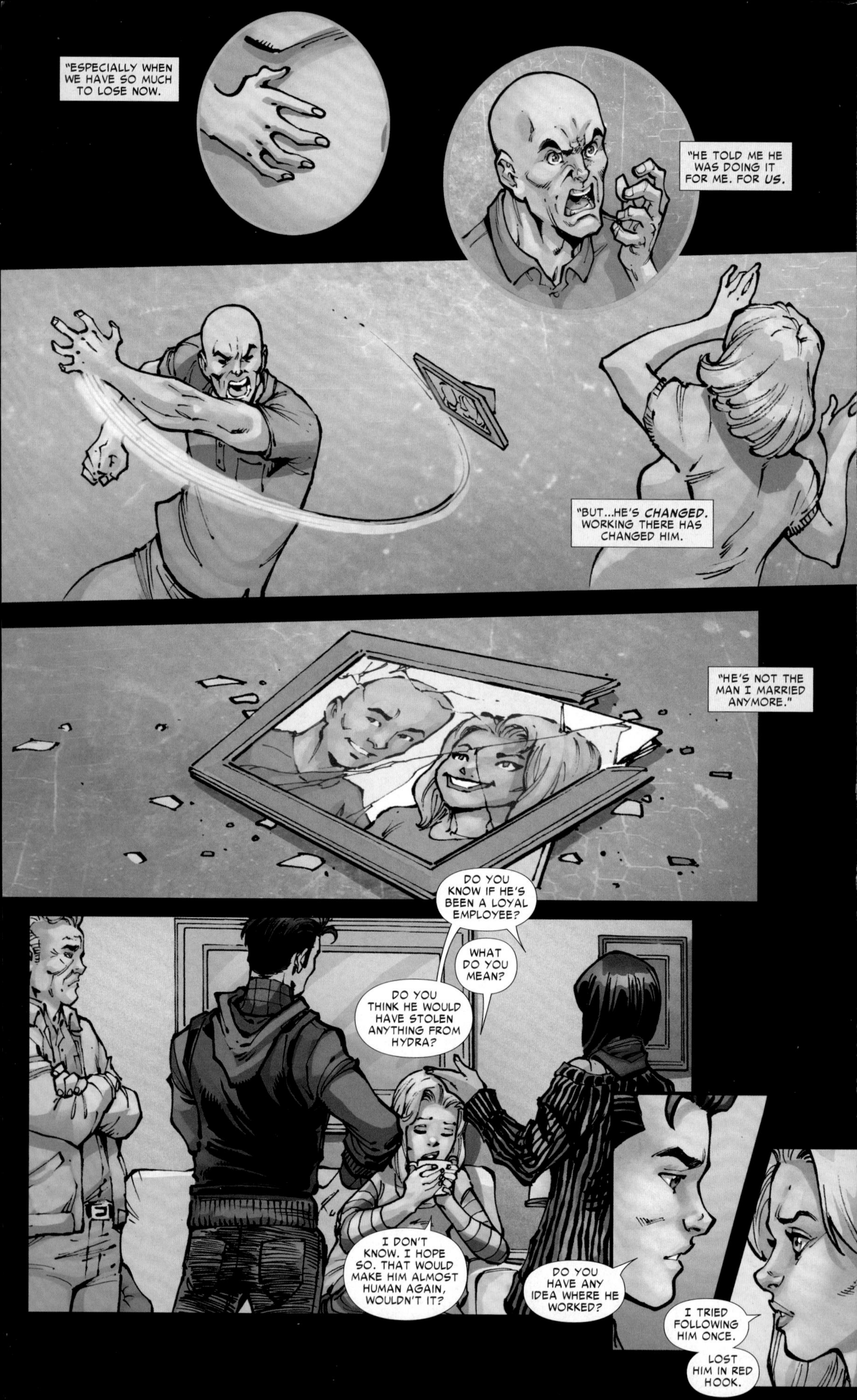
"ESPECIALLY WHEN WE HAVE SO MUCH TO LOSE NOW.
"HE TOLD ME HE WAS DOING IT FOR ME. FOR US.
"BUT...HE'S CHANGED. WORKING THERE HAS CHANGED HIM.
"HE'S NOT THE MAN I MARRIED ANYMORE."
DO YOU KNOW IF HE'S BEEN A LOYAL EMPLOYEE?
WHAT DO YOU MEAN?
DO YOU THINK HE WOULD HAVE STOLEN ANYTHING FROM HYDRA?
I DON'T KNOW. I HOPE SO. THAT WOULD MAKE HIM ALMOST HUMAN AGAIN, WOULDN'T IT?
DO YOU HAVE ANY IDEA WHERE HE WORKED?
I TRIED FOLLOWING HIM ONCE.
LOST HIM IN RED HOOK.

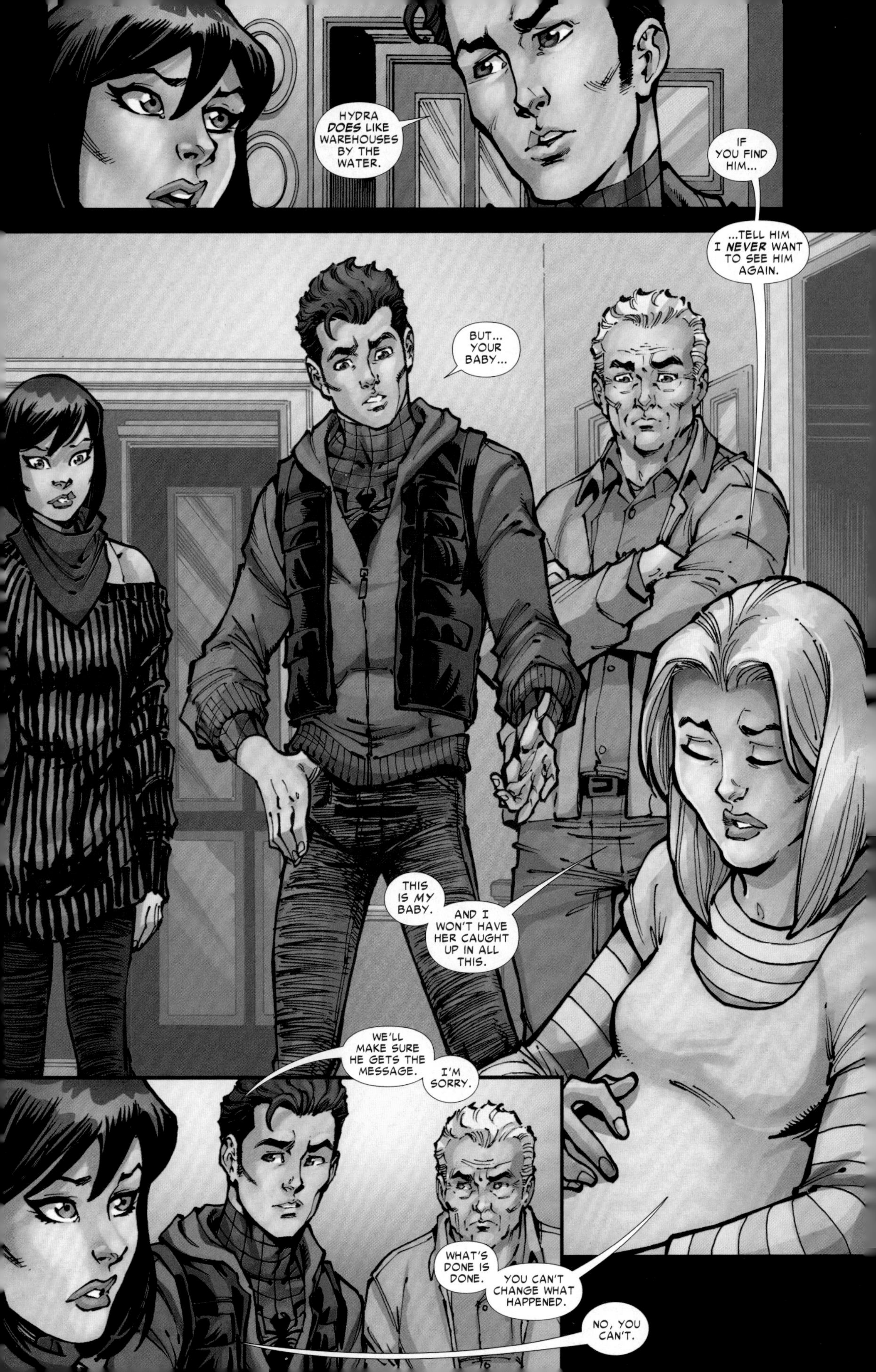
HYDRA DOES LIKE WAREHOUSES BY THE WATER.
IF YOU FIND HIM...
...TELL HIM I NEVER WANT TO SEE HIM AGAIN.
BUT... YOUR BABY...
THIS IS MY BABY.
AND I WON'T HAVE HER CAUGHT UP IN ALL THIS.
WE'LL MAKE SURE HE GETS THE MESSAGE.
I'M SORRY.
WHAT'S DONE IS DONE.
YOU CAN'T CHANGE WHAT HAPPENED.
NO, YOU CAN'T.

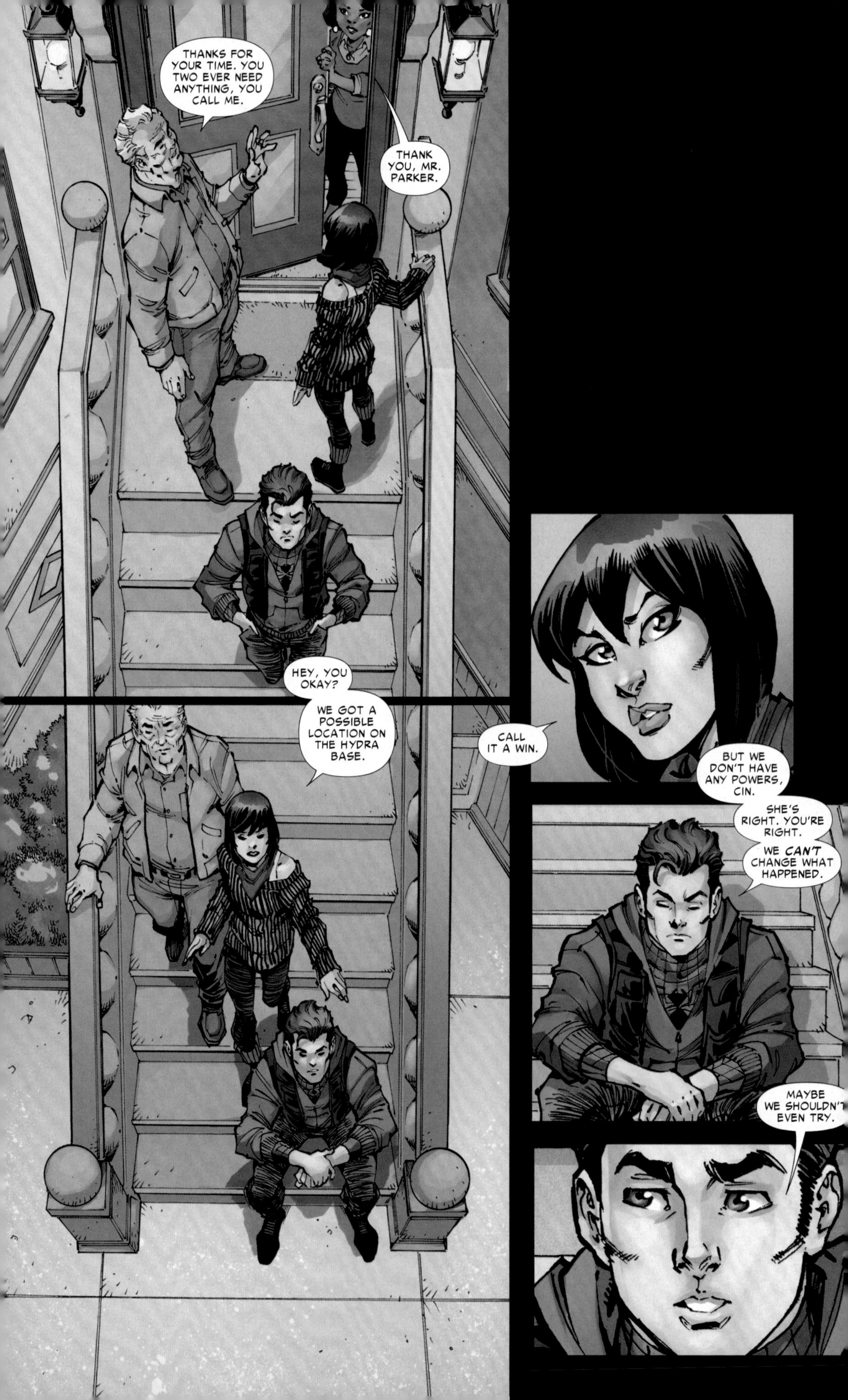
THANKS FOR YOUR TIME. YOU TWO EVER NEED ANYTHING, YOU CALL ME.
THANK YOU, MR. PARKER.
HEY, YOU OKAY?
WE GOT A POSSIBLE LOCATION ON THE HYDRA BASE.
CALL IT A WIN.
BUT WE DON'T HAVE ANY POWERS, CIN.
SHE'S RIGHT. YOU'RE RIGHT.
WE *CAN'T* CHANGE WHAT HAPPENED.
MAYBE WE SHOULDN'T EVEN TRY.

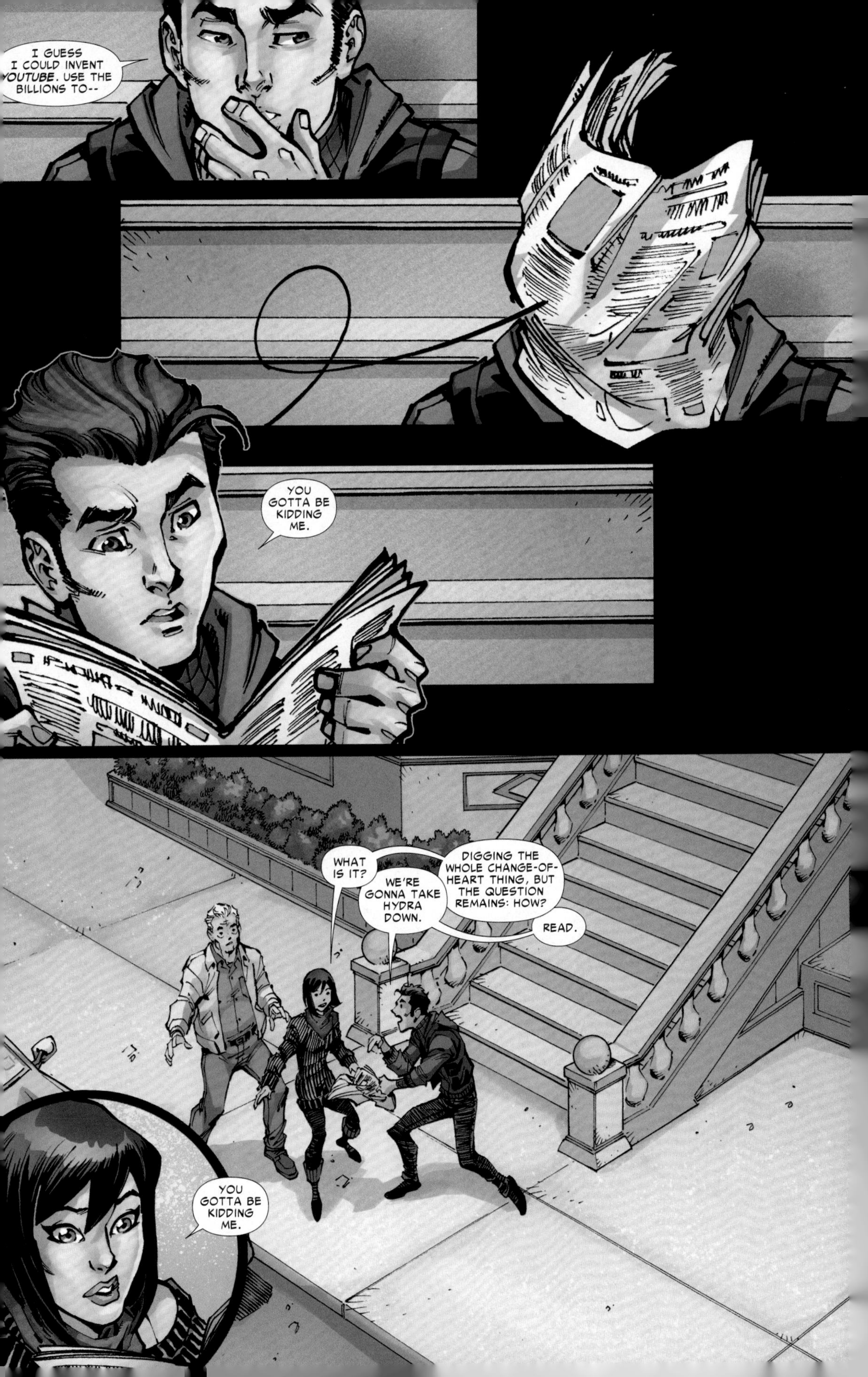
I GUESS I COULD INVENT YOUTUBE. USE THE BILLIONS TO--
YOU GOTTA BE KIDDING ME.
WHAT IS IT?
DIGGING THE WHOLE CHANGE-OF-HEART THING, BUT THE QUESTION REMAINS: HOW?
WE'RE GONNA TAKE HYDRA DOWN.
READ.
YOU GOTTA BE KIDDING ME.

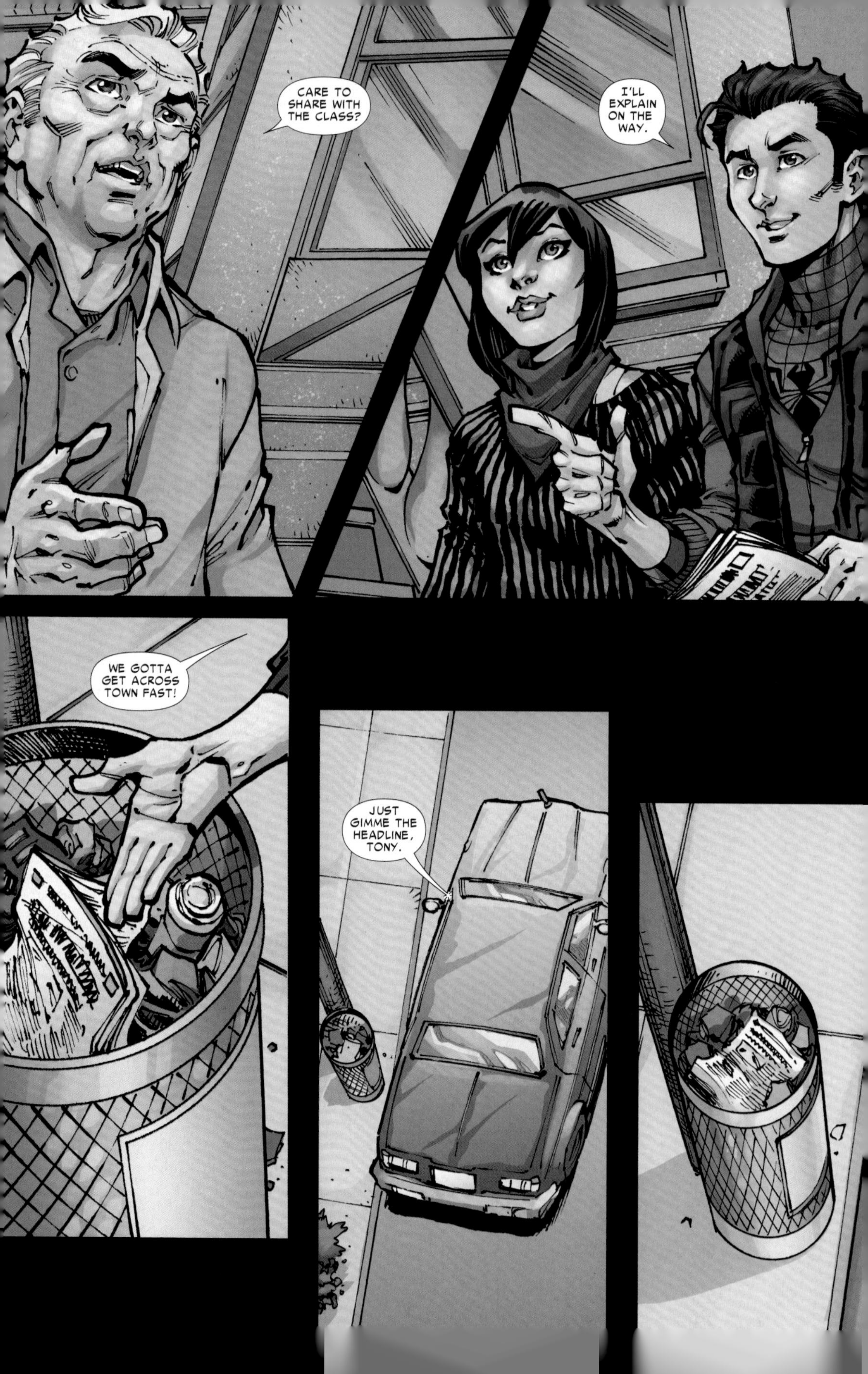
CARE TO SHARE WITH THE CLASS?
I'LL EXPLAIN ON THE WAY.
WE GOTTA GET ACROSS TOWN FAST!
JUST GIMME THE HEADLINE, TONY.

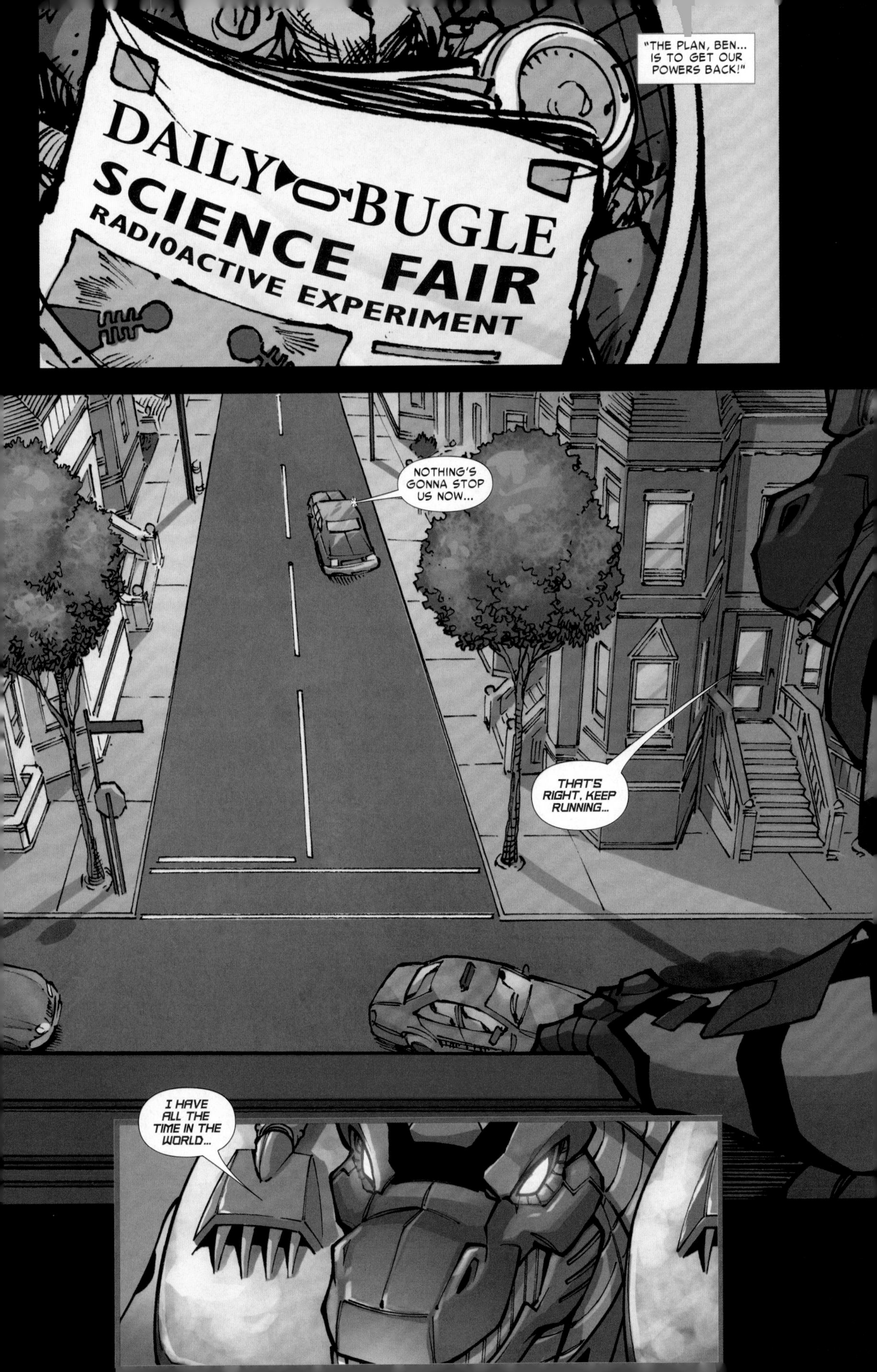
DAILY BUGLE
SCIENCE FAIR
RADIOACTIVE EXPERIMENT
"THE PLAN, BEN... IS TO GET OUR POWERS BACK!"
NOTHING'S GONNA STOP US NOW...
THAT'S RIGHT, KEEP RUNNING...
I HAVE ALL THE TIME IN THE WORLD...

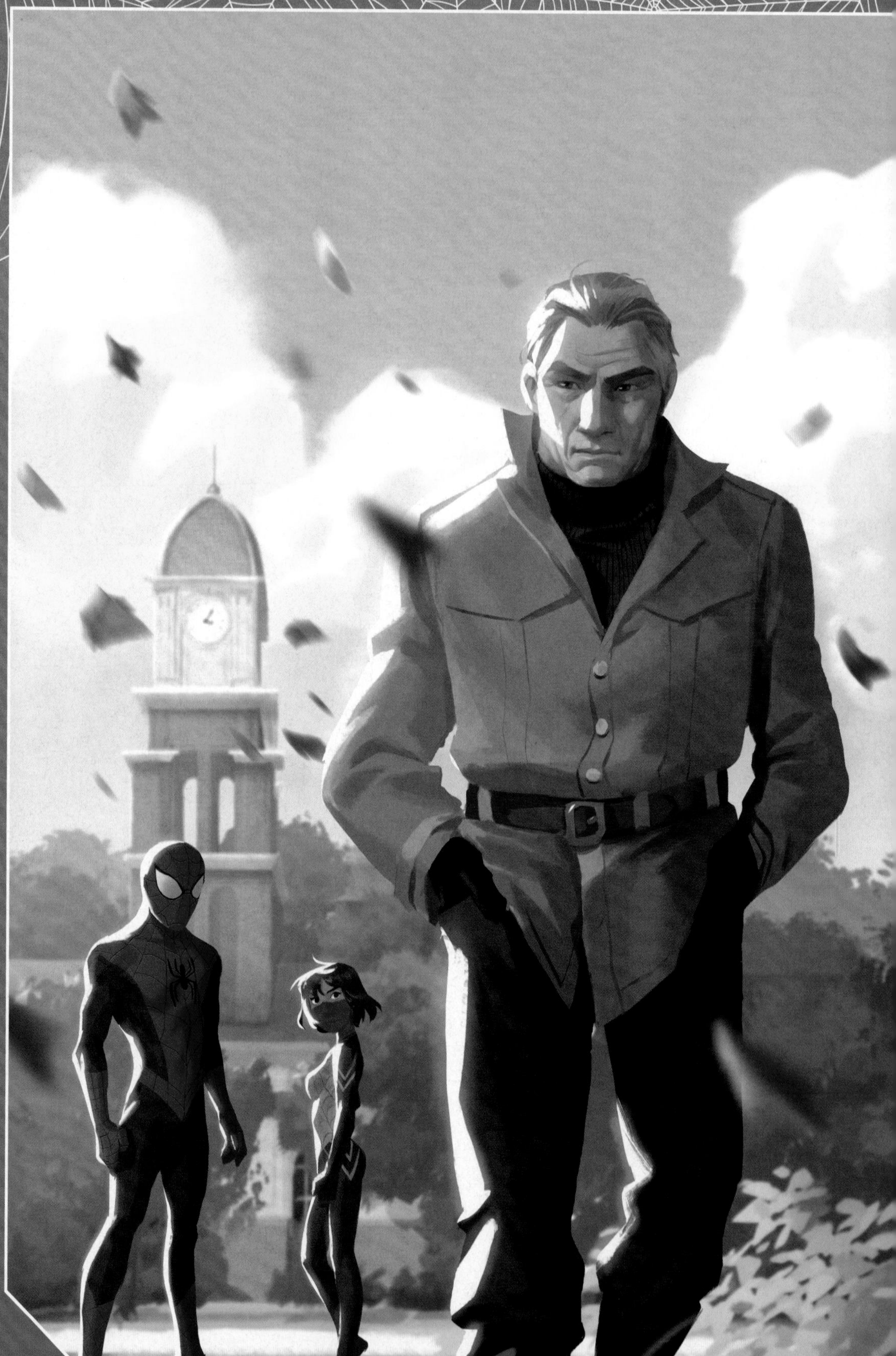

3

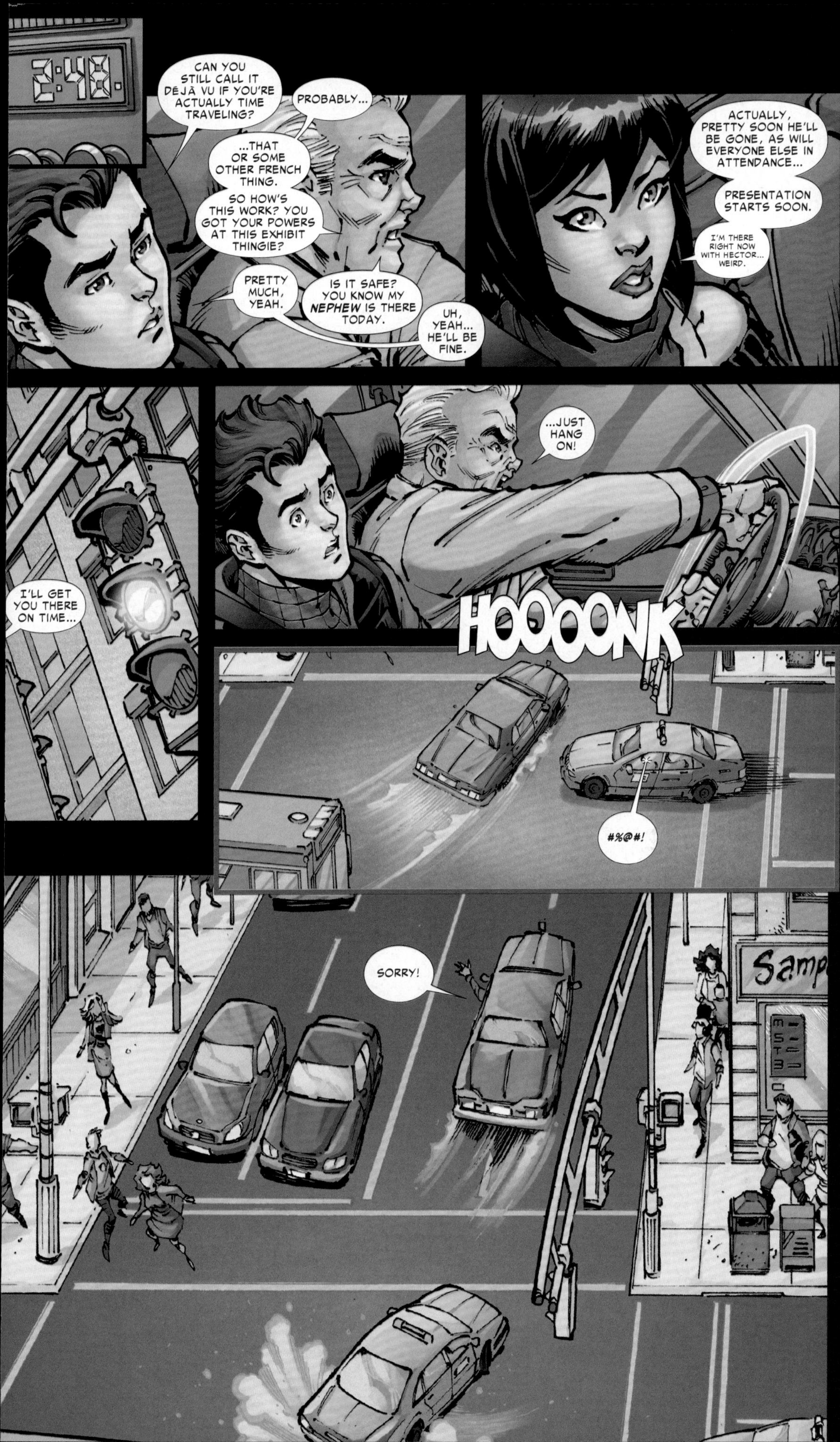
2:48
CAN YOU STILL CALL IT DÉJÀ VU IF YOU'RE ACTUALLY TIME TRAVELING?
PROBABLY...
...THAT OR SOME OTHER FRENCH THING.
SO HOW'S THIS WORK? YOU GOT YOUR POWERS AT THIS EXHIBIT THINGIE?
PRETTY MUCH, YEAH.
IS IT SAFE? YOU KNOW MY NEPHEW IS THERE TODAY.
UH, YEAH... HE'LL BE FINE.
ACTUALLY, PRETTY SOON HE'LL BE GONE, AS WILL EVERYONE ELSE IN ATTENDANCE...
PRESENTATION STARTS SOON.
I'M THERE RIGHT NOW WITH HECTOR... WEIRD.
I'LL GET YOU THERE ON TIME...
...JUST HANG ON!
HOOOONK
#%@#!
SORRY!

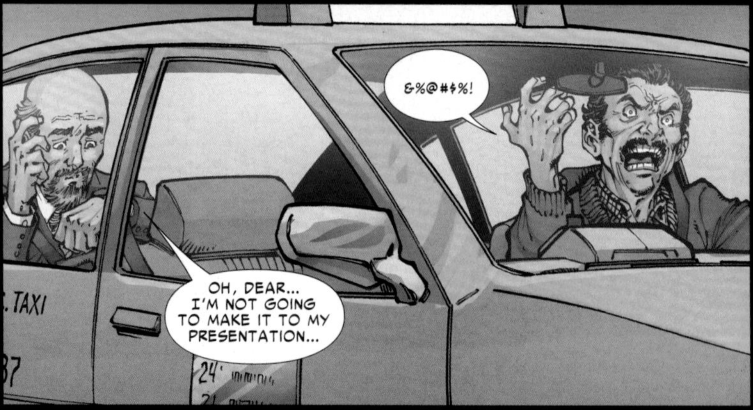
&%@#$%!
OH, DEAR... I'M NOT GOING TO MAKE IT TO MY PRESENTATION...

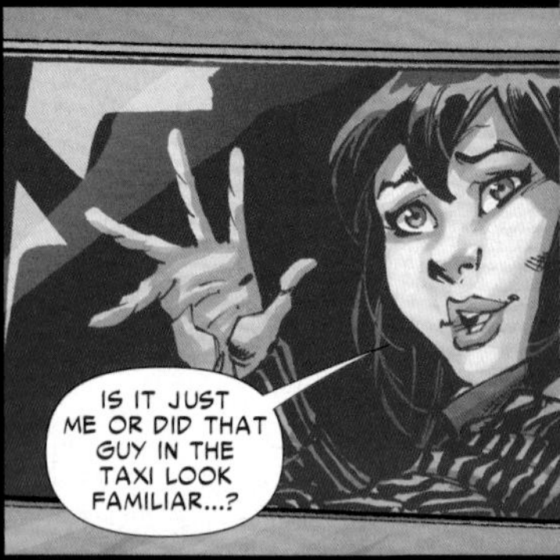
IS IT JUST ME OR DID THAT GUY IN THE TAXI LOOK FAMILIAR...?

THE SPIDER (FLY) EFFECT
CHAPTER FIVE & SIX

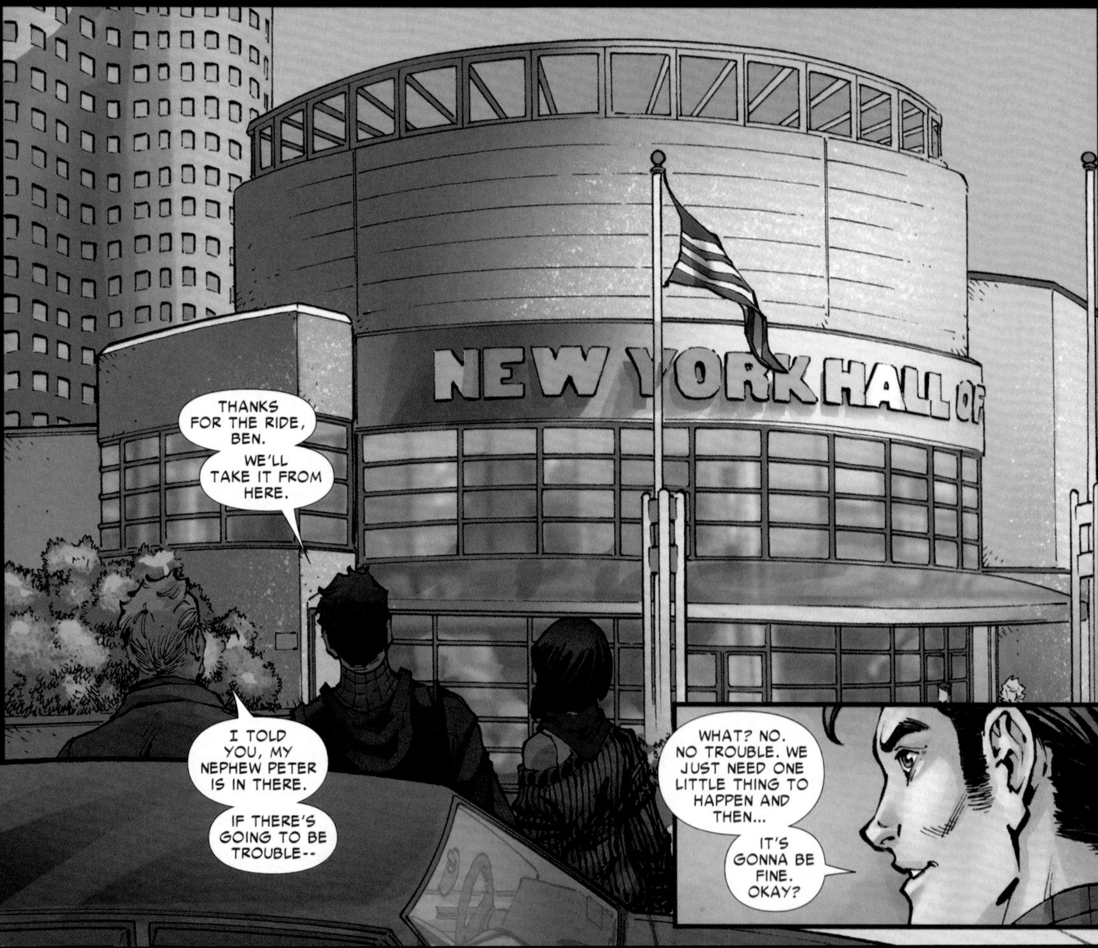
NEW YORK HALL OF
THANKS FOR THE RIDE, BEN.
WE'LL TAKE IT FROM HERE.
I TOLD YOU, MY NEPHEW PETER IS IN THERE.
IF THERE'S GOING TO BE TROUBLE--
WHAT? NO. NO TROUBLE. WE JUST NEED ONE LITTLE THING TO HAPPEN AND THEN...
IT'S GONNA BE FINE. OKAY?

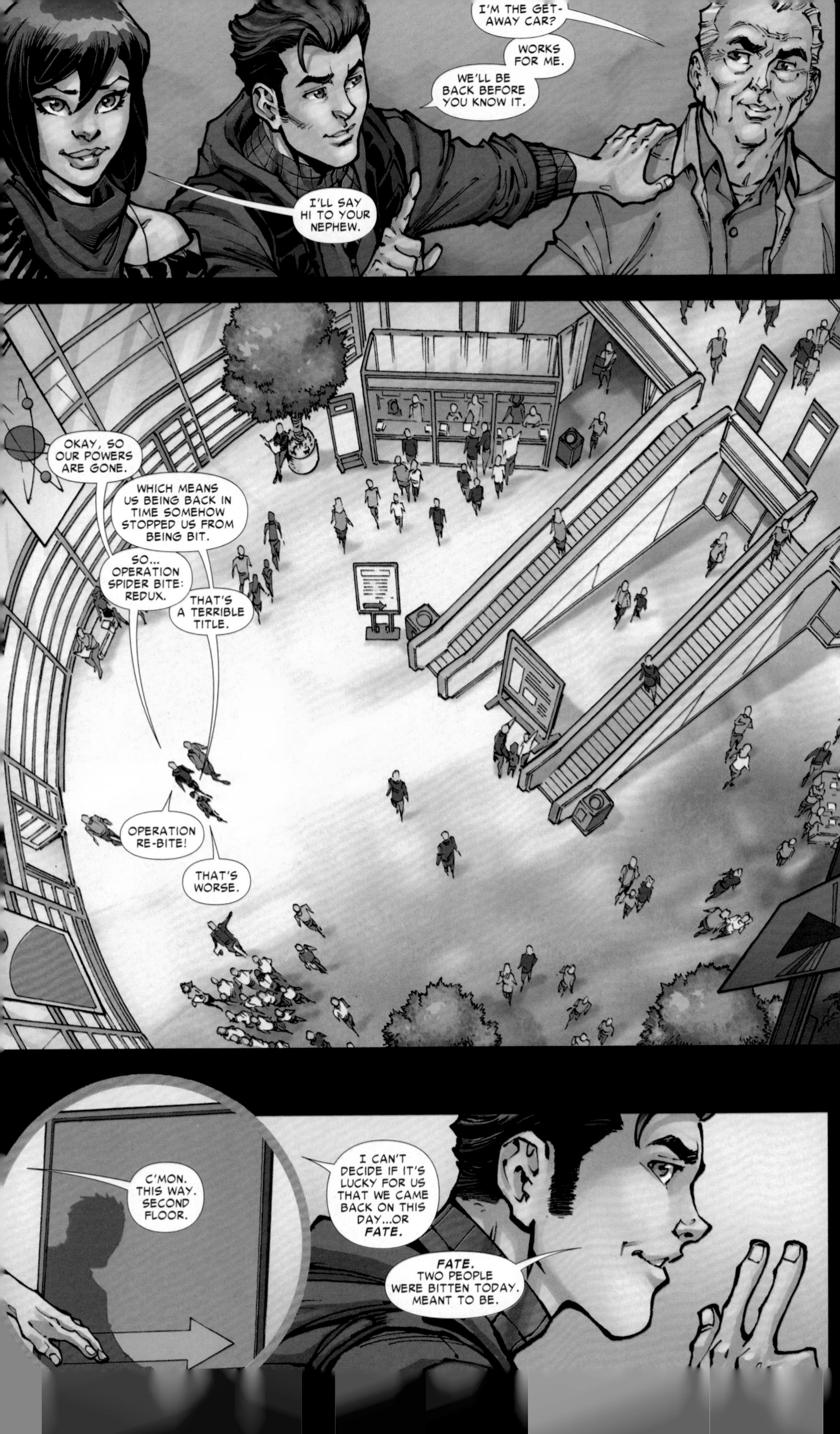
I'M THE GET-AWAY CAR?
WORKS FOR ME.
WE'LL BE BACK BEFORE YOU KNOW IT.
I'LL SAY HI TO YOUR NEPHEW.
OKAY, SO OUR POWERS ARE GONE.
WHICH MEANS US BEING BACK IN TIME SOMEHOW STOPPED US FROM BEING BIT.
SO... OPERATION SPIDER BITE: REDUX.
THAT'S A TERRIBLE TITLE.
OPERATION RE-BITE!
THAT'S WORSE.
C'MON. THIS WAY. SECOND FLOOR.
I CAN'T DECIDE IF IT'S LUCKY FOR US THAT WE CAME BACK ON THIS DAY...OR *FATE.*
FATE. TWO PEOPLE WERE BITTEN TODAY. MEANT TO BE.

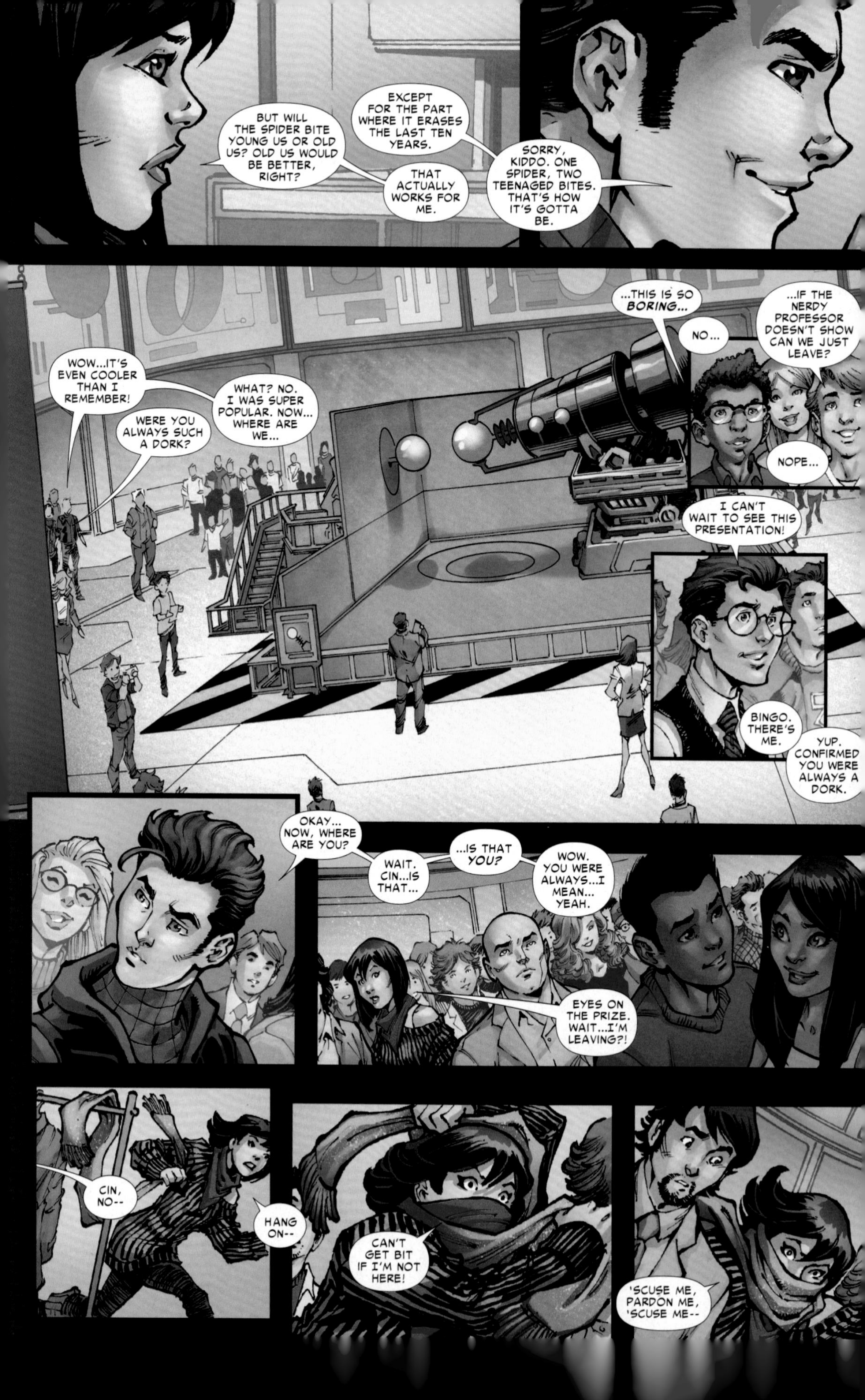

BUT WILL THE SPIDER BITE YOUNG US OR OLD US? OLD US WOULD BE BETTER, RIGHT?
EXCEPT FOR THE PART WHERE IT ERASES THE LAST TEN YEARS.
THAT ACTUALLY WORKS FOR ME.
SORRY, KIDDO. ONE SPIDER, TWO TEENAGED BITES. THAT'S HOW IT'S GOTTA BE.
WOW...IT'S EVEN COOLER THAN I REMEMBER!
WERE YOU ALWAYS SUCH A DORK?
WHAT? NO. I WAS SUPER POPULAR. NOW... WHERE ARE WE...
...THIS IS SO BORING...
NO...
...IF THE NERDY PROFESSOR DOESN'T SHOW CAN WE JUST LEAVE?
NOPE...
I CAN'T WAIT TO SEE THIS PRESENTATION!
BINGO. THERE'S ME.
YUP. CONFIRMED YOU WERE ALWAYS A DORK.
OKAY... NOW, WHERE ARE YOU?
WAIT. CIN...IS THAT...
...IS THAT YOU?
WOW. YOU WERE ALWAYS...I MEAN... YEAH.
EYES ON THE PRIZE. WAIT...I'M LEAVING?!
CIN, NO--
HANG ON--
CAN'T GET BIT IF I'M NOT HERE!
'SCUSE ME, PARDON ME, 'SCUSE ME--

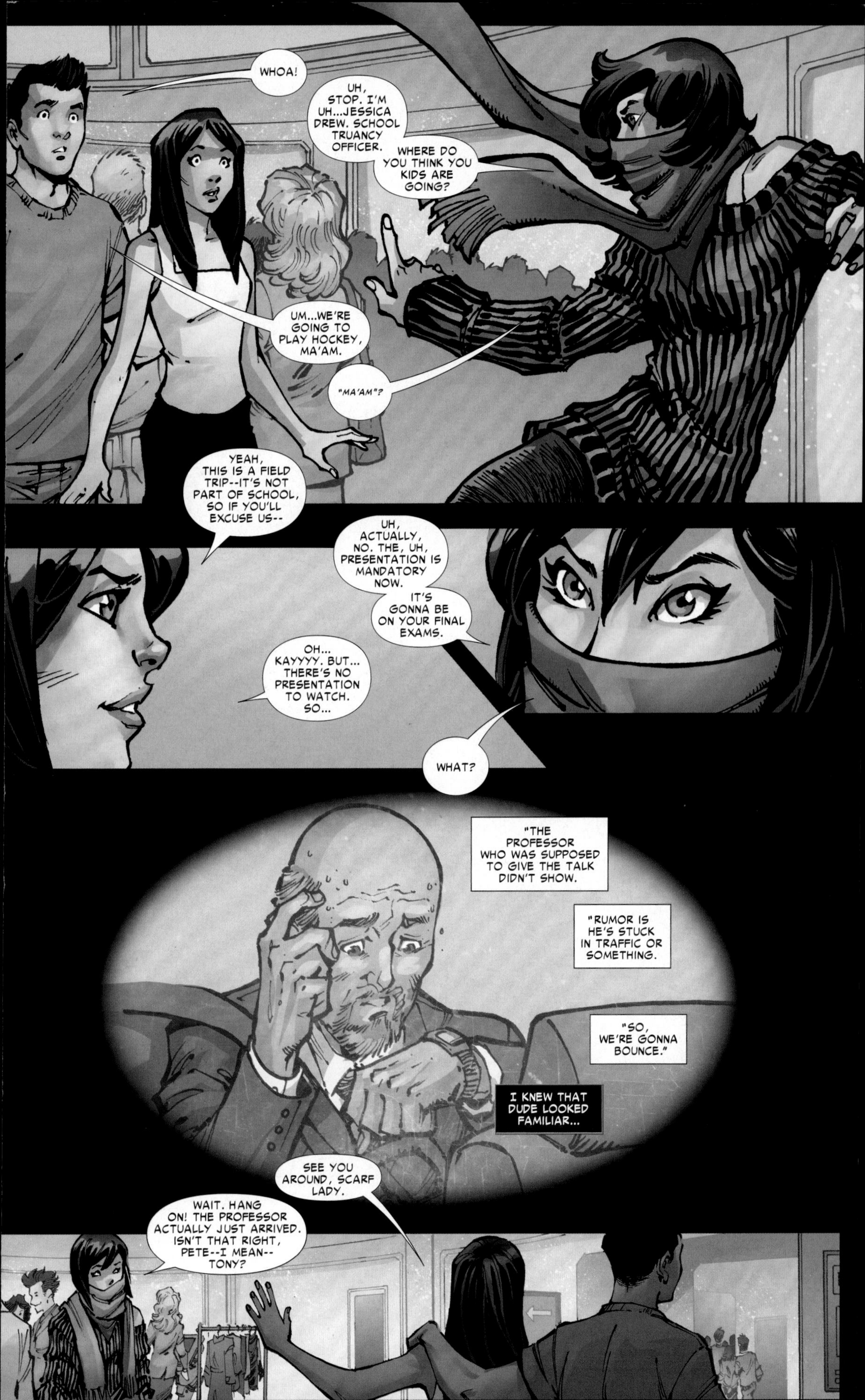
WHOA!
UH, STOP. I'M UH...JESSICA DREW. SCHOOL TRUANCY OFFICER.
WHERE DO YOU THINK YOU KIDS ARE GOING?
UM...WE'RE GOING TO PLAY HOCKEY, MA'AM.
"MA'AM"?
YEAH, THIS IS A FIELD TRIP--IT'S NOT PART OF SCHOOL, SO IF YOU'LL EXCUSE US--
UH, ACTUALLY, NO. THE, UH, PRESENTATION IS MANDATORY NOW.
IT'S GONNA BE ON YOUR FINAL EXAMS.
OH... KAYYYY. BUT... THERE'S NO PRESENTATION TO WATCH. SO...
WHAT?
"THE PROFESSOR WHO WAS SUPPOSED TO GIVE THE TALK DIDN'T SHOW.
"RUMOR IS HE'S STUCK IN TRAFFIC OR SOMETHING.
"SO, WE'RE GONNA BOUNCE."
I KNEW THAT DUDE LOOKED FAMILIAR...
SEE YOU AROUND, SCARF LADY.
WAIT. HANG ON! THE PROFESSOR ACTUALLY JUST ARRIVED. ISN'T THAT RIGHT, PETE--I MEAN--TONY?

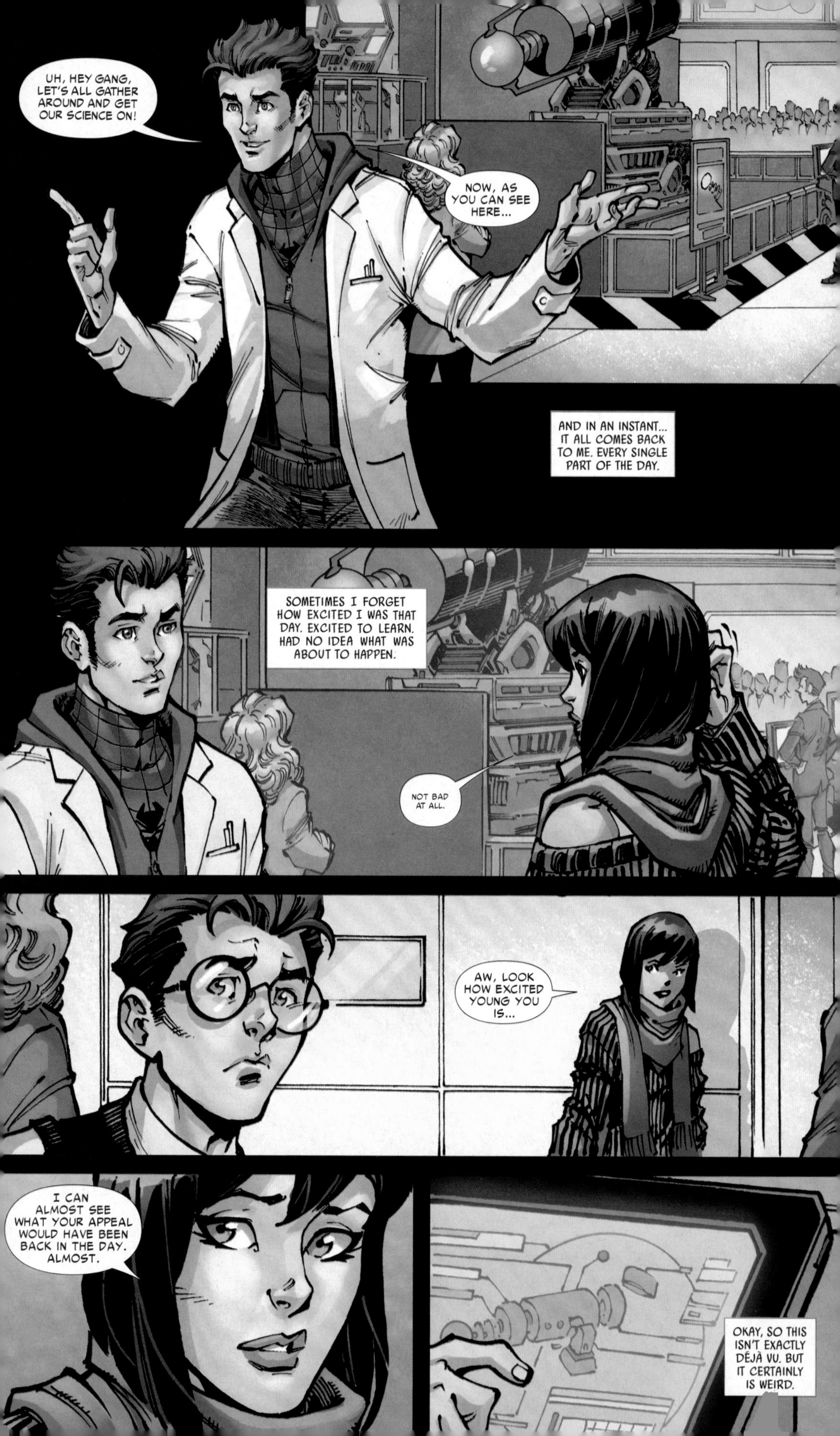
UH, HEY GANG, LET'S ALL GATHER AROUND AND GET OUR SCIENCE ON!
NOW, AS YOU CAN SEE HERE...
AND IN AN INSTANT... IT ALL COMES BACK TO ME. EVERY SINGLE PART OF THE DAY.
SOMETIMES I FORGET HOW EXCITED I WAS THAT DAY. EXCITED TO LEARN. HAD NO IDEA WHAT WAS ABOUT TO HAPPEN.
NOT BAD AT ALL.
AW, LOOK HOW EXCITED YOUNG YOU IS...
I CAN ALMOST SEE WHAT YOUR APPEAL WOULD HAVE BEEN BACK IN THE DAY. ALMOST.
OKAY, SO THIS ISN'T EXACTLY DÉJÀ VU. BUT IT CERTAINLY IS WEIRD.

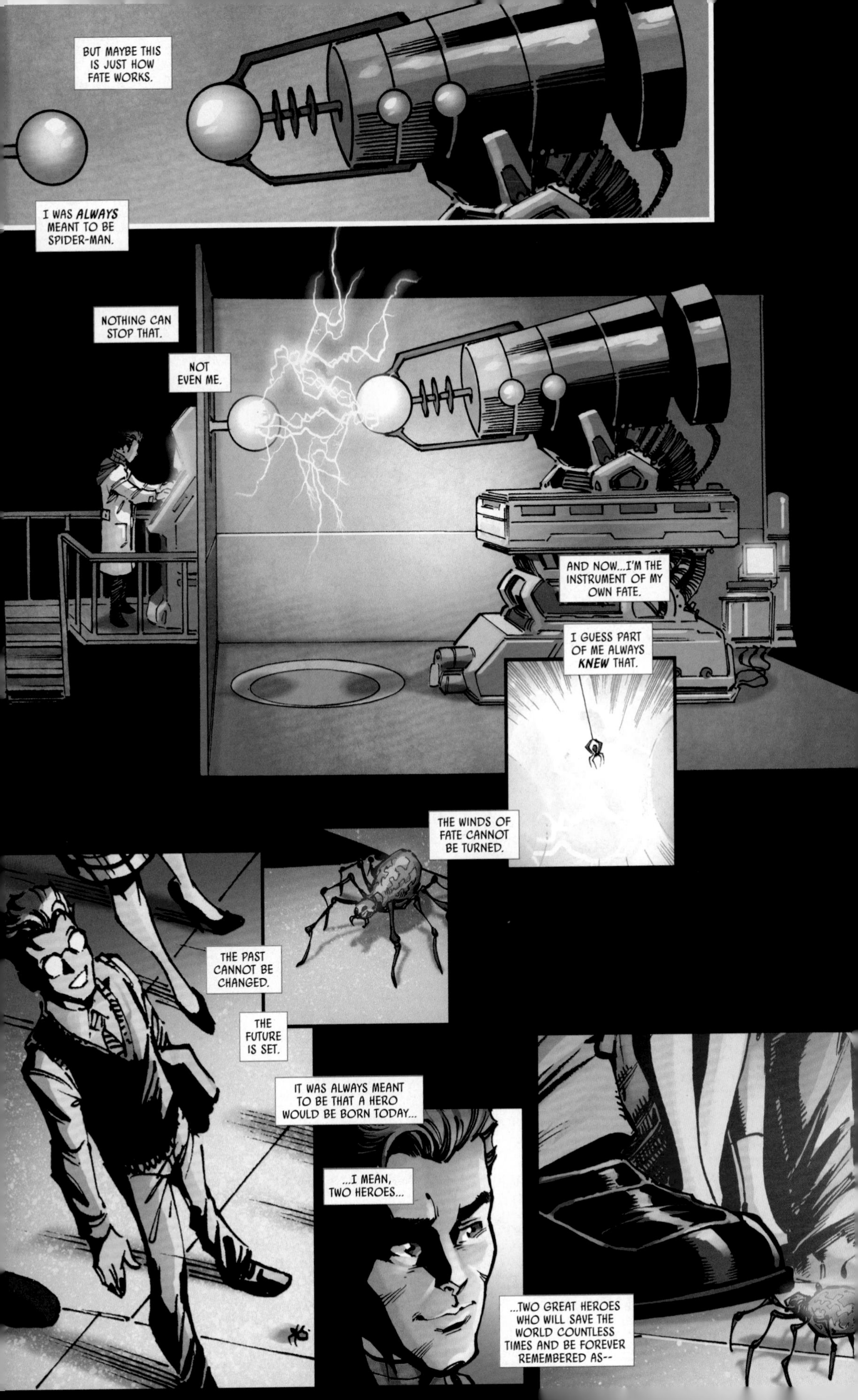
BUT MAYBE THIS IS JUST HOW FATE WORKS.
I WAS ALWAYS MEANT TO BE SPIDER-MAN.
NOTHING CAN STOP THAT.
NOT EVEN ME.
AND NOW...I'M THE INSTRUMENT OF MY OWN FATE.
I GUESS PART OF ME ALWAYS KNEW THAT.
THE WINDS OF FATE CANNOT BE TURNED.
THE PAST CANNOT BE CHANGED.
THE FUTURE IS SET.
IT WAS ALWAYS MEANT TO BE THAT A HERO WOULD BE BORN TODAY...
...I MEAN, TWO HEROES...
...TWO GREAT HEROES WHO WILL SAVE THE WORLD COUNTLESS TIMES AND BE FOREVER REMEMBERED AS--

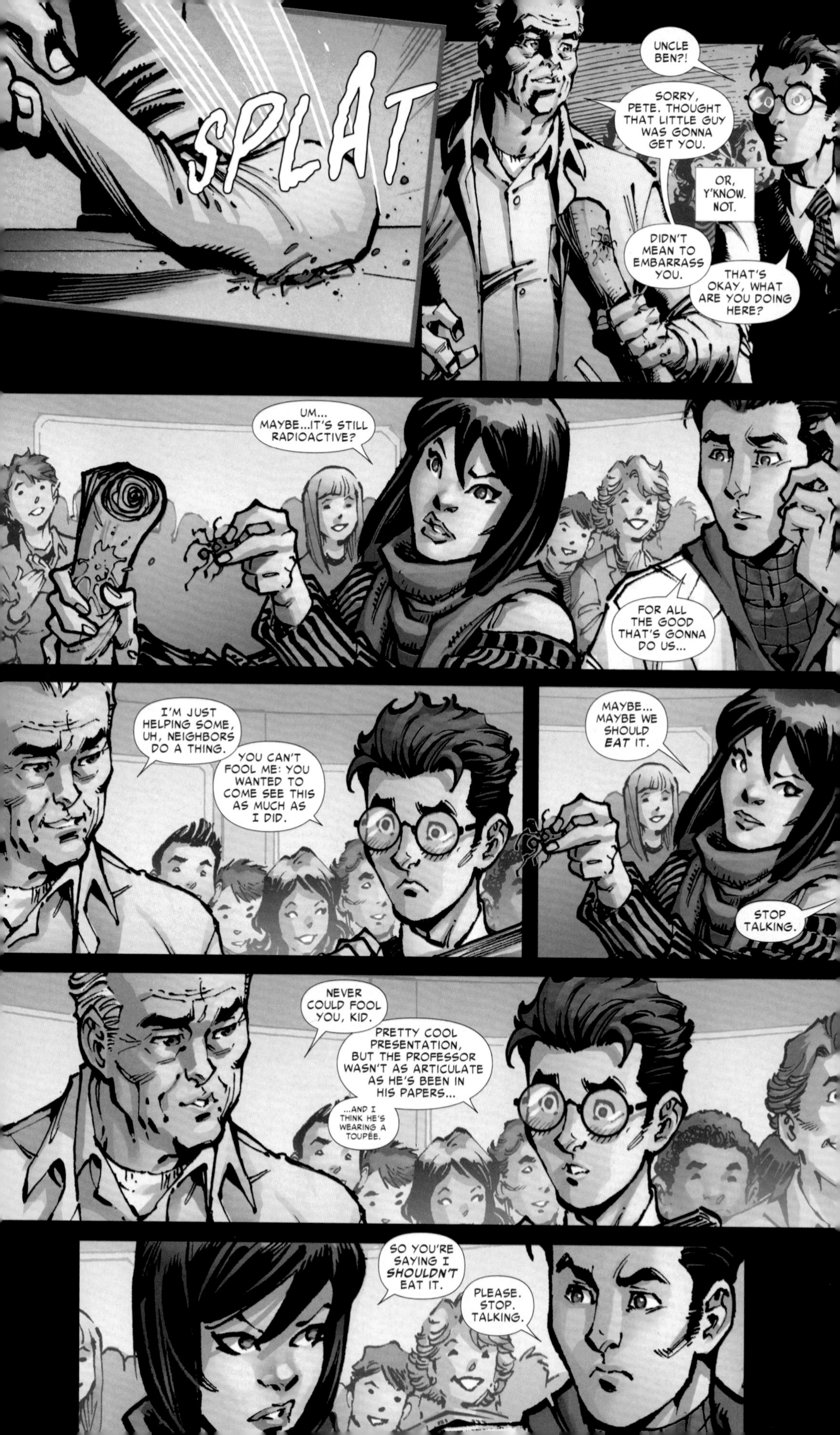
SPLAT
UNCLE BEN?!
SORRY, PETE. THOUGHT THAT LITTLE GUY WAS GONNA GET YOU.
OR, Y'KNOW. NOT.
DIDN'T MEAN TO EMBARRASS YOU.
THAT'S OKAY, WHAT ARE YOU DOING HERE?
UM... MAYBE...IT'S STILL RADIOACTIVE?
FOR ALL THE GOOD THAT'S GONNA DO US...
I'M JUST HELPING SOME, UH, NEIGHBORS DO A THING.
YOU CAN'T FOOL ME: YOU WANTED TO COME SEE THIS AS MUCH AS I DID.
MAYBE... MAYBE WE SHOULD EAT IT.
STOP TALKING.
NEVER COULD FOOL YOU, KID.
PRETTY COOL PRESENTATION, BUT THE PROFESSOR WASN'T AS ARTICULATE AS HE'S BEEN IN HIS PAPERS...
...AND I THINK HE'S WEARING A TOUPÉE.
SO YOU'RE SAYING I SHOULDN'T EAT IT.
PLEASE. STOP. TALKING.

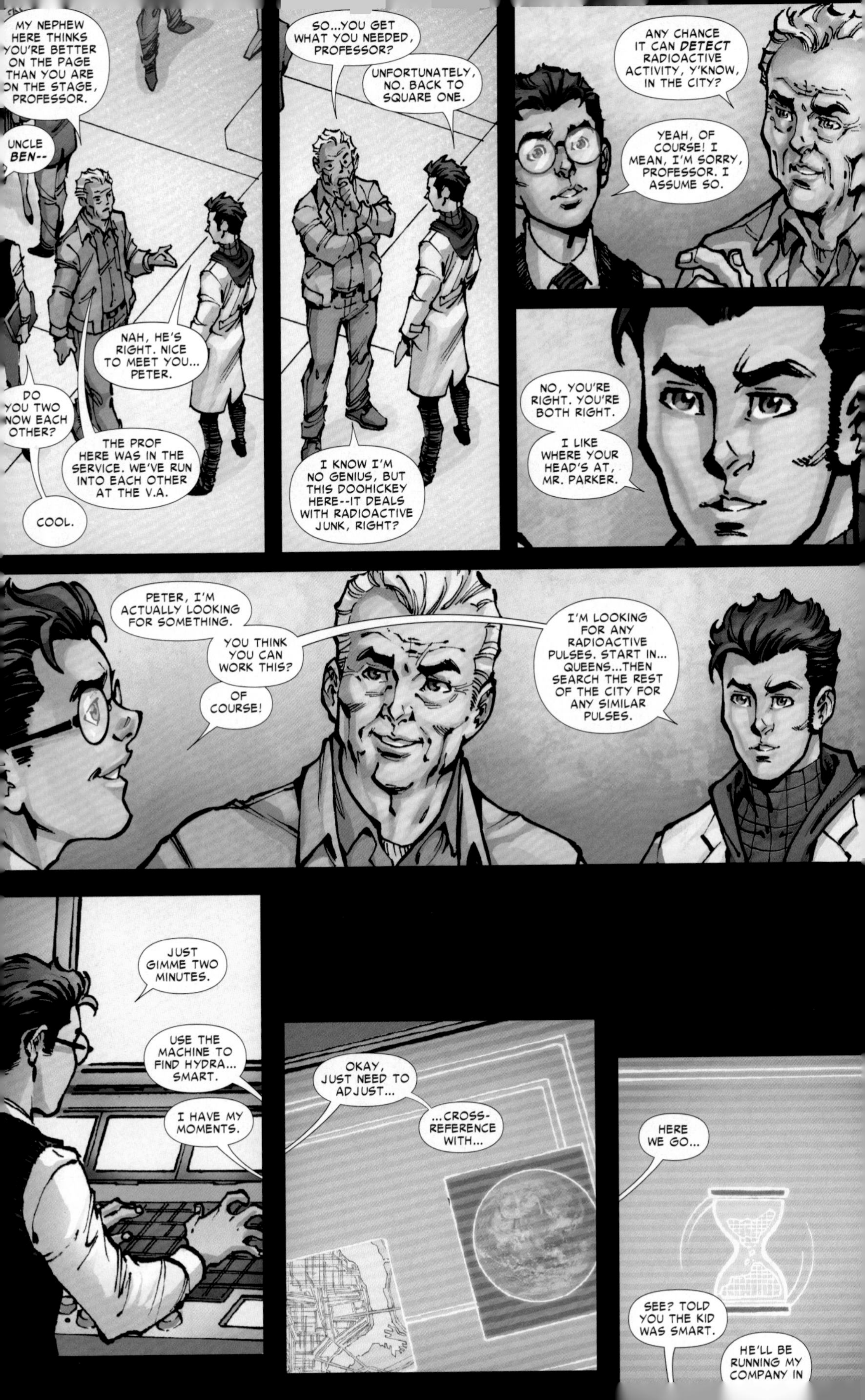
MY NEPHEW HERE THINKS YOU'RE BETTER ON THE PAGE THAN YOU ARE ON THE STAGE, PROFESSOR.
UNCLE BEN--
NAH, HE'S RIGHT. NICE TO MEET YOU... PETER.
DO YOU TWO KNOW EACH OTHER?
THE PROF HERE WAS IN THE SERVICE. WE'VE RUN INTO EACH OTHER AT THE V.A.
COOL.
SO...YOU GET WHAT YOU NEEDED, PROFESSOR?
UNFORTUNATELY, NO. BACK TO SQUARE ONE.
I KNOW I'M NO GENIUS, BUT THIS DOOHICKEY HERE--IT DEALS WITH RADIOACTIVE JUNK, RIGHT?
ANY CHANCE IT CAN DETECT RADIOACTIVE ACTIVITY, Y'KNOW, IN THE CITY?
YEAH, OF COURSE! I MEAN, I'M SORRY, PROFESSOR. I ASSUME SO.
NO, YOU'RE RIGHT. YOU'RE BOTH RIGHT.
I LIKE WHERE YOUR HEAD'S AT, MR. PARKER.
PETER, I'M ACTUALLY LOOKING FOR SOMETHING.
YOU THINK YOU CAN WORK THIS?
OF COURSE!
I'M LOOKING FOR ANY RADIOACTIVE PULSES. START IN... QUEENS...THEN SEARCH THE REST OF THE CITY FOR ANY SIMILAR PULSES.
JUST GIMME TWO MINUTES.
USE THE MACHINE TO FIND HYDRA... SMART.
I HAVE MY MOMENTS.
OKAY, JUST NEED TO ADJUST...
...CROSS-REFERENCE WITH...
HERE WE GO...
SEE? TOLD YOU THE KID WAS SMART.
HE'LL BE RUNNING MY COMPANY IN

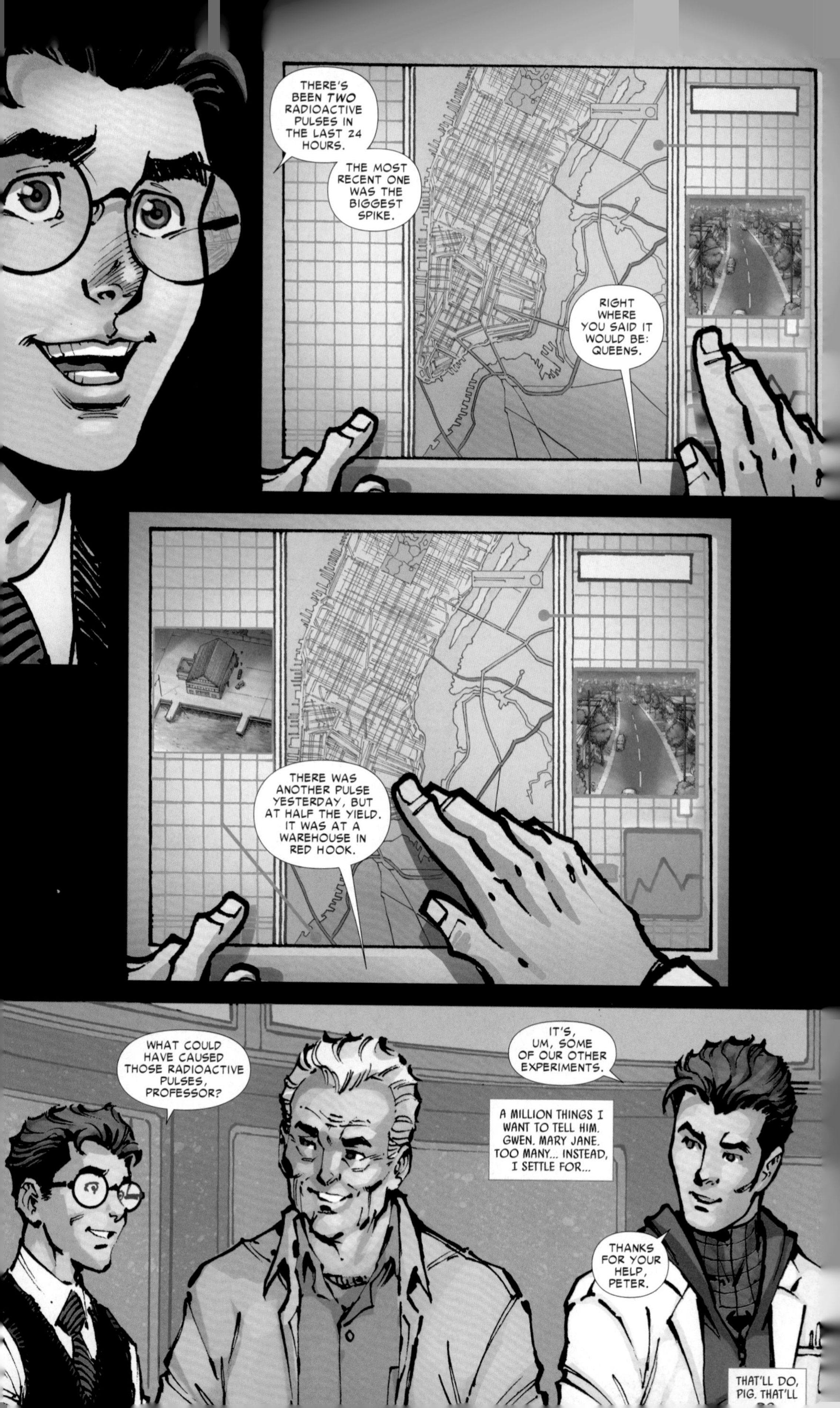
THERE'S BEEN TWO RADIOACTIVE PULSES IN THE LAST 24 HOURS.
THE MOST RECENT ONE WAS THE BIGGEST SPIKE.
RIGHT WHERE YOU SAID IT WOULD BE: QUEENS.
THERE WAS ANOTHER PULSE YESTERDAY, BUT AT HALF THE YIELD. IT WAS AT A WAREHOUSE IN RED HOOK.
WHAT COULD HAVE CAUSED THOSE RADIOACTIVE PULSES, PROFESSOR?
IT'S, UM, SOME OF OUR OTHER EXPERIMENTS.
A MILLION THINGS I WANT TO TELL HIM. GWEN. MARY JANE. TOO MANY... INSTEAD, I SETTLE FOR...
THANKS FOR YOUR HELP, PETER.
THAT'LL DO, PIG. THAT'LL

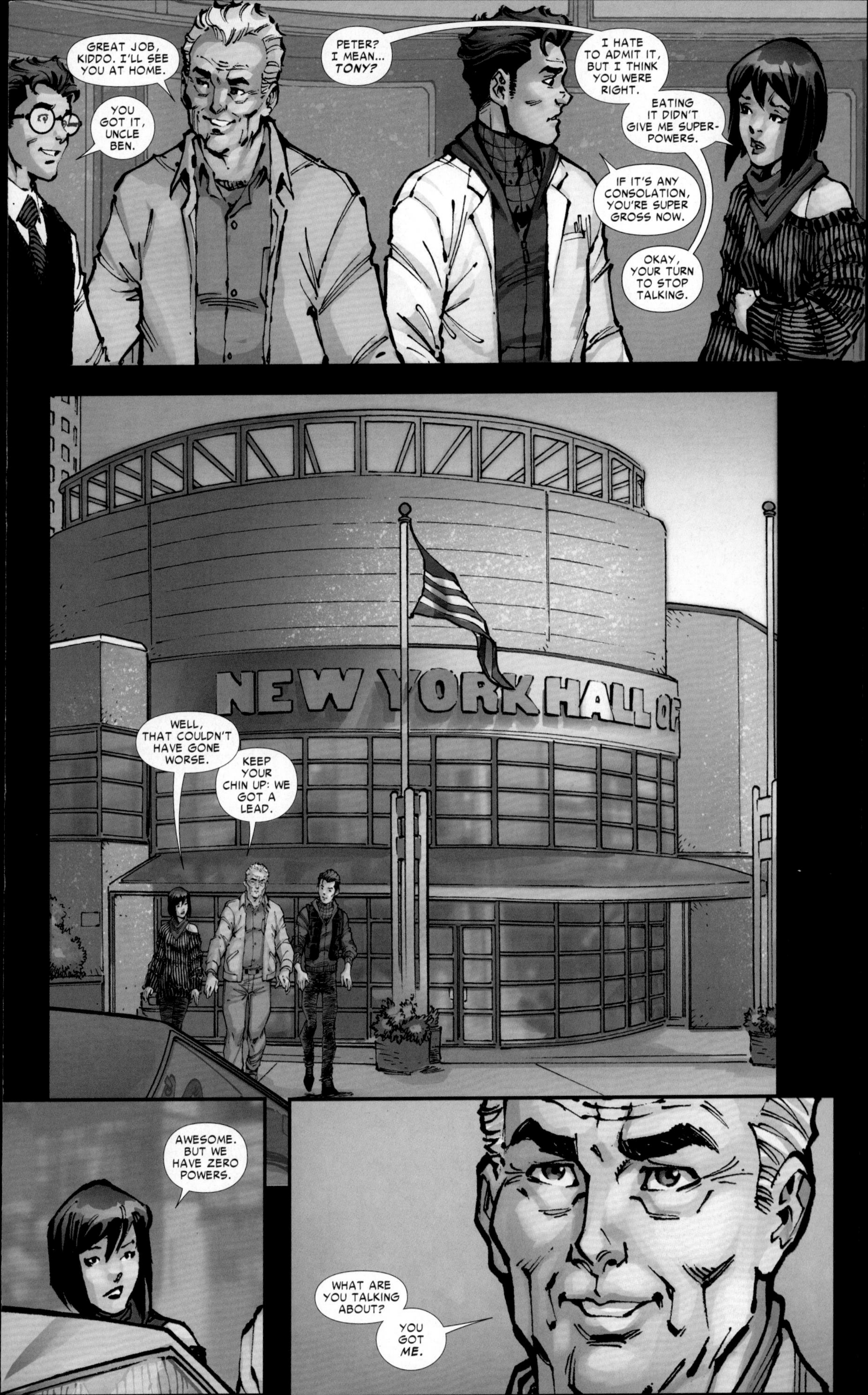
GREAT JOB, KIDDO. I'LL SEE YOU AT HOME.
YOU GOT IT, UNCLE BEN.
PETER? I MEAN... *TONY?*
I HATE TO ADMIT IT, BUT I THINK YOU WERE RIGHT.
EATING IT DIDN'T GIVE ME SUPER-POWERS.
IF IT'S ANY CONSOLATION, YOU'RE SUPER GROSS NOW.
OKAY, YOUR TURN TO STOP TALKING.
NEW YORK HALL OF
WELL, THAT COULDN'T HAVE GONE WORSE.
KEEP YOUR CHIN UP: WE GOT A LEAD.
AWESOME. BUT WE HAVE ZERO POWERS.
WHAT ARE YOU TALKING ABOUT?
YOU GOT *ME.*

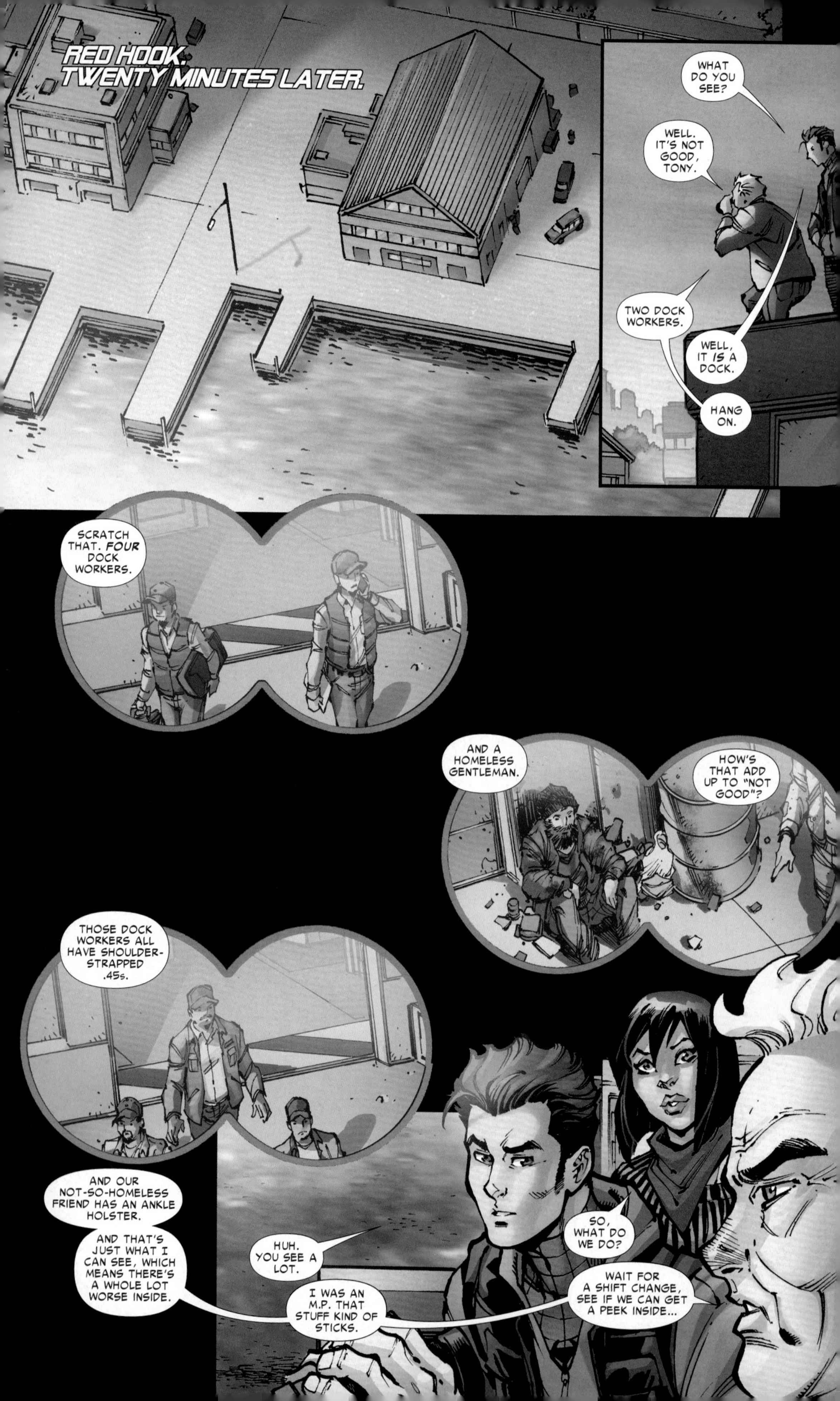
RED HOOK. TWENTY MINUTES LATER.
WHAT DO YOU SEE?
WELL. IT'S NOT GOOD, TONY.
TWO DOCK WORKERS.
WELL, IT *IS* A DOCK.
HANG ON.
SCRATCH THAT. *FOUR* DOCK WORKERS.
AND A HOMELESS GENTLEMAN.
HOW'S THAT ADD UP TO "NOT GOOD"?
THOSE DOCK WORKERS ALL HAVE SHOULDER-STRAPPED .45s.
AND OUR NOT-SO-HOMELESS FRIEND HAS AN ANKLE HOLSTER.
AND THAT'S JUST WHAT I CAN SEE, WHICH MEANS THERE'S A WHOLE LOT WORSE INSIDE.
HUH. YOU SEE A LOT.
I WAS AN M.P. THAT STUFF KIND OF STICKS.
SO, WHAT DO WE DO?
WAIT FOR A SHIFT CHANGE, SEE IF WE CAN GET A PEEK INSIDE...

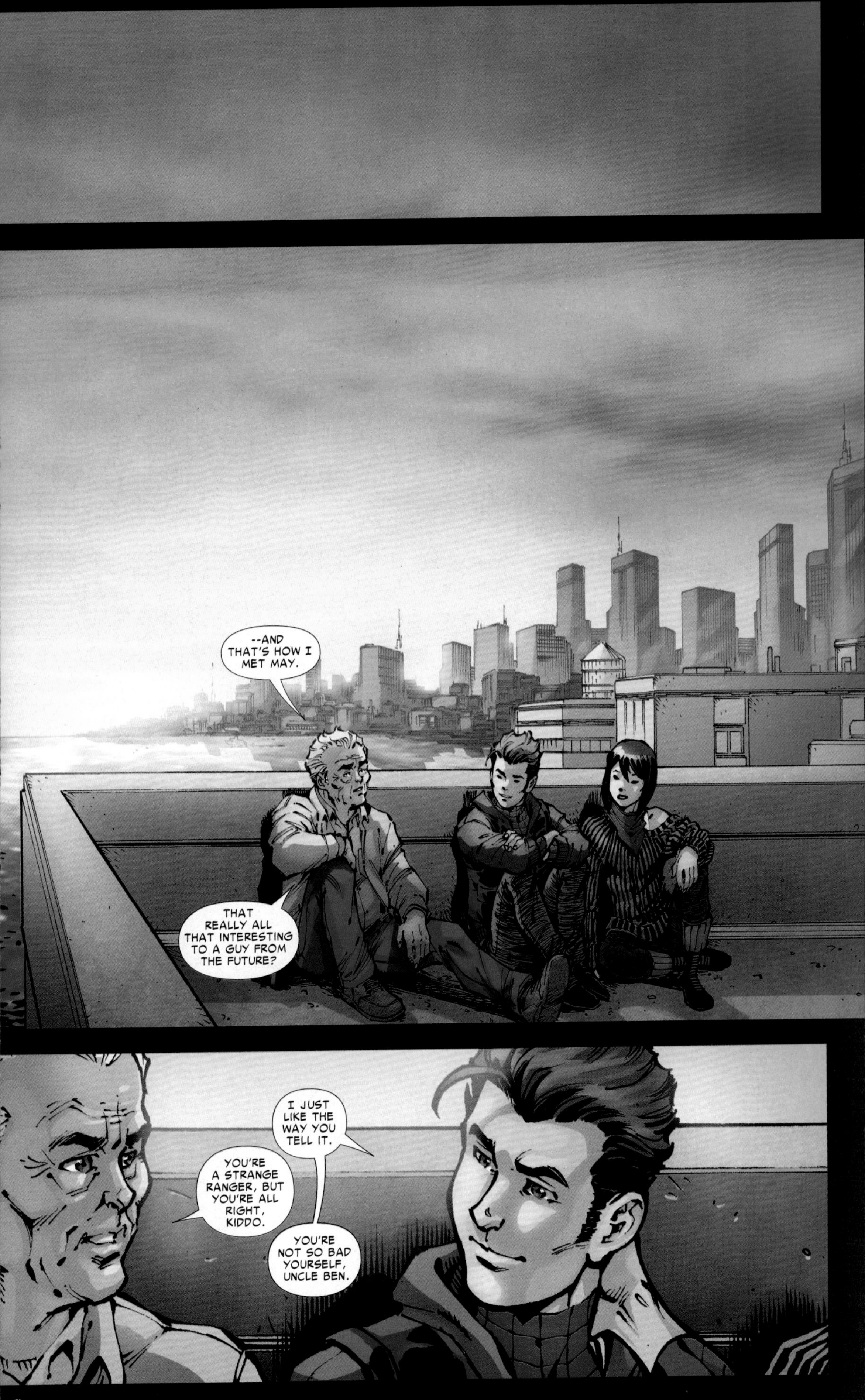
--AND THAT'S HOW I MET MAY.
THAT REALLY ALL THAT INTERESTING TO A GUY FROM THE FUTURE?
I JUST LIKE THE WAY YOU TELL IT.
YOU'RE A STRANGE RANGER, BUT YOU'RE ALL RIGHT, KIDDO.
YOU'RE NOT SO BAD YOURSELF, UNCLE BEN.

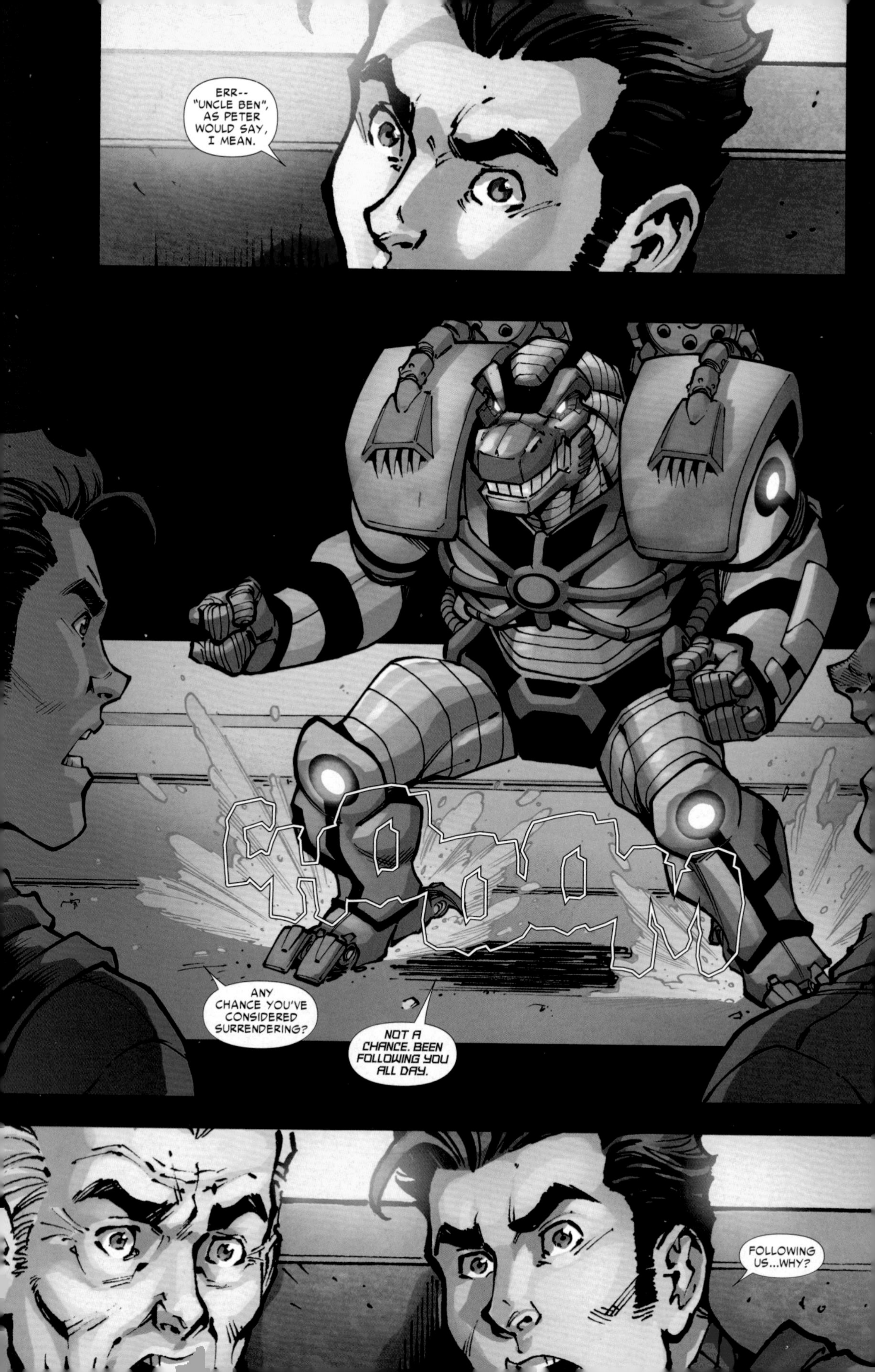
ERR-- "UNCLE BEN", AS PETER WOULD SAY, I MEAN.
CHOOOOM
ANY CHANCE YOU'VE CONSIDERED SURRENDERING?
NOT A CHANCE. BEEN FOLLOWING YOU ALL DAY.
FOLLOWING US...WHY?

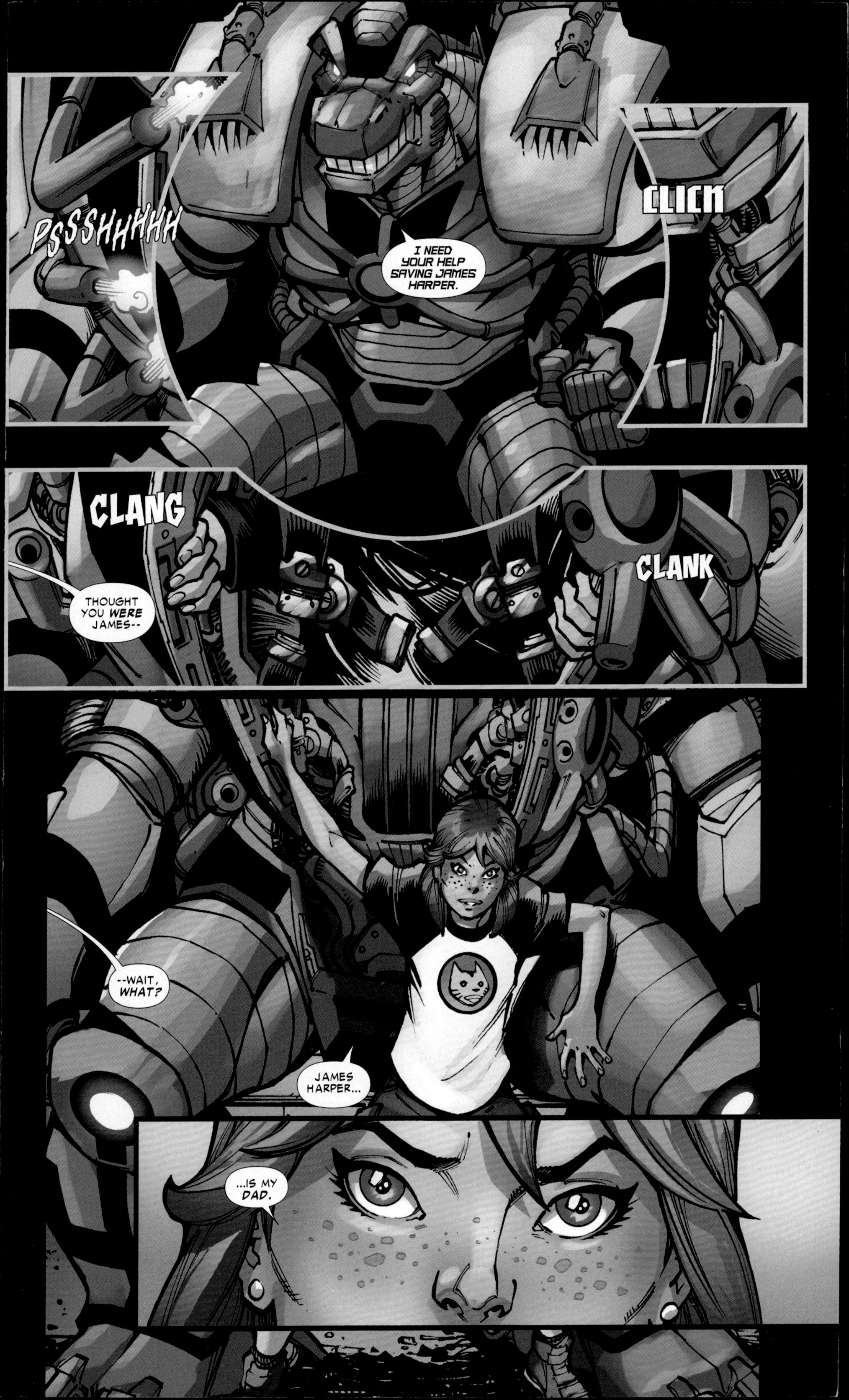
PSSSHHHHH
CLICK
I NEED YOUR HELP SAVING JAMES HARPER.
CLANG
CLANK
THOUGHT YOU WERE JAMES--
--WAIT, WHAT?
JAMES HARPER...
...IS MY DAD.

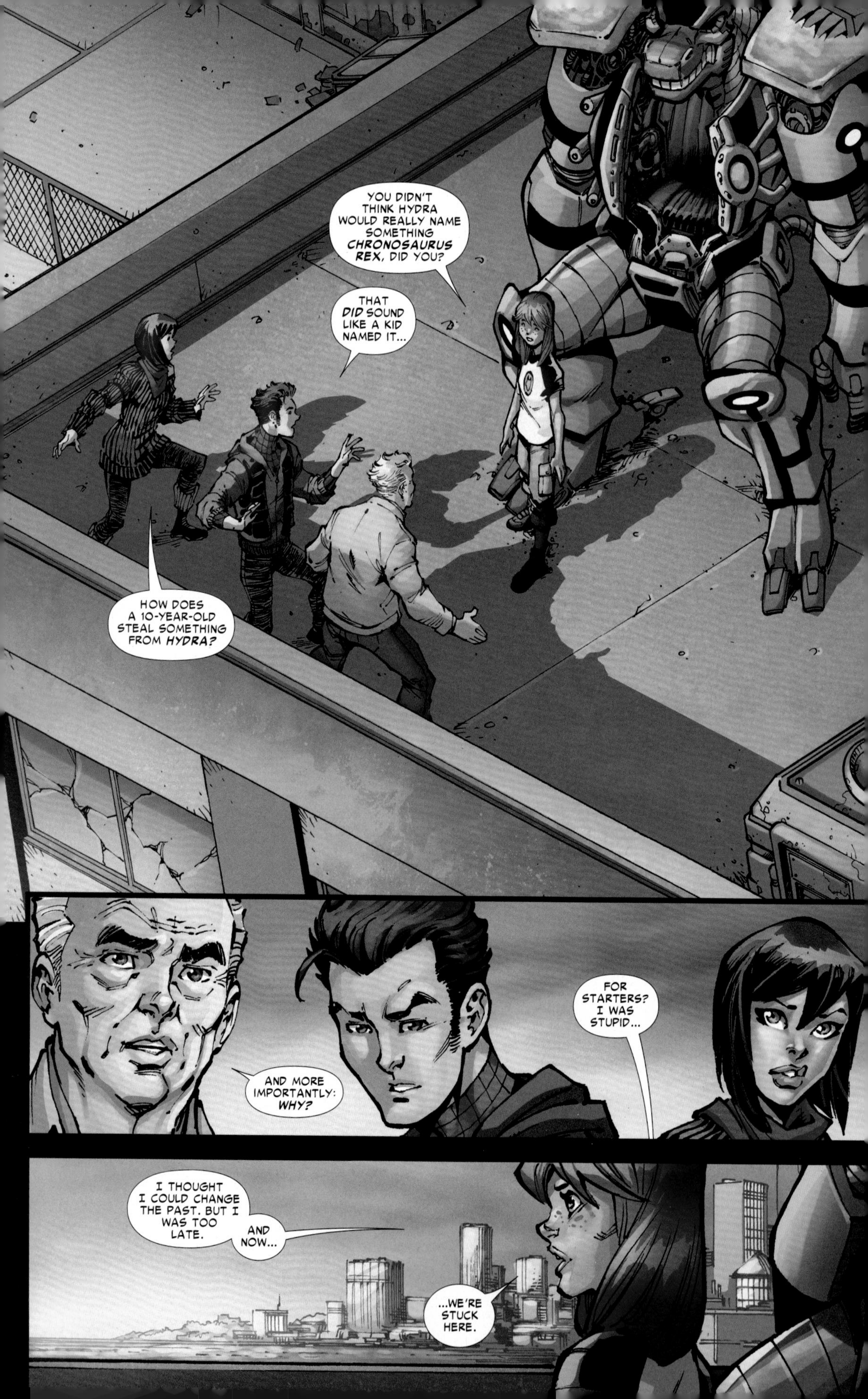
YOU DIDN'T THINK HYDRA WOULD REALLY NAME SOMETHING CHRONOSAURUS REX, DID YOU?
THAT DID SOUND LIKE A KID NAMED IT...
HOW DOES A 10-YEAR-OLD STEAL SOMETHING FROM HYDRA?
AND MORE IMPORTANTLY: WHY?
FOR STARTERS? I WAS STUPID...
I THOUGHT I COULD CHANGE THE PAST. BUT I WAS TOO LATE.
AND NOW...
...WE'RE STUCK HERE.

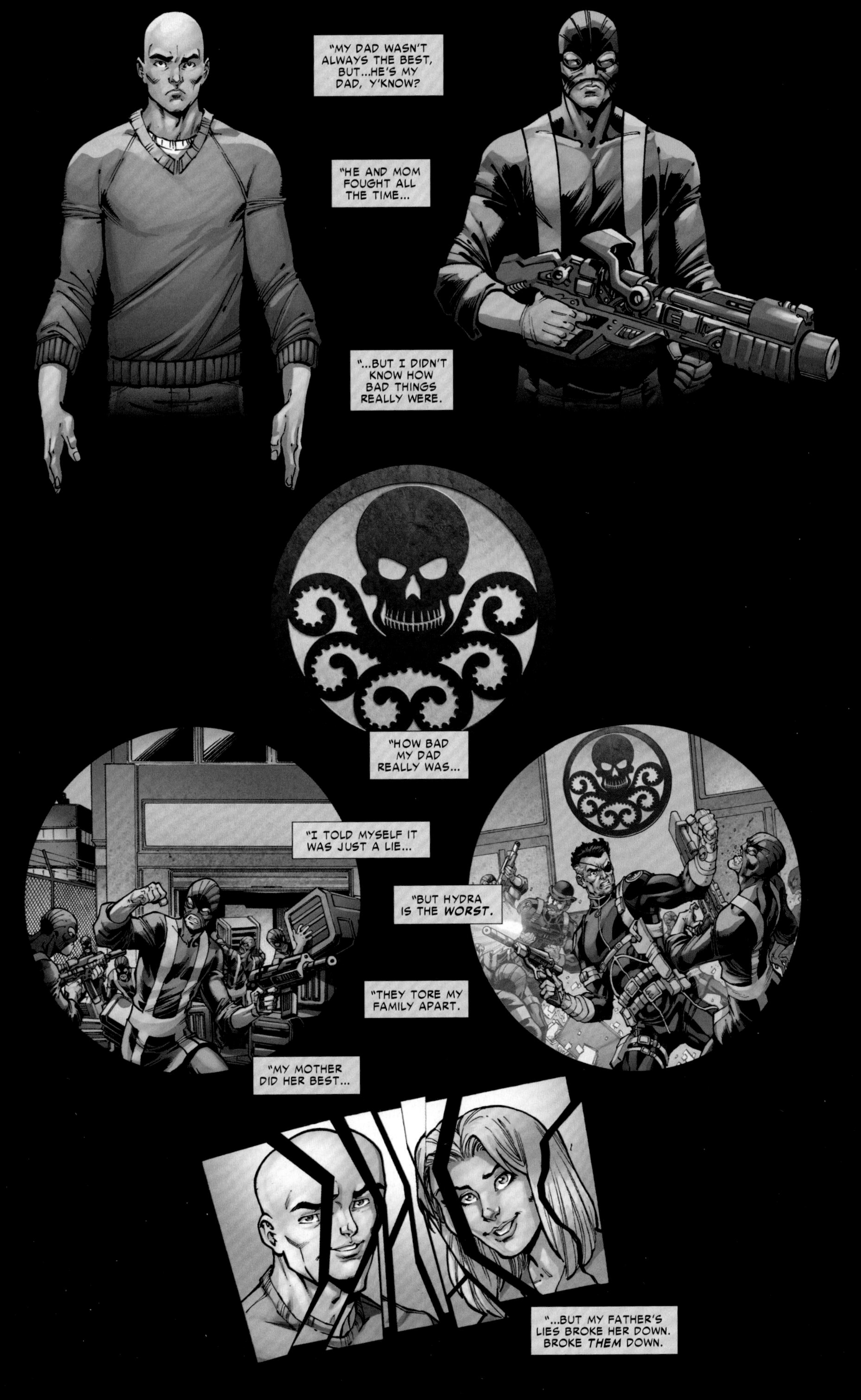
"MY DAD WASN'T ALWAYS THE BEST, BUT...HE'S MY DAD, Y'KNOW?
"HE AND MOM FOUGHT ALL THE TIME...
"...BUT I DIDN'T KNOW HOW BAD THINGS REALLY WERE.
"HOW BAD MY DAD REALLY WAS...
"I TOLD MYSELF IT WAS JUST A LIE...
"BUT HYDRA IS THE *WORST*.
"THEY TORE MY FAMILY APART.
"MY MOTHER DID HER BEST...
"...BUT MY FATHER'S LIES BROKE HER DOWN. BROKE *THEM* DOWN.

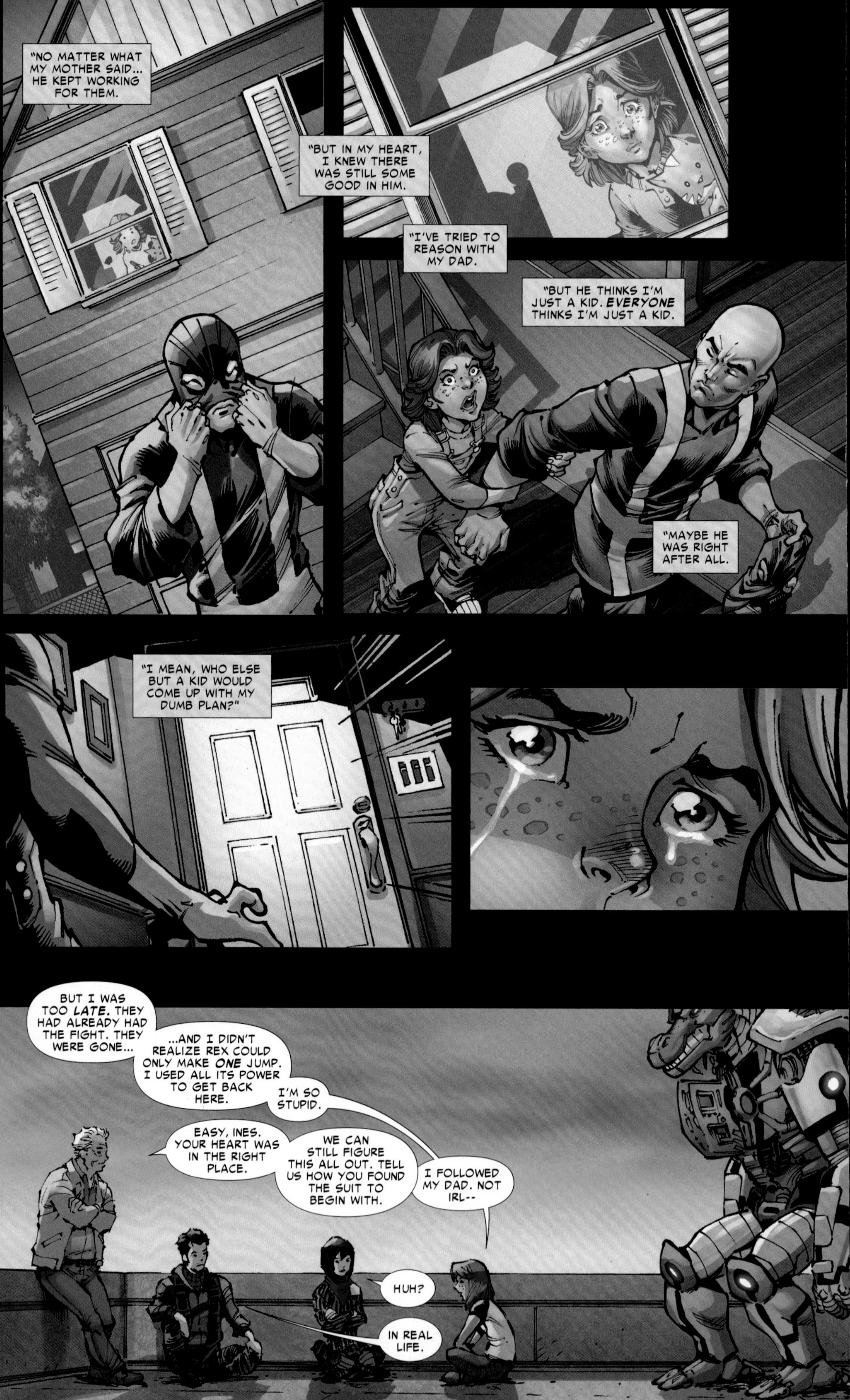
"NO MATTER WHAT MY MOTHER SAID... HE KEPT WORKING FOR THEM.
"BUT IN MY HEART, I KNEW THERE WAS STILL SOME GOOD IN HIM.
"I'VE TRIED TO REASON WITH MY DAD.
"BUT HE THINKS I'M JUST A KID. EVERYONE THINKS I'M JUST A KID.
"MAYBE HE WAS RIGHT AFTER ALL.
"I MEAN, WHO ELSE BUT A KID WOULD COME UP WITH MY DUMB PLAN?"
BUT I WAS TOO LATE. THEY HAD ALREADY HAD THE FIGHT. THEY WERE GONE...
...AND I DIDN'T REALIZE REX COULD ONLY MAKE ONE JUMP. I USED ALL ITS POWER TO GET BACK HERE.
I'M SO STUPID.
EASY, INES. YOUR HEART WAS IN THE RIGHT PLACE.
WE CAN STILL FIGURE THIS ALL OUT. TELL US HOW YOU FOUND THE SUIT TO BEGIN WITH.
I FOLLOWED MY DAD. NOT IRL--
HUH?
IN REAL LIFE.

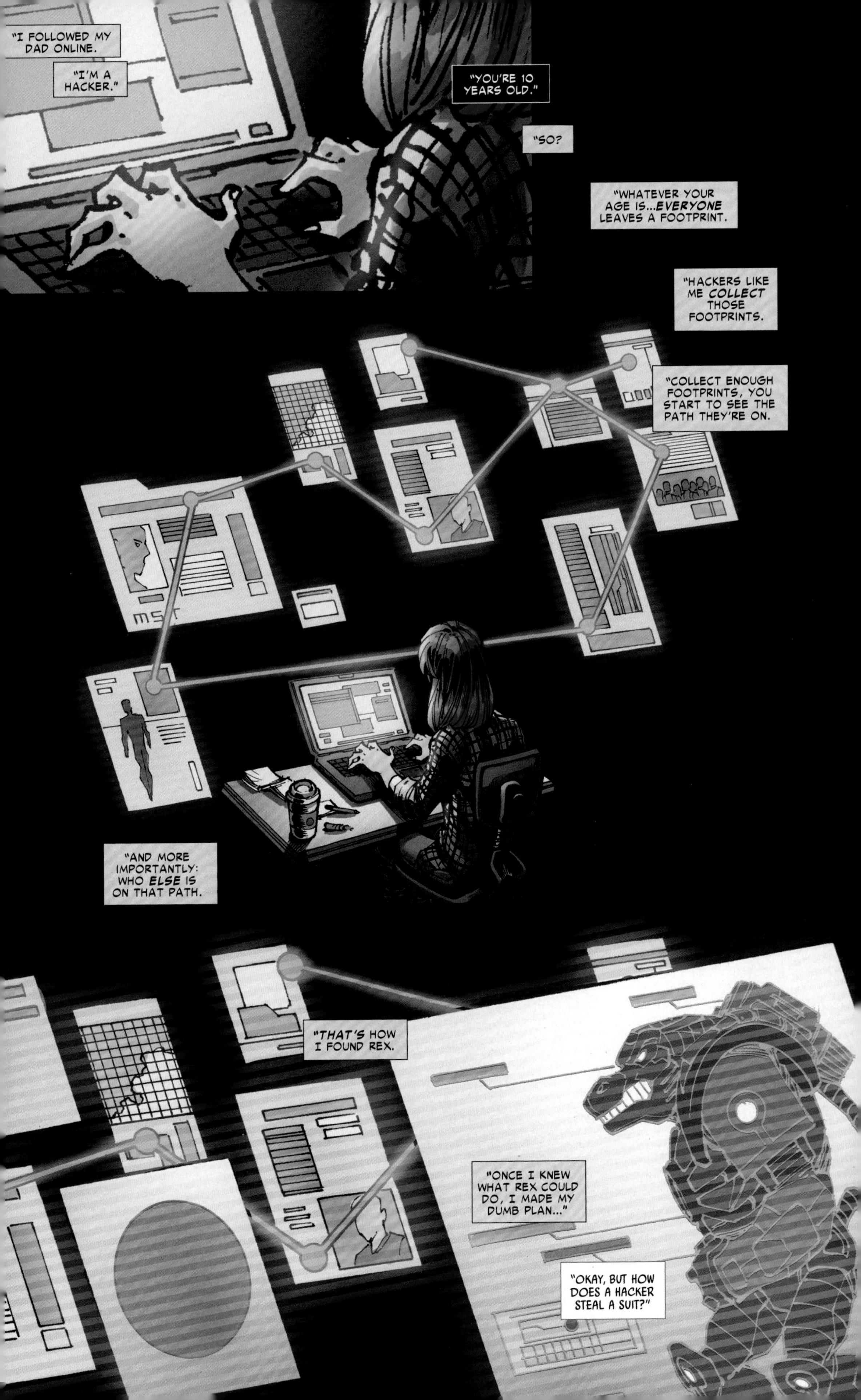
"I FOLLOWED MY DAD ONLINE.
"I'M A HACKER."
"YOU'RE 10 YEARS OLD."
"SO?
"WHATEVER YOUR AGE IS...EVERYONE LEAVES A FOOTPRINT.
"HACKERS LIKE ME COLLECT THOSE FOOTPRINTS.
"COLLECT ENOUGH FOOTPRINTS, YOU START TO SEE THE PATH THEY'RE ON.
"AND MORE IMPORTANTLY: WHO ELSE IS ON THAT PATH.
"THAT'S HOW I FOUND REX.
"ONCE I KNEW WHAT REX COULD DO, I MADE MY DUMB PLAN..."
"OKAY, BUT HOW DOES A HACKER STEAL A SUIT?"

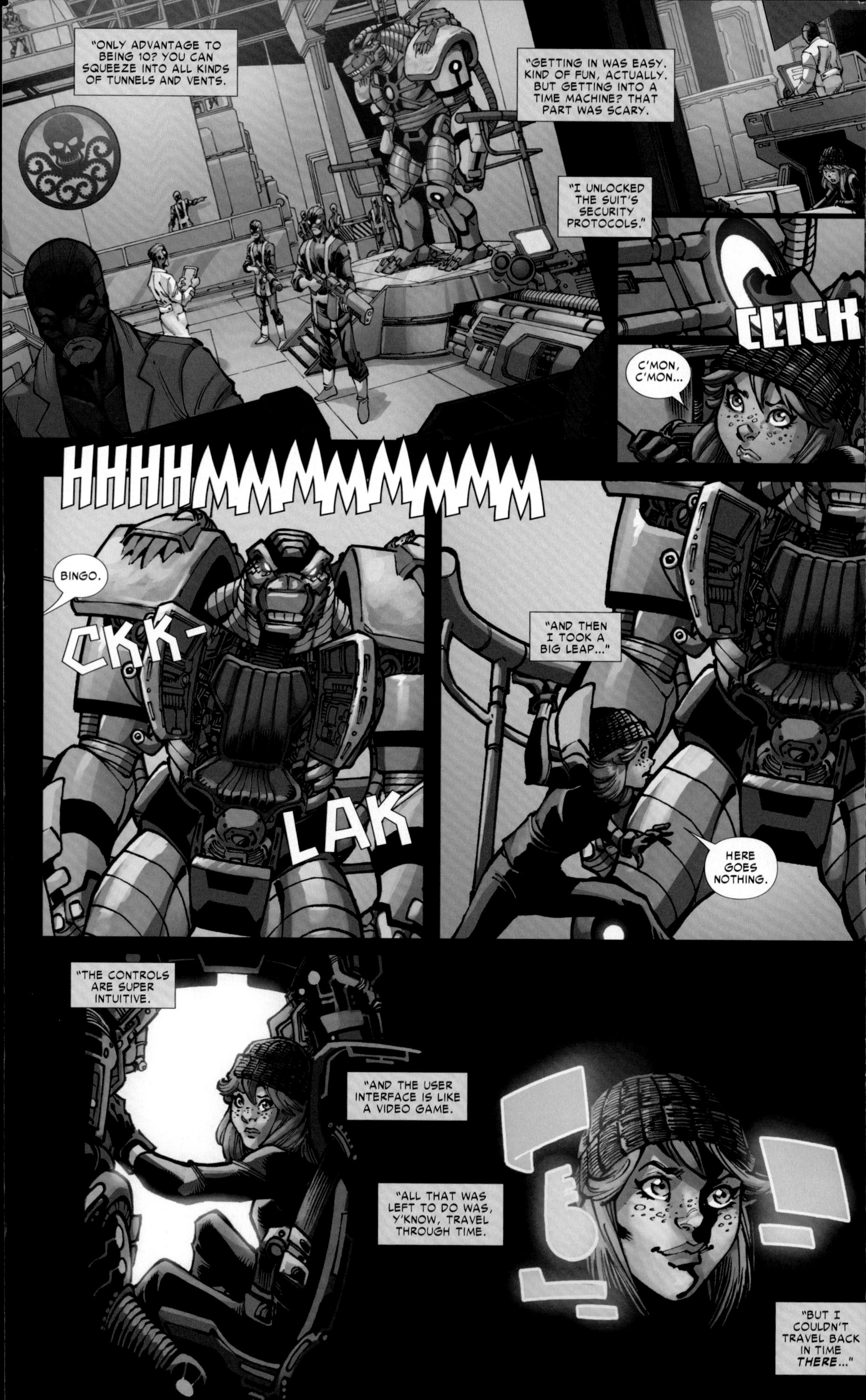

"ONLY ADVANTAGE TO BEING 10? YOU CAN SQUEEZE INTO ALL KINDS OF TUNNELS AND VENTS.
"GETTING IN WAS EASY. KIND OF FUN, ACTUALLY. BUT GETTING INTO A TIME MACHINE? THAT PART WAS SCARY.
"I UNLOCKED THE SUIT'S SECURITY PROTOCOLS."
CLICK
C'MON, C'MON...
HHHHMMMMMMMMMM
BINGO.
CKK-
LAK
"AND THEN I TOOK A BIG LEAP..."
HERE GOES NOTHING.
"THE CONTROLS ARE SUPER INTUITIVE.
"AND THE USER INTERFACE IS LIKE A VIDEO GAME.
"ALL THAT WAS LEFT TO DO WAS, Y'KNOW, TRAVEL THROUGH TIME.
"BUT I COULDN'T TRAVEL BACK IN TIME *THERE*..."

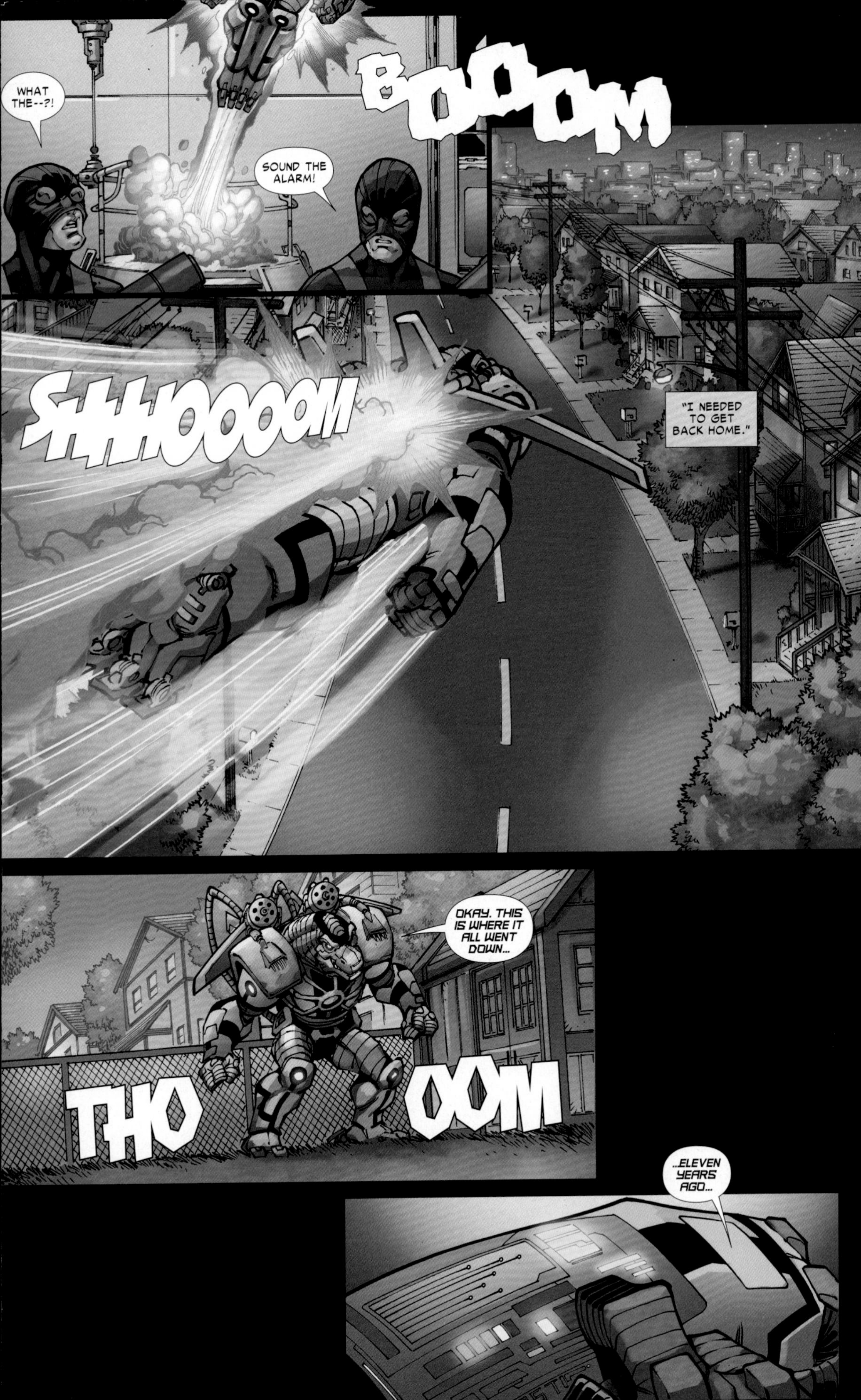
BOOOOM
WHAT THE--?!
SOUND THE ALARM!
SHHOOOOM
"I NEEDED TO GET BACK HOME."
OKAY. THIS IS WHERE IT ALL WENT DOWN...
THOOOM
...ELEVEN YEARS AGO...

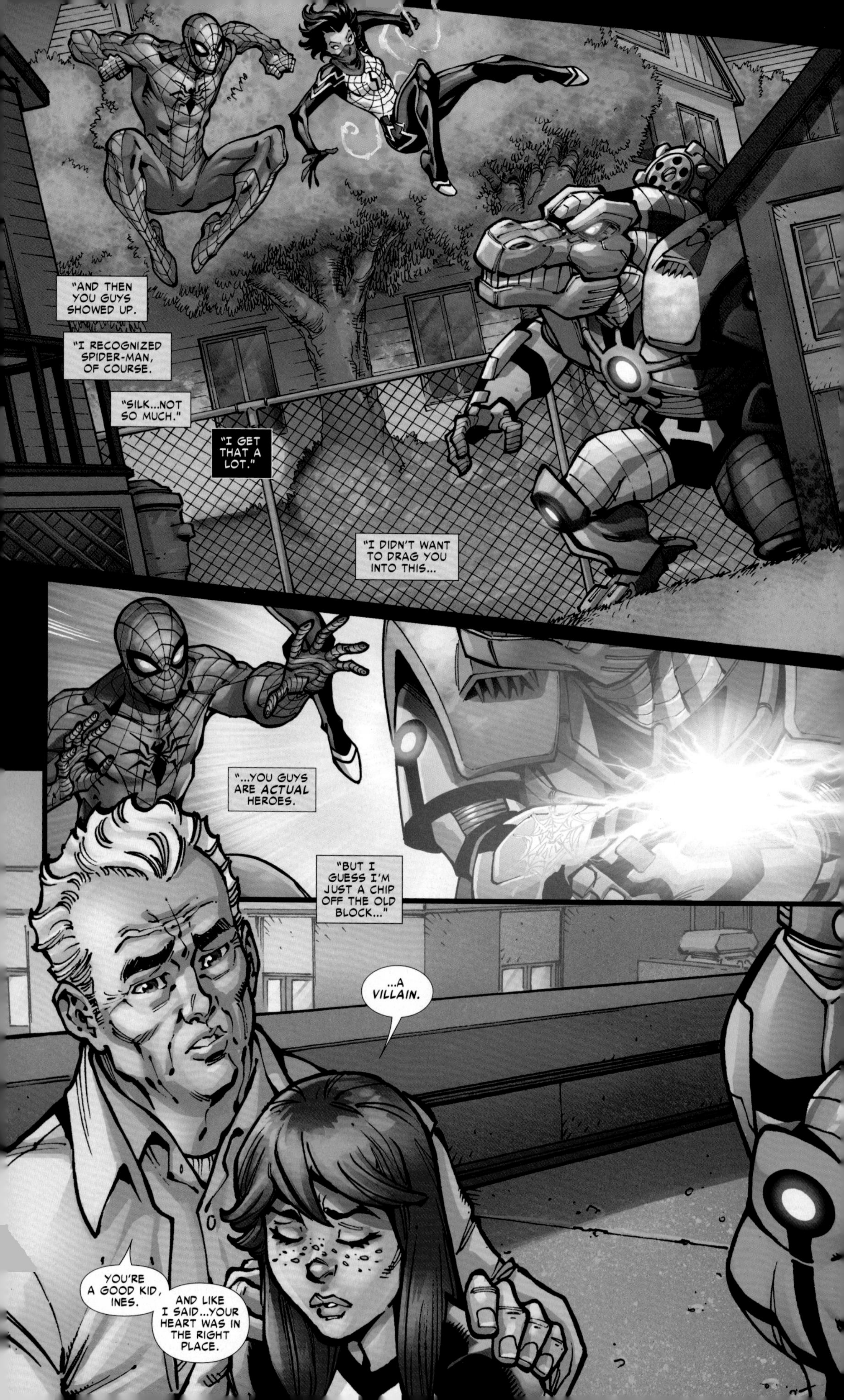
"AND THEN YOU GUYS SHOWED UP.
"I RECOGNIZED SPIDER-MAN, OF COURSE.
"SILK...NOT SO MUCH."
"I GET THAT A LOT."
"I DIDN'T WANT TO DRAG YOU INTO THIS...
"...YOU GUYS ARE ACTUAL HEROES.
"BUT I GUESS I'M JUST A CHIP OFF THE OLD BLOCK..."
...A VILLAIN.
YOU'RE A GOOD KID, INES.
AND LIKE I SAID...YOUR HEART WAS IN THE RIGHT PLACE.

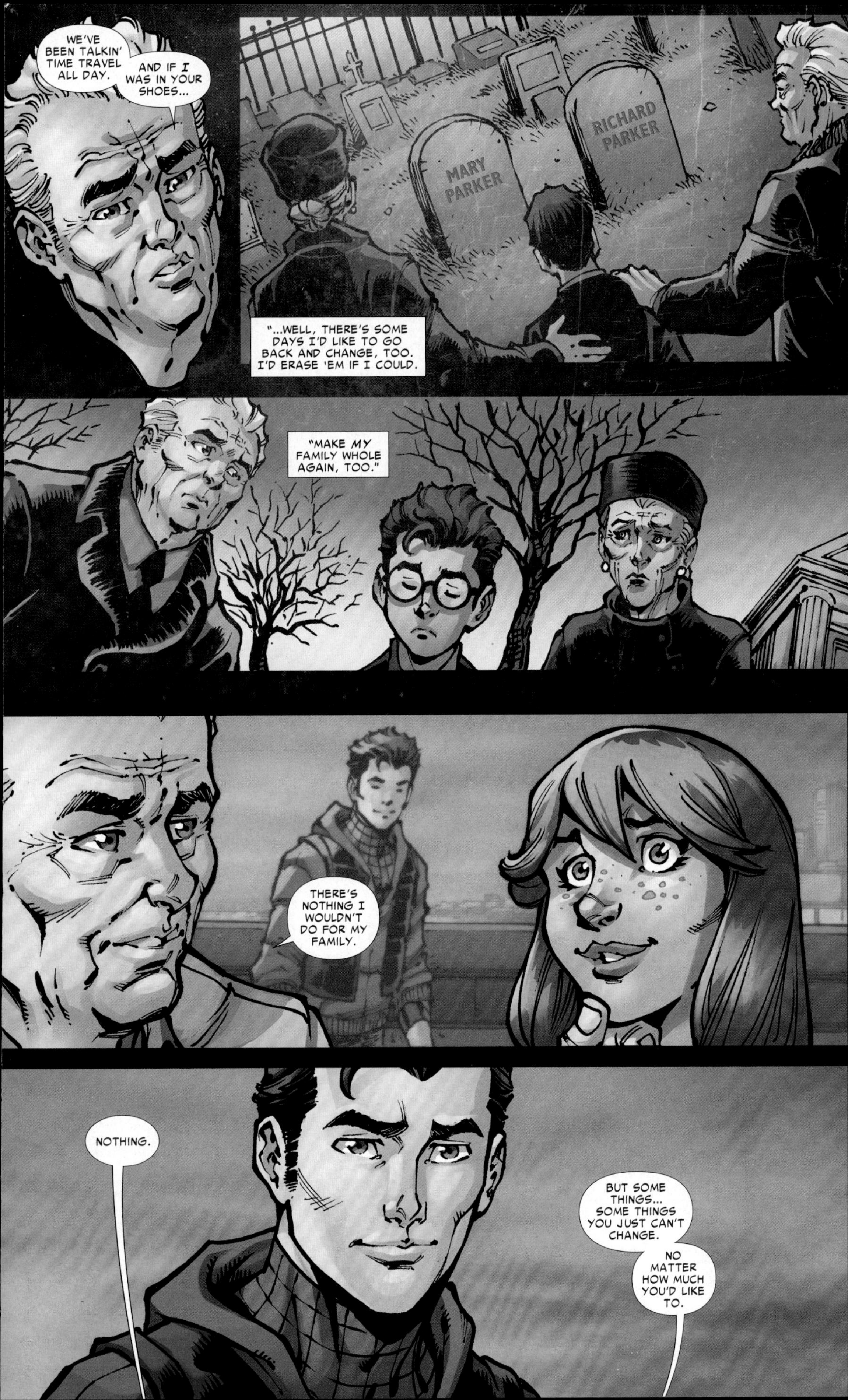
WE'VE BEEN TALKIN' TIME TRAVEL ALL DAY.
AND IF I WAS IN YOUR SHOES...
RICHARD PARKER
MARY PARKER
"...WELL, THERE'S SOME DAYS I'D LIKE TO GO BACK AND CHANGE, TOO. I'D ERASE 'EM IF I COULD.
"MAKE MY FAMILY WHOLE AGAIN, TOO."
THERE'S NOTHING I WOULDN'T DO FOR MY FAMILY.
NOTHING.
BUT SOME THINGS... SOME THINGS YOU JUST CAN'T CHANGE.
NO MATTER HOW MUCH YOU'D LIKE TO.

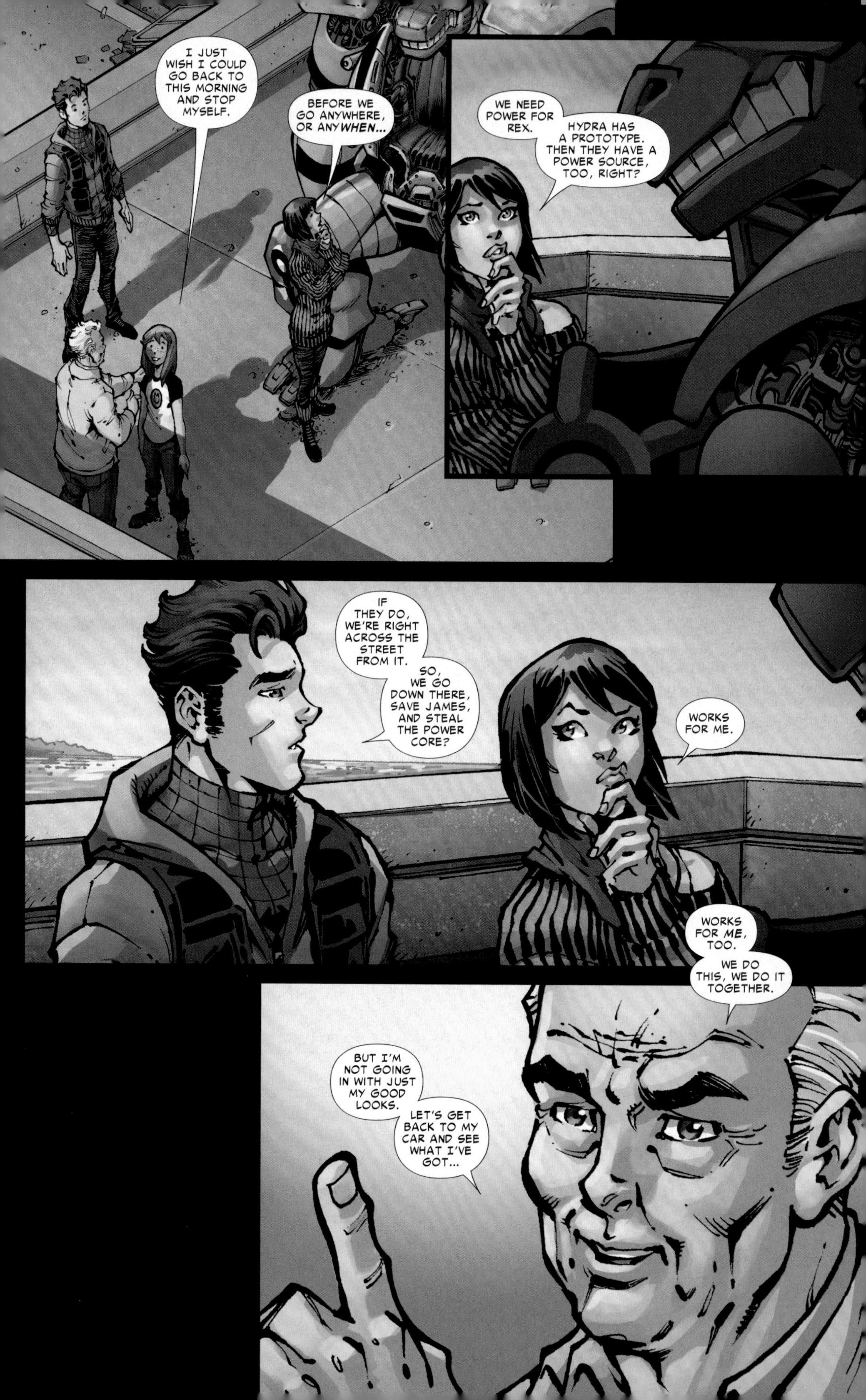
I JUST WISH I COULD GO BACK TO THIS MORNING AND STOP MYSELF.
BEFORE WE GO ANYWHERE, OR ANY*WHEN*...
WE NEED POWER FOR REX.
HYDRA HAS A PROTOTYPE. THEN THEY HAVE A POWER SOURCE, TOO, RIGHT?
IF THEY DO, WE'RE RIGHT ACROSS THE STREET FROM IT.
SO, WE GO DOWN THERE, SAVE JAMES, AND STEAL THE POWER CORE?
WORKS FOR ME.
WORKS FOR *ME*, TOO.
WE DO THIS, WE DO IT TOGETHER.
BUT I'M NOT GOING IN WITH JUST MY GOOD LOOKS.
LET'S GET BACK TO MY CAR AND SEE WHAT I'VE GOT...

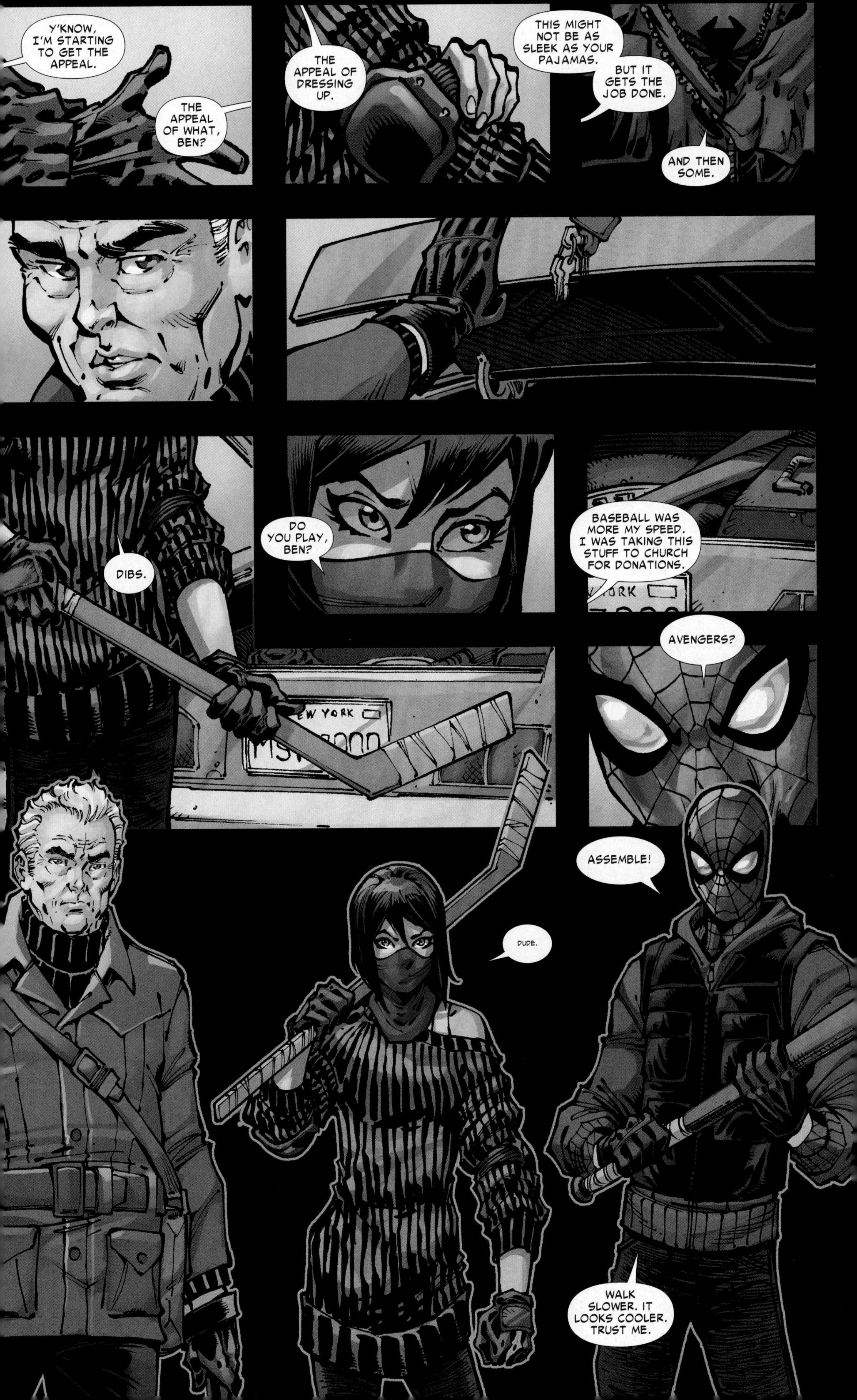
Y'KNOW, I'M STARTING TO GET THE APPEAL.
THE APPEAL OF WHAT, BEN?
THE APPEAL OF DRESSING UP.
THIS MIGHT NOT BE AS SLEEK AS YOUR PAJAMAS.
BUT IT GETS THE JOB DONE.
AND THEN SOME.
DIBS.
DO YOU PLAY, BEN?
BASEBALL WAS MORE MY SPEED. I WAS TAKING THIS STUFF TO CHURCH FOR DONATIONS.
NEW YORK
AVENGERS?
ASSEMBLE!
DUDE.
WALK SLOWER. IT LOOKS COOLER. TRUST ME.

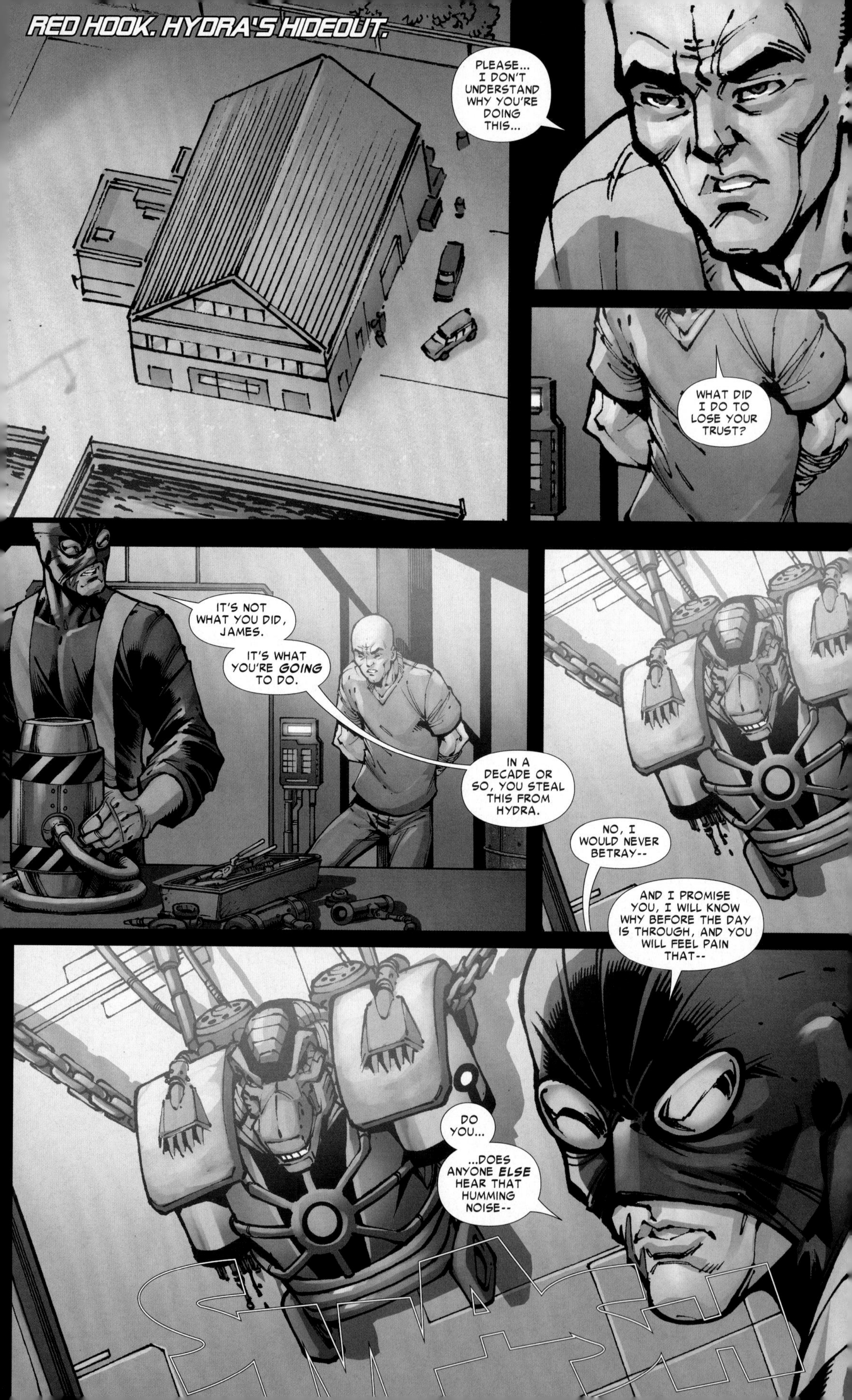
RED HOOK. HYDRA'S HIDEOUT.
PLEASE... I DON'T UNDERSTAND WHY YOU'RE DOING THIS...
WHAT DID I DO TO LOSE YOUR TRUST?
IT'S NOT WHAT YOU DID, JAMES.
IT'S WHAT YOU'RE *GOING* TO DO.
IN A DECADE OR SO, YOU STEAL THIS FROM HYDRA.
NO, I WOULD NEVER BETRAY--
AND I PROMISE YOU, I WILL KNOW WHY BEFORE THE DAY IS THROUGH, AND YOU WILL FEEL PAIN THAT--
DO YOU...
...DOES ANYONE *ELSE* HEAR THAT HUMMING NOISE--

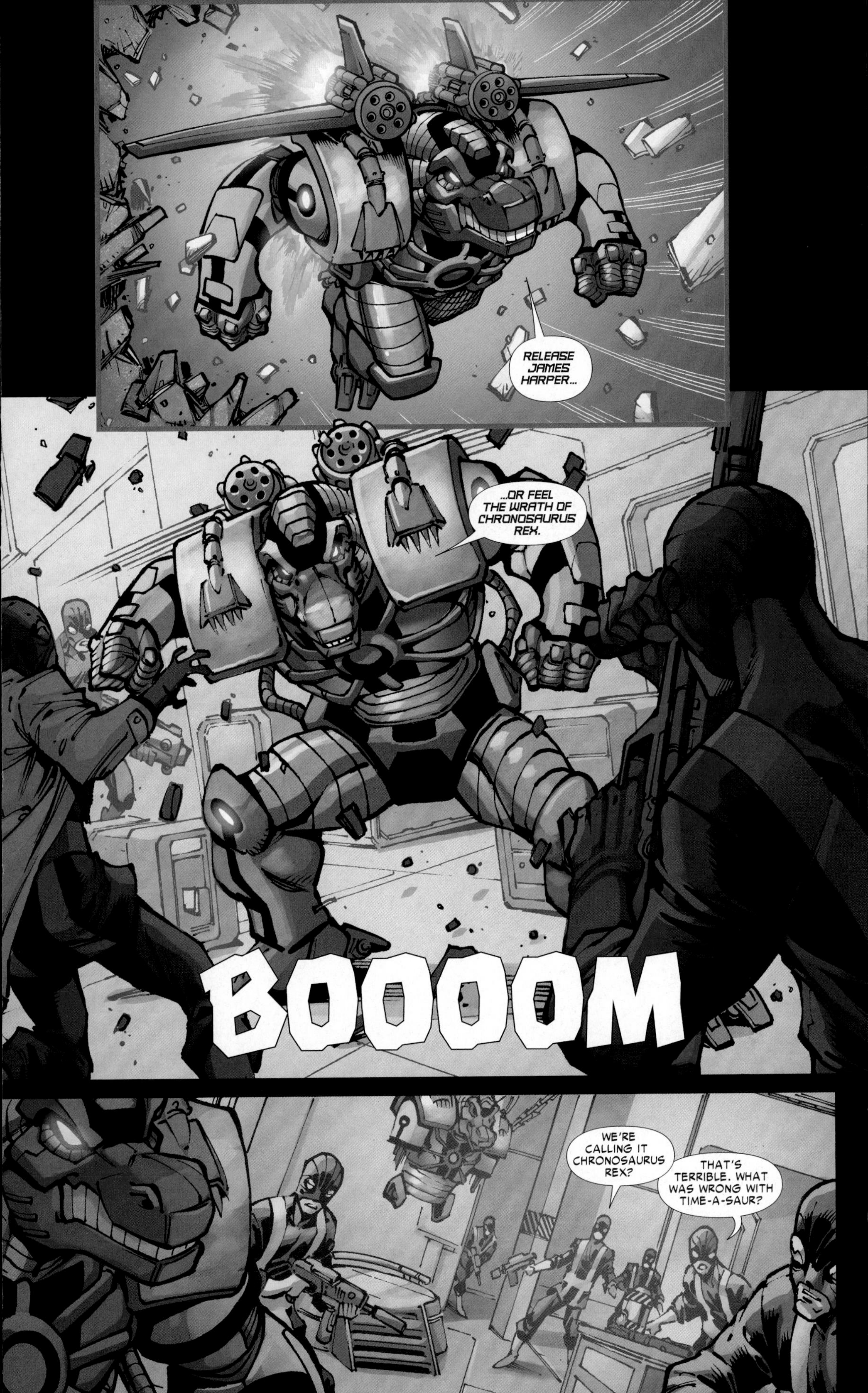
RELEASE JAMES HARPER...
...OR FEEL THE WRATH OF CHRONOSAURUS REX.
BOOOOM
WE'RE CALLING IT CHRONOSAURUS REX?
THAT'S TERRIBLE. WHAT WAS WRONG WITH TIME-A-SAUR?

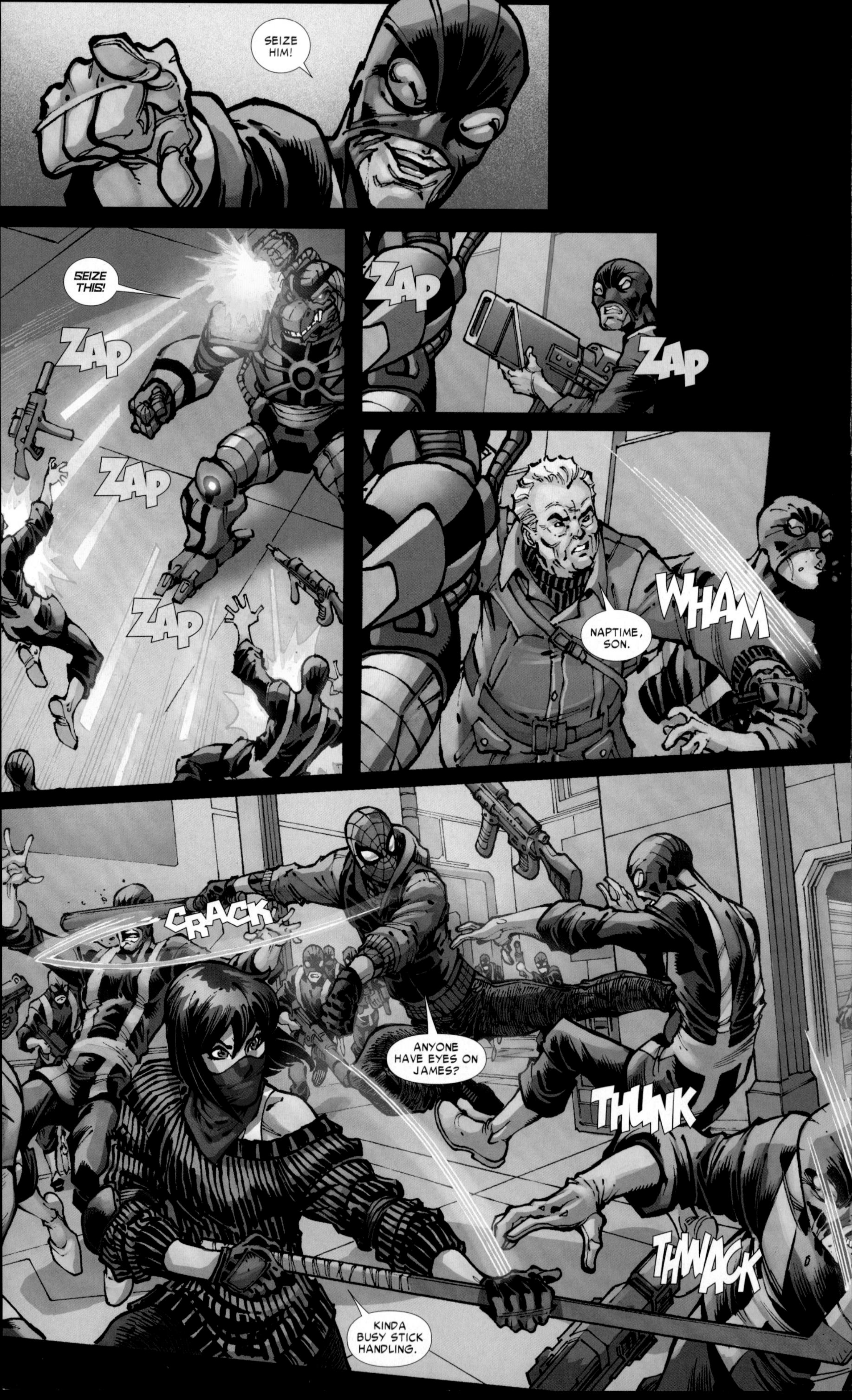
SEIZE HIM!
SEIZE THIS!
ZAP
ZAP
ZAP
ZAP
ZAP
NAPTIME, SON.
WHAM
CRACK
ANYONE HAVE EYES ON JAMES?
THUNK
KINDA BUSY STICK HANDLING.
THWACK

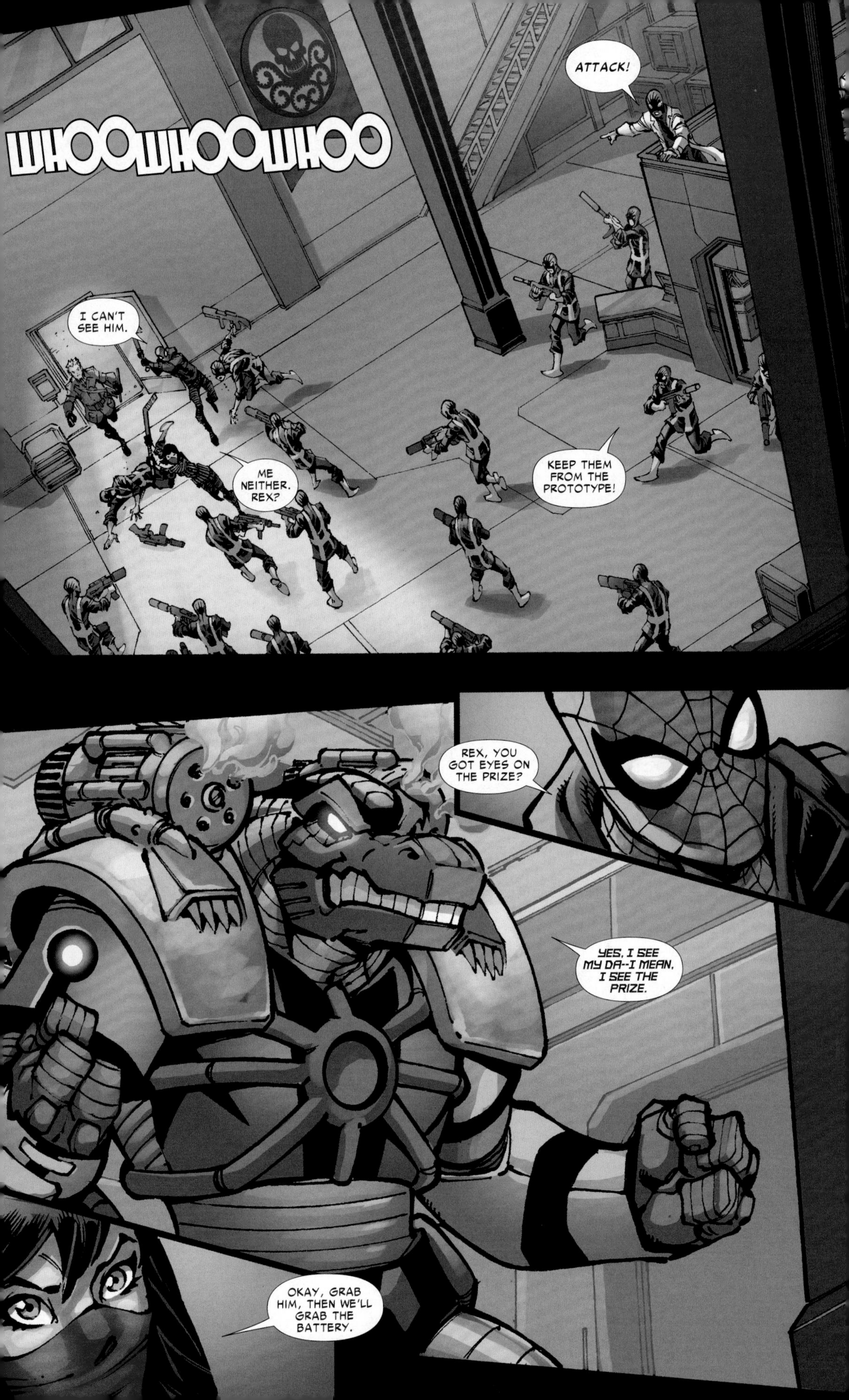
WHOOWHOOWHOO
ATTACK!
I CAN'T SEE HIM.
ME NEITHER. REX?
KEEP THEM FROM THE PROTOTYPE!
REX, YOU GOT EYES ON THE PRIZE?
YES, I SEE MY DA--I MEAN, I SEE THE PRIZE.
OKAY, GRAB HIM, THEN WE'LL GRAB THE BATTERY.

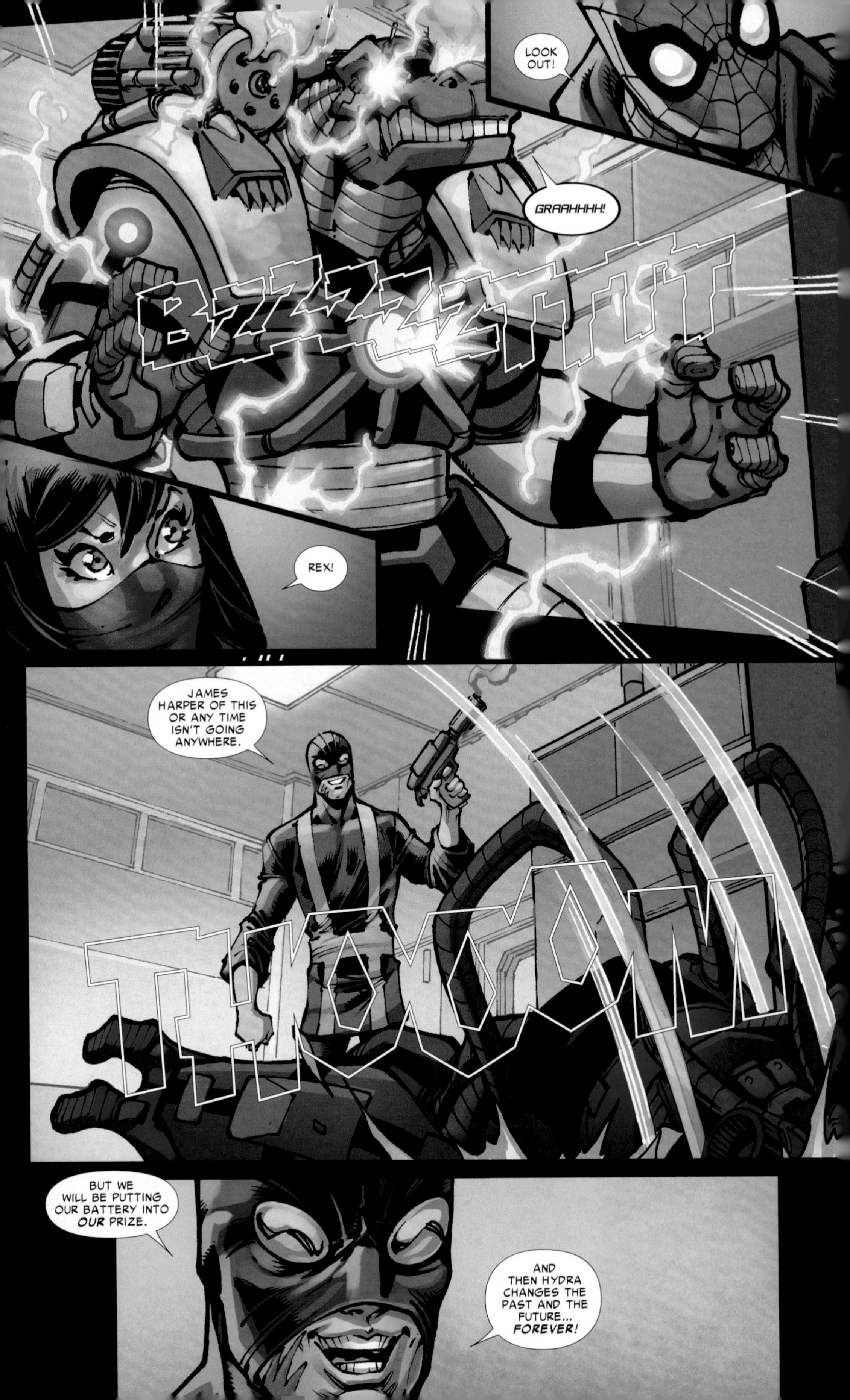
LOOK OUT!
GRAAHHHH!
BZZZZZTTTT
REX!
JAMES HARPER OF THIS OR ANY TIME ISN'T GOING ANYWHERE.
THOOOOM
BUT WE WILL BE PUTTING OUR BATTERY INTO *OUR* PRIZE.
AND THEN HYDRA CHANGES THE PAST AND THE FUTURE... *FOREVER!*

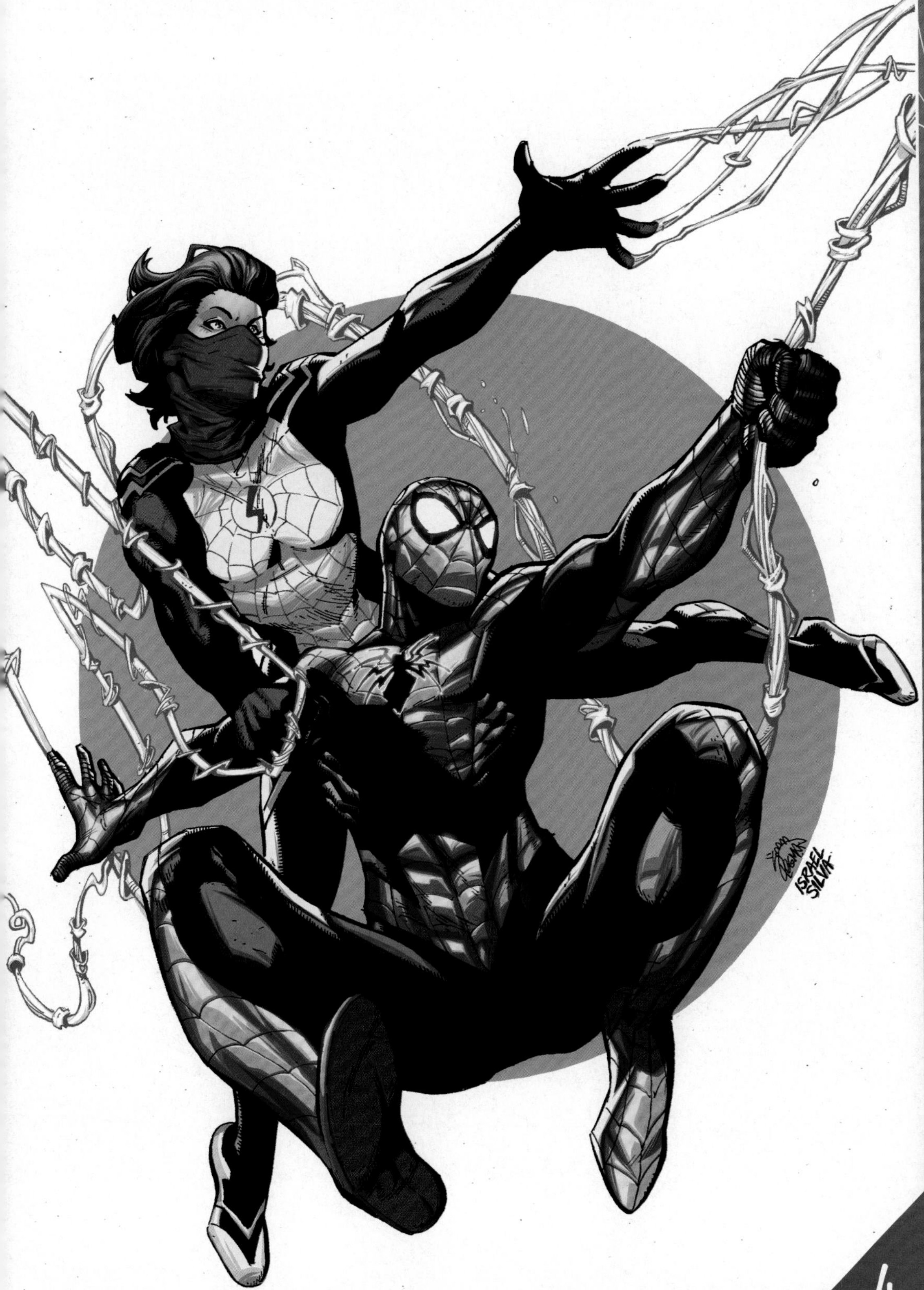

ISRAEL SILVA

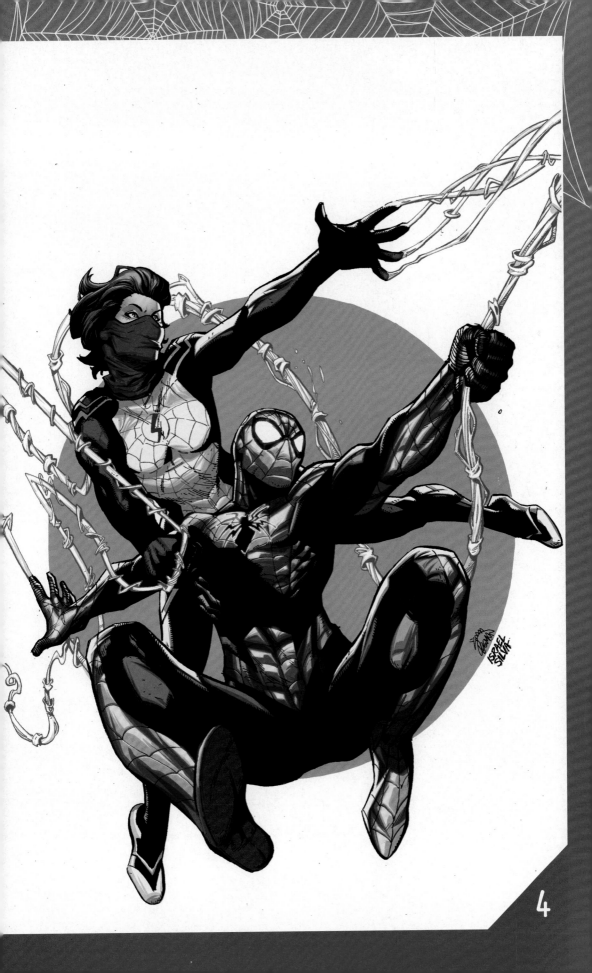

4

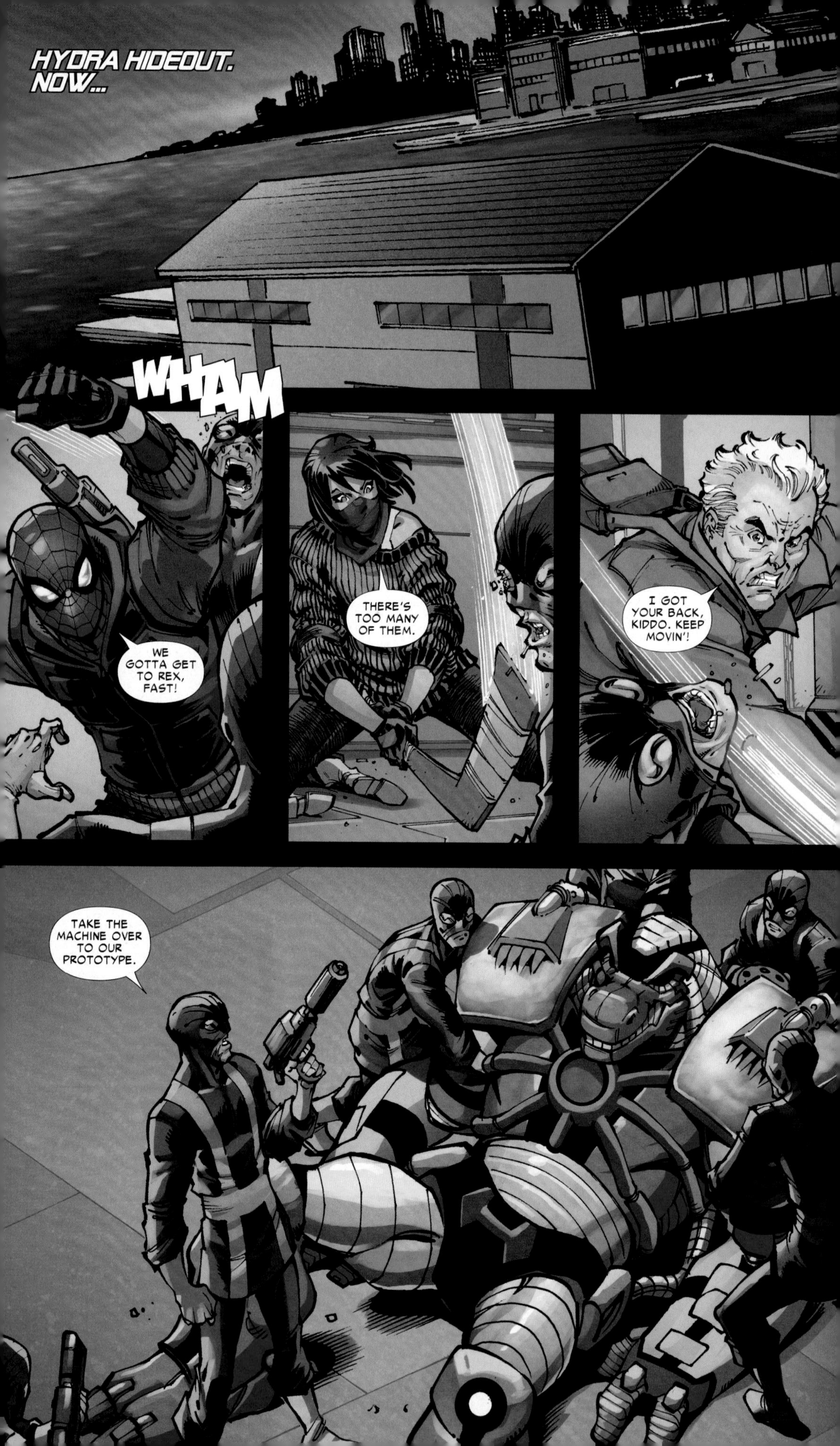
HYDRA HIDEOUT. NOW...
WHAM
WE GOTTA GET TO REX, FAST!
THERE'S TOO MANY OF THEM.
I GOT YOUR BACK, KIDDO. KEEP MOVIN'!
TAKE THE MACHINE OVER TO OUR PROTOTYPE.

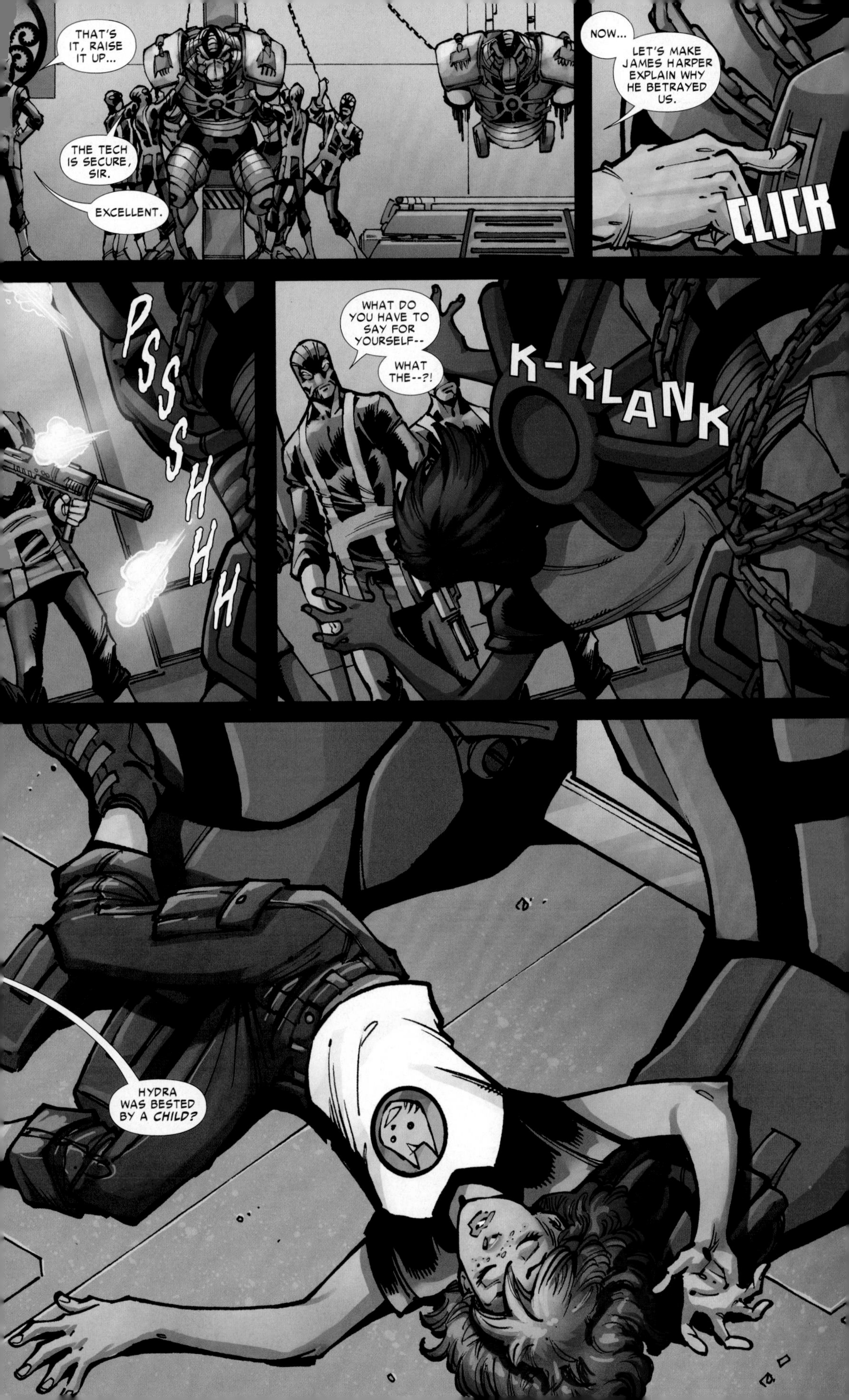
THAT'S IT, RAISE IT UP...
THE TECH IS SECURE, SIR.
EXCELLENT.
NOW...
LET'S MAKE JAMES HARPER EXPLAIN WHY HE BETRAYED US.
CLICK
PSSSHHH
WHAT DO YOU HAVE TO SAY FOR YOURSELF--
WHAT THE--?!
K-KLANK
HYDRA WAS BESTED BY A *CHILD?*

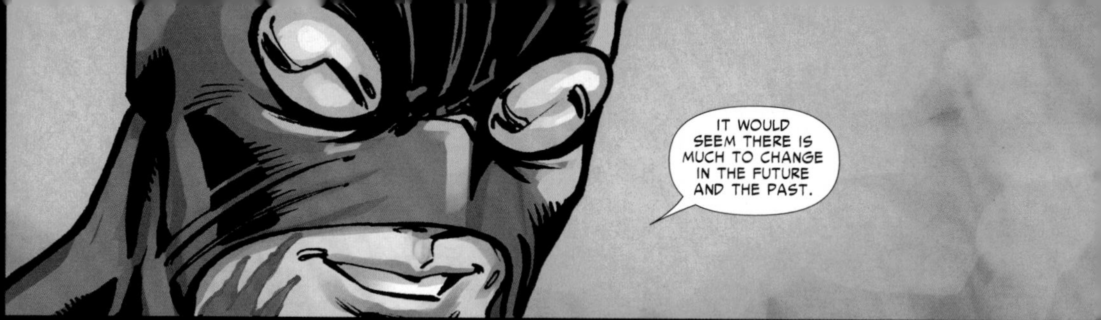
IT WOULD SEEM THERE IS MUCH TO CHANGE IN THE FUTURE AND THE PAST.

THE SPIDER(FLY) EFFECT
CHAPTERS SEVEN & EIGHT

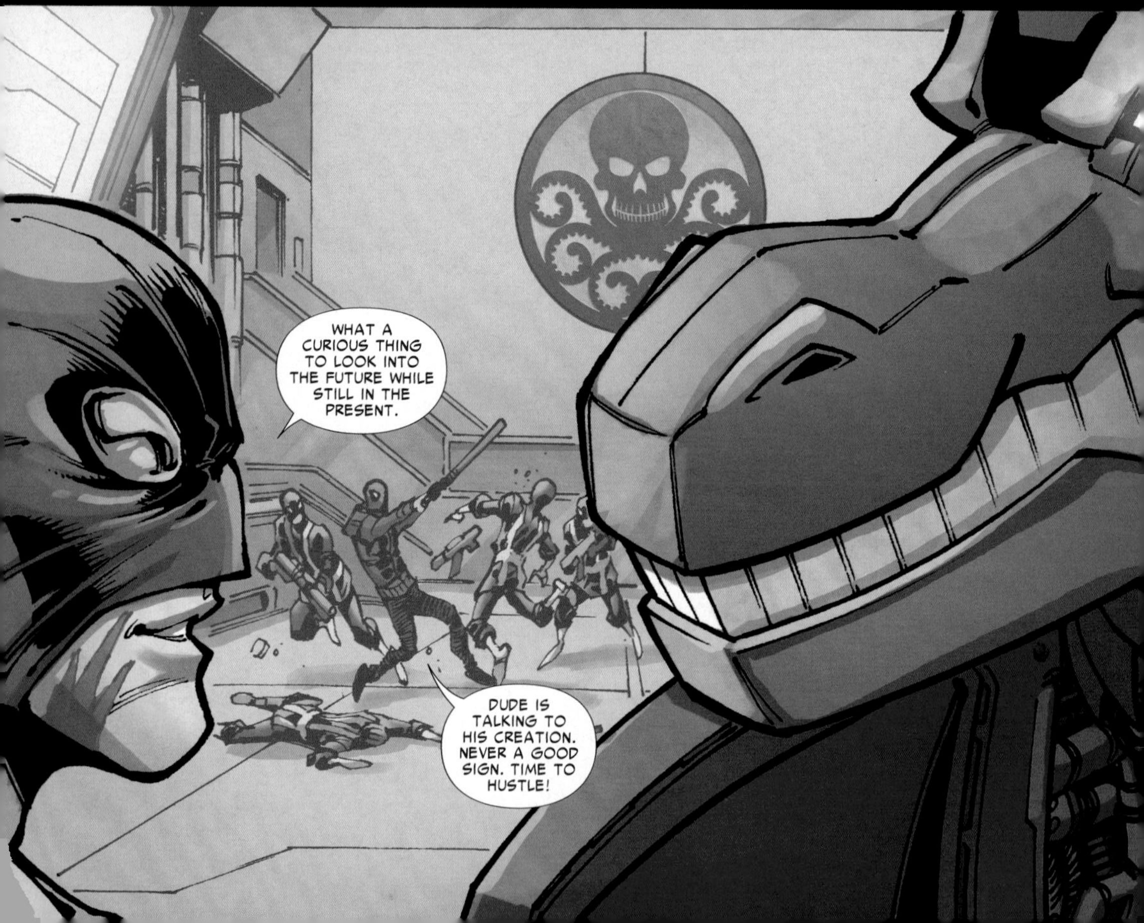
WHAT A CURIOUS THING TO LOOK INTO THE FUTURE WHILE STILL IN THE PRESENT.
DUDE IS TALKING TO HIS CREATION. NEVER A GOOD SIGN. TIME TO HUSTLE!

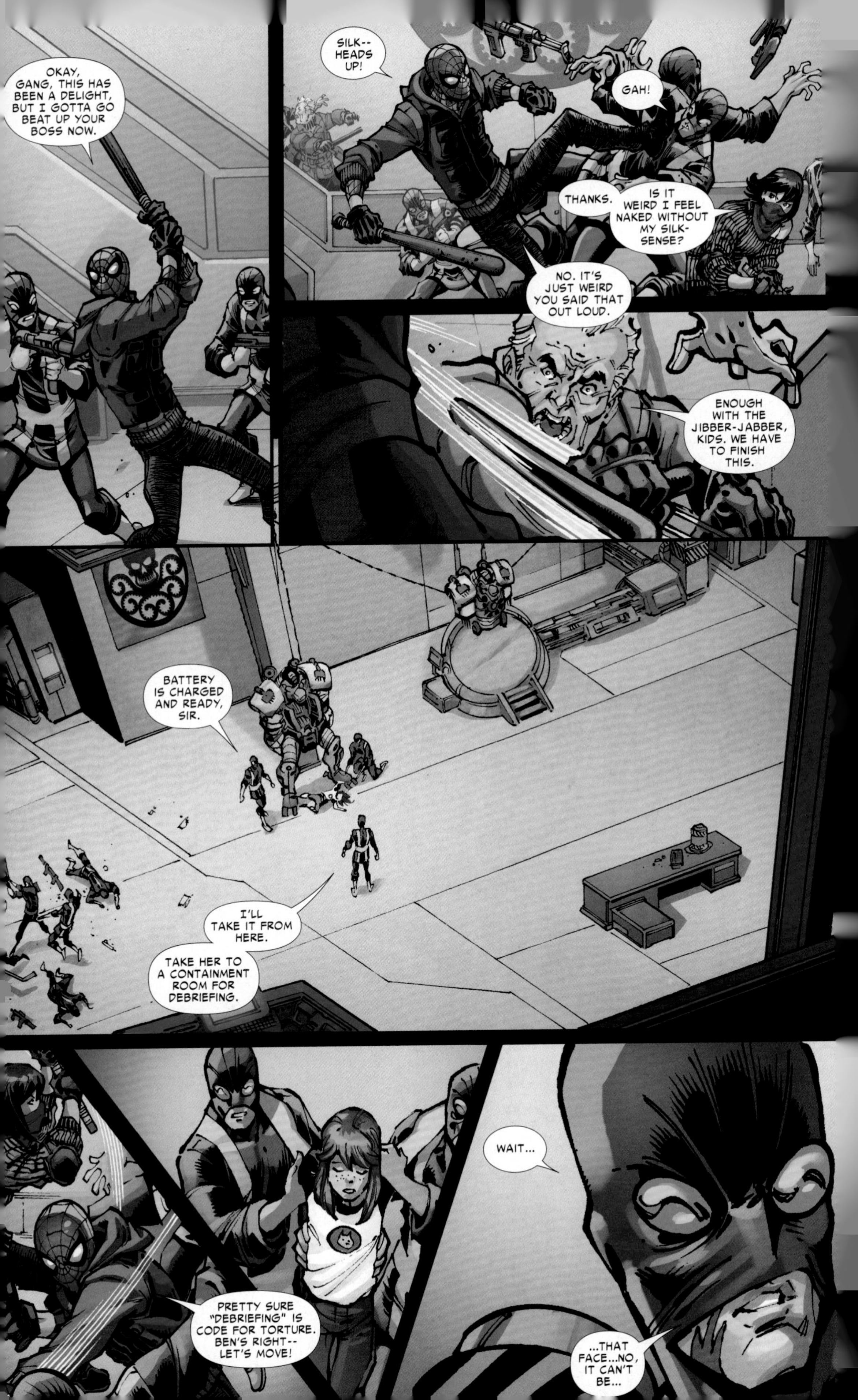
OKAY, GANG, THIS HAS BEEN A DELIGHT, BUT I GOTTA GO BEAT UP YOUR BOSS NOW.
SILK-- HEADS UP!
GAH!
THANKS.
IS IT WEIRD I FEEL NAKED WITHOUT MY SILK-SENSE?
NO. IT'S JUST WEIRD YOU SAID THAT OUT LOUD.
ENOUGH WITH THE JIBBER-JABBER, KIDS. WE HAVE TO FINISH THIS.
BATTERY IS CHARGED AND READY, SIR.
I'LL TAKE IT FROM HERE.
TAKE HER TO A CONTAINMENT ROOM FOR DEBRIEFING.
PRETTY SURE "DEBRIEFING" IS CODE FOR TORTURE. BEN'S RIGHT-- LET'S MOVE!
WAIT...
...THAT FACE...NO, IT CAN'T BE...

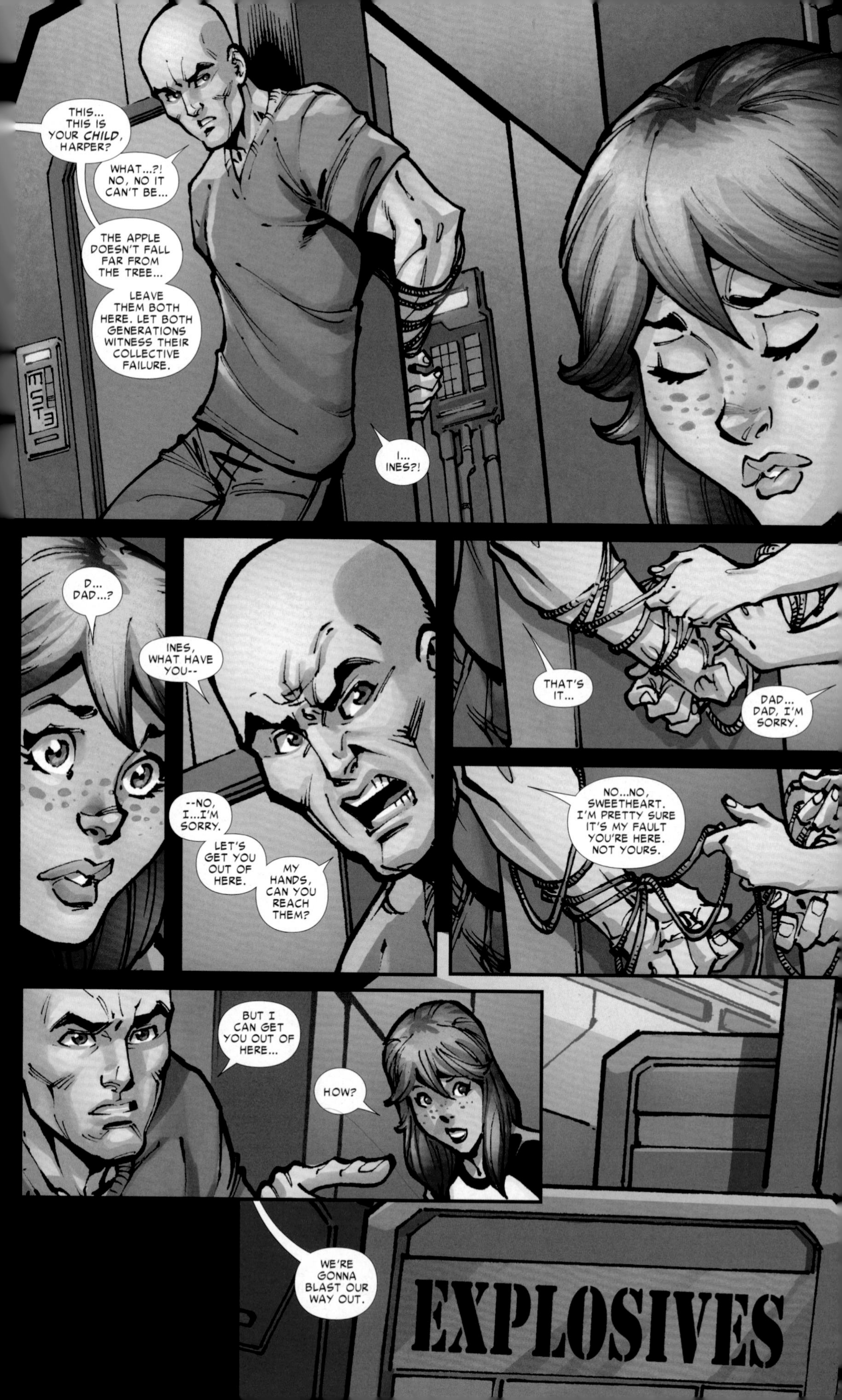

THIS... THIS IS YOUR CHILD, HARPER?
WHAT...?! NO, NO IT CAN'T BE...
THE APPLE DOESN'T FALL FAR FROM THE TREE...
LEAVE THEM BOTH HERE. LET BOTH GENERATIONS WITNESS THEIR COLLECTIVE FAILURE.
I... INES?!
D... DAD...?
INES, WHAT HAVE YOU--
--NO, I...I'M SORRY.
LET'S GET YOU OUT OF HERE.
MY HANDS, CAN YOU REACH THEM?
THAT'S IT...
DAD... DAD, I'M SORRY.
NO...NO, SWEETHEART. I'M PRETTY SURE IT'S MY FAULT YOU'RE HERE. NOT YOURS.
BUT I CAN GET YOU OUT OF HERE...
HOW?
WE'RE GONNA BLAST OUR WAY OUT.
EXPLOSIVES

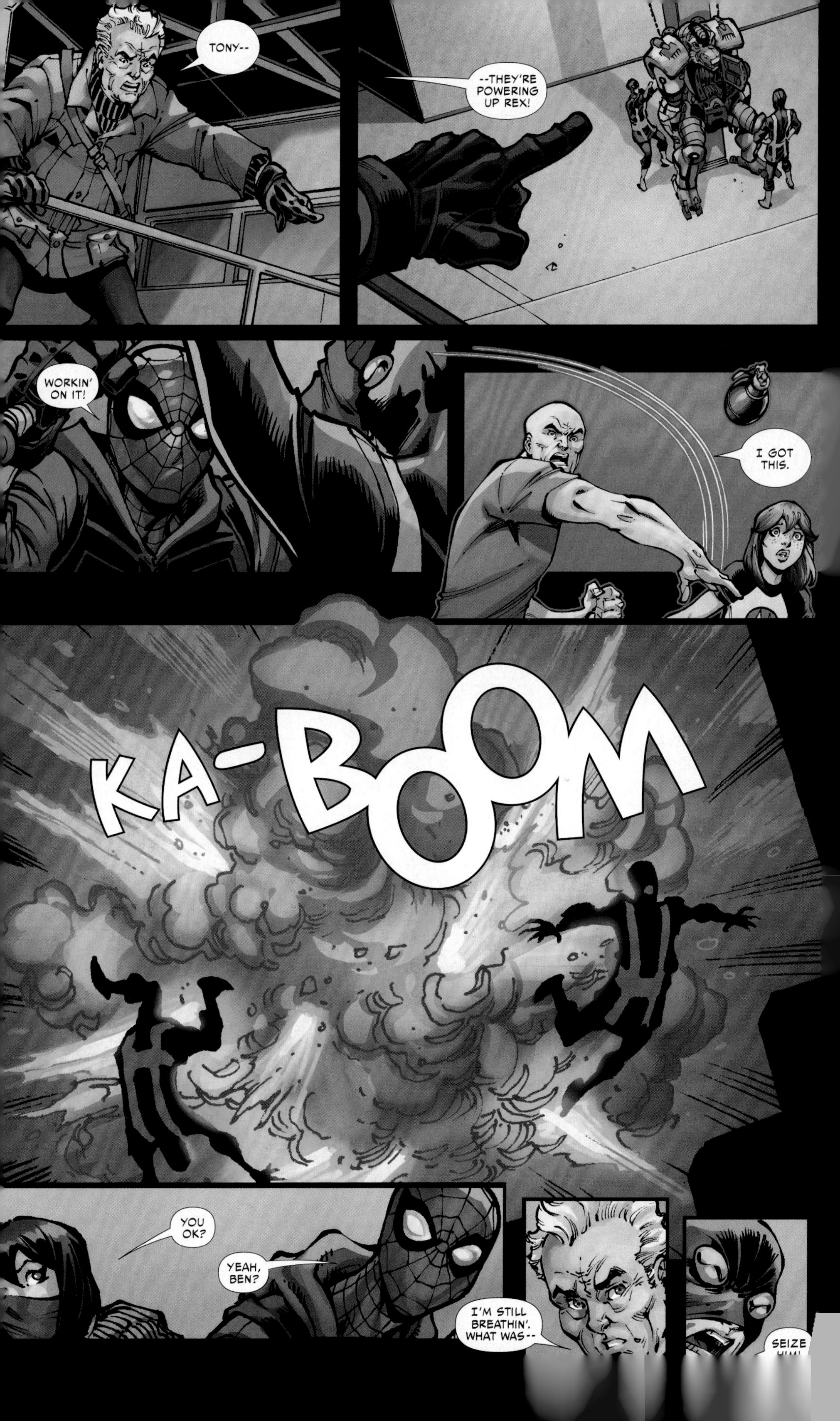
TONY--
--THEY'RE POWERING UP REX!
WORKIN' ON IT!
I GOT THIS.
KA-BOOM
YOU OK?
YEAH, BEN?
I'M STILL BREATHIN'. WHAT WAS--
SEIZE

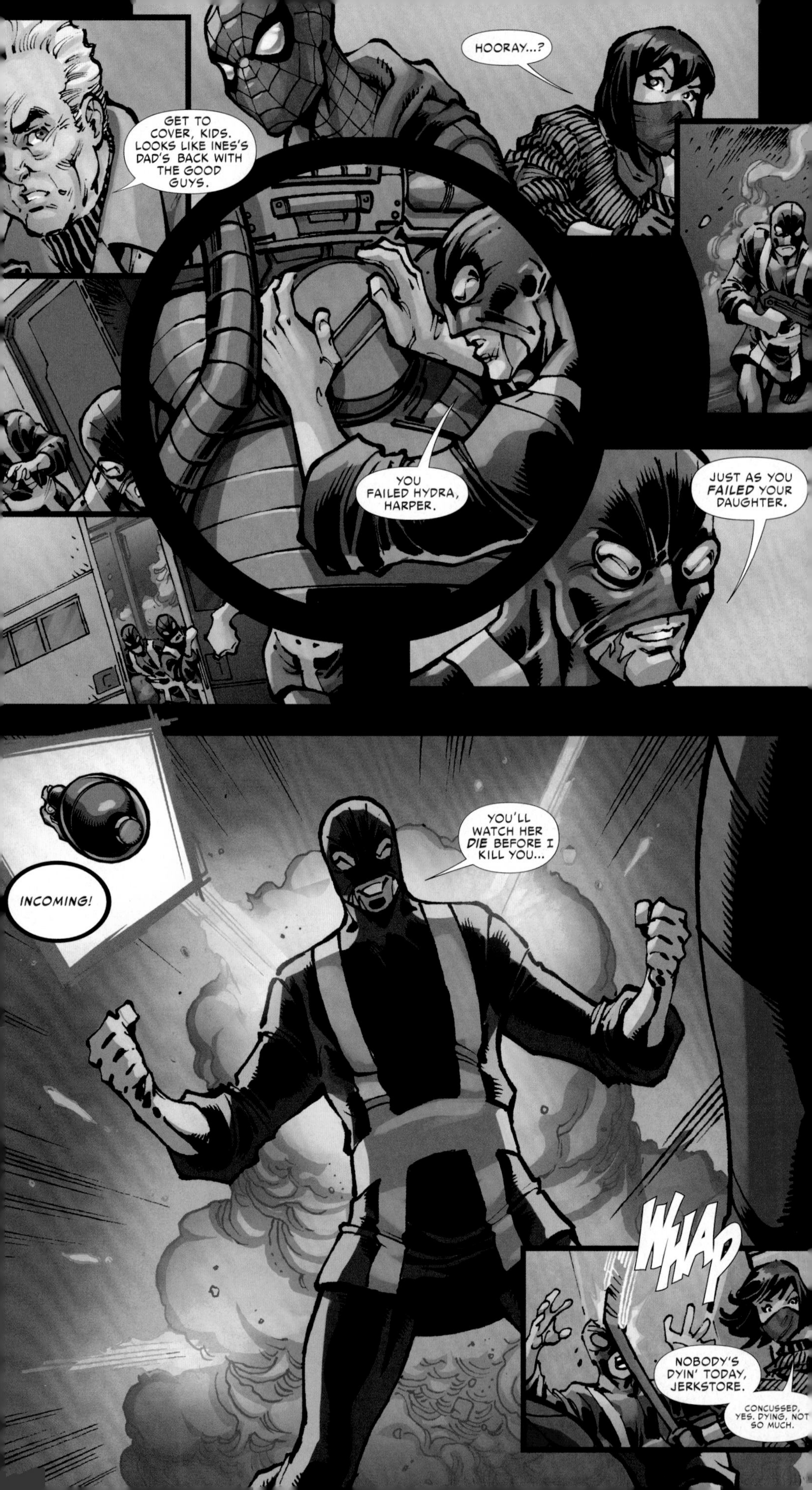
GET TO COVER, KIDS. LOOKS LIKE INES'S DAD'S BACK WITH THE GOOD GUYS.
HOORAY...?
YOU FAILED HYDRA, HARPER.
JUST AS YOU FAILED YOUR DAUGHTER.
INCOMING!
YOU'LL WATCH HER DIE BEFORE I KILL YOU...
WHAP
NOBODY'S DYIN' TODAY, JERKSTORE.
CONCUSSED, YES. DYING, NOT SO MUCH.

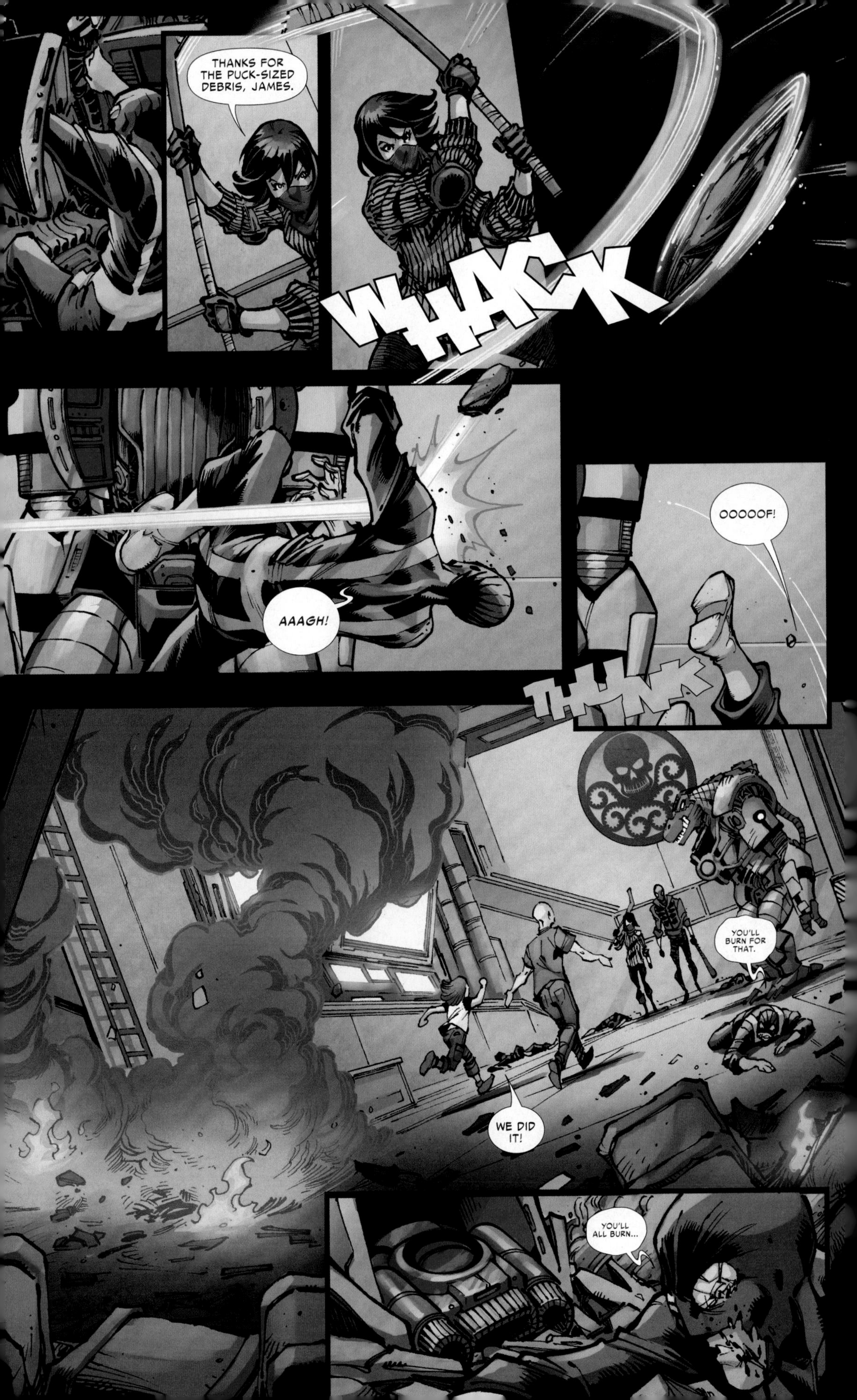
THANKS FOR THE PUCK-SIZED DEBRIS, JAMES.
WHACK
AAAGH!
OOOOOF!
THUNK
YOU'LL BURN FOR THAT.
WE DID IT!
YOU'LL ALL BURN...

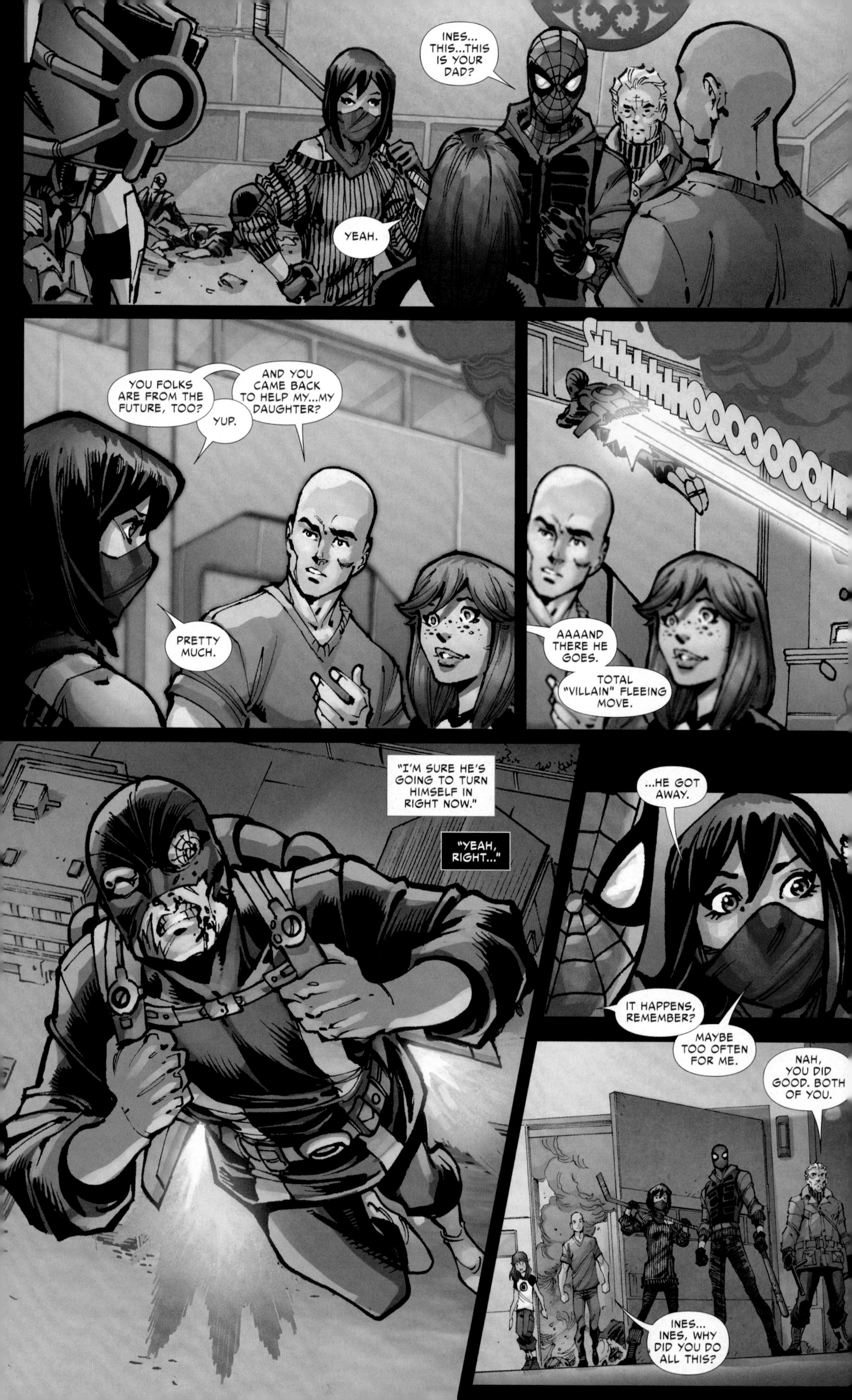

INES... THIS...THIS IS YOUR DAD?
YEAH.
YOU FOLKS ARE FROM THE FUTURE, TOO?
AND YOU CAME BACK TO HELP MY...MY DAUGHTER?
YUP.
PRETTY MUCH.
SHHHHHHHOOOOOOOOM
AAAAND THERE HE GOES.
TOTAL "VILLAIN" FLEEING MOVE.
"I'M SURE HE'S GOING TO TURN HIMSELF IN RIGHT NOW."
"YEAH, RIGHT..."
...HE GOT AWAY.
IT HAPPENS, REMEMBER?
MAYBE TOO OFTEN FOR ME.
NAH, YOU DID GOOD. BOTH OF YOU.
INES... INES, WHY DID YOU DO ALL THIS?

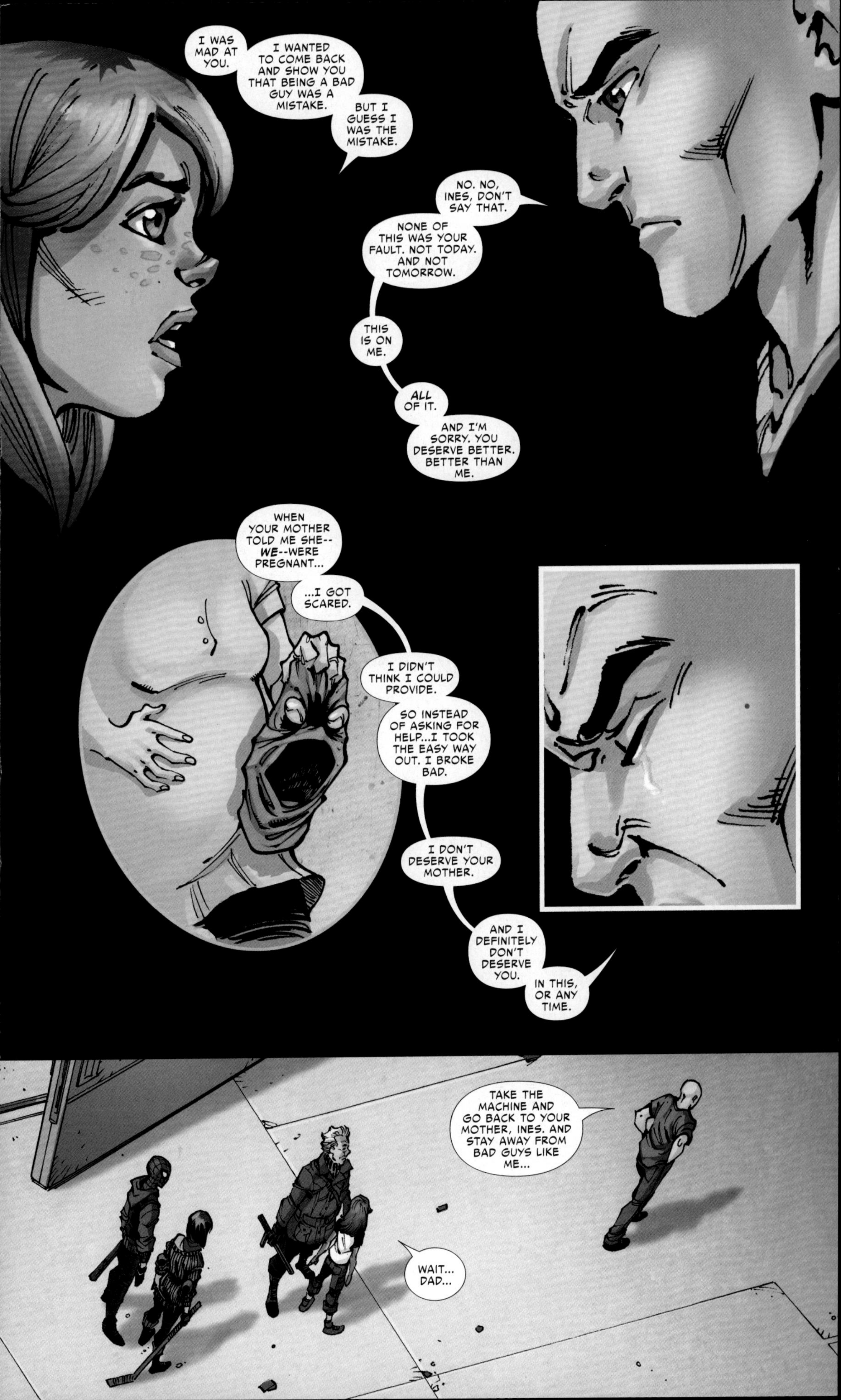
I WAS MAD AT YOU.
I WANTED TO COME BACK AND SHOW YOU THAT BEING A BAD GUY WAS A MISTAKE.
BUT I GUESS I WAS THE MISTAKE.
NO. NO, INES, DON'T SAY THAT.
NONE OF THIS WAS YOUR FAULT. NOT TODAY. AND NOT TOMORROW.
THIS IS ON ME.
ALL OF IT.
AND I'M SORRY. YOU DESERVE BETTER. BETTER THAN ME.
WHEN YOUR MOTHER TOLD ME SHE-- WE--WERE PREGNANT...
...I GOT SCARED.
I DIDN'T THINK I COULD PROVIDE.
SO INSTEAD OF ASKING FOR HELP...I TOOK THE EASY WAY OUT. I BROKE BAD.
I DON'T DESERVE YOUR MOTHER.
AND I DEFINITELY DON'T DESERVE YOU.
IN THIS, OR ANY TIME.
TAKE THE MACHINE AND GO BACK TO YOUR MOTHER, INES. AND STAY AWAY FROM BAD GUYS LIKE ME...
WAIT... DAD...

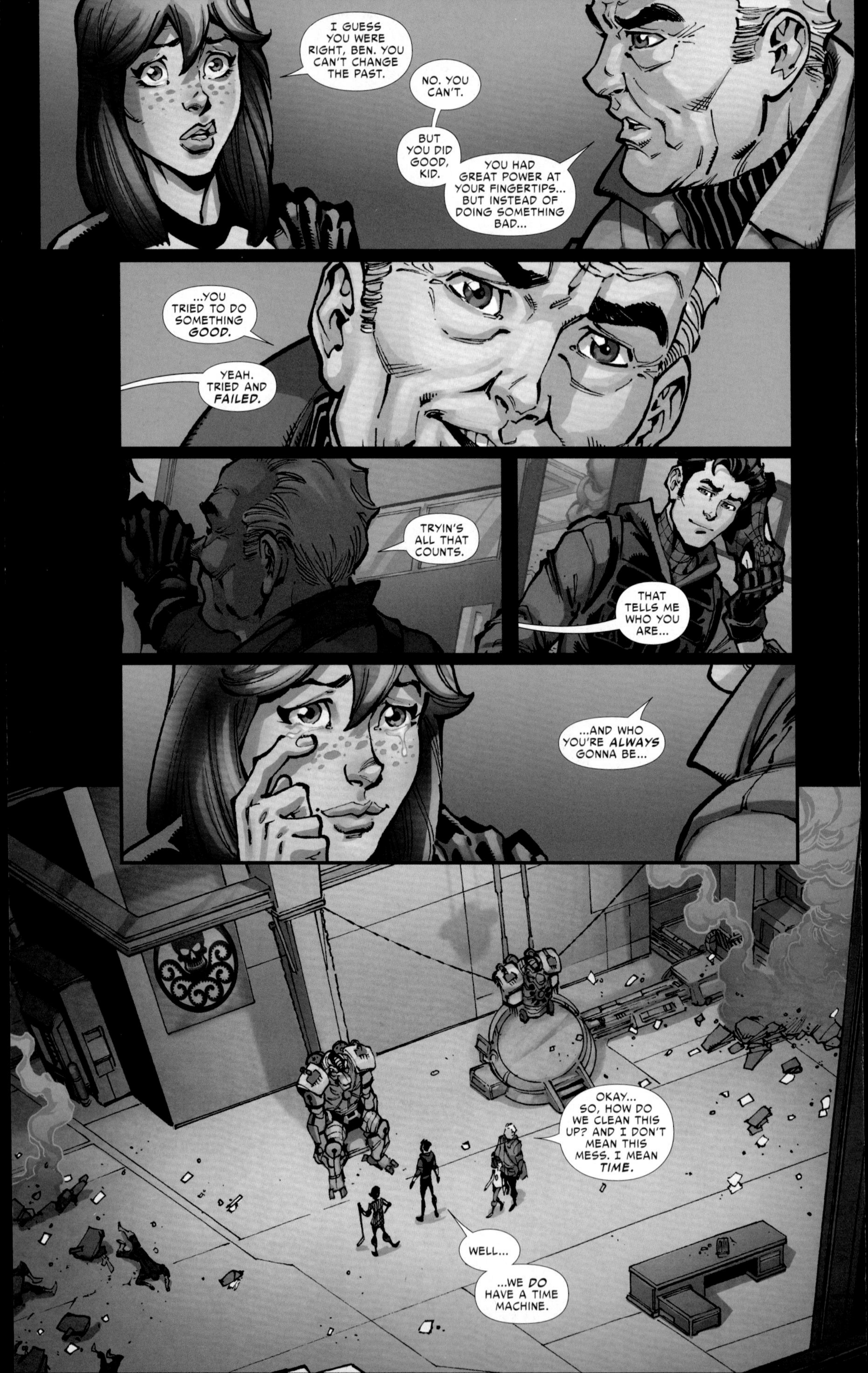
I GUESS YOU WERE RIGHT, BEN. YOU CAN'T CHANGE THE PAST.
NO. YOU CAN'T.
BUT YOU DID GOOD, KID.
YOU HAD GREAT POWER AT YOUR FINGERTIPS... BUT INSTEAD OF DOING SOMETHING BAD...
...YOU TRIED TO DO SOMETHING GOOD.
YEAH. TRIED AND FAILED.
TRYIN'S ALL THAT COUNTS.
THAT TELLS ME WHO YOU ARE...
...AND WHO YOU'RE ALWAYS GONNA BE...
OKAY... SO, HOW DO WE CLEAN THIS UP? AND I DON'T MEAN THIS MESS. I MEAN TIME.
WELL...
...WE DO HAVE A TIME MACHINE.

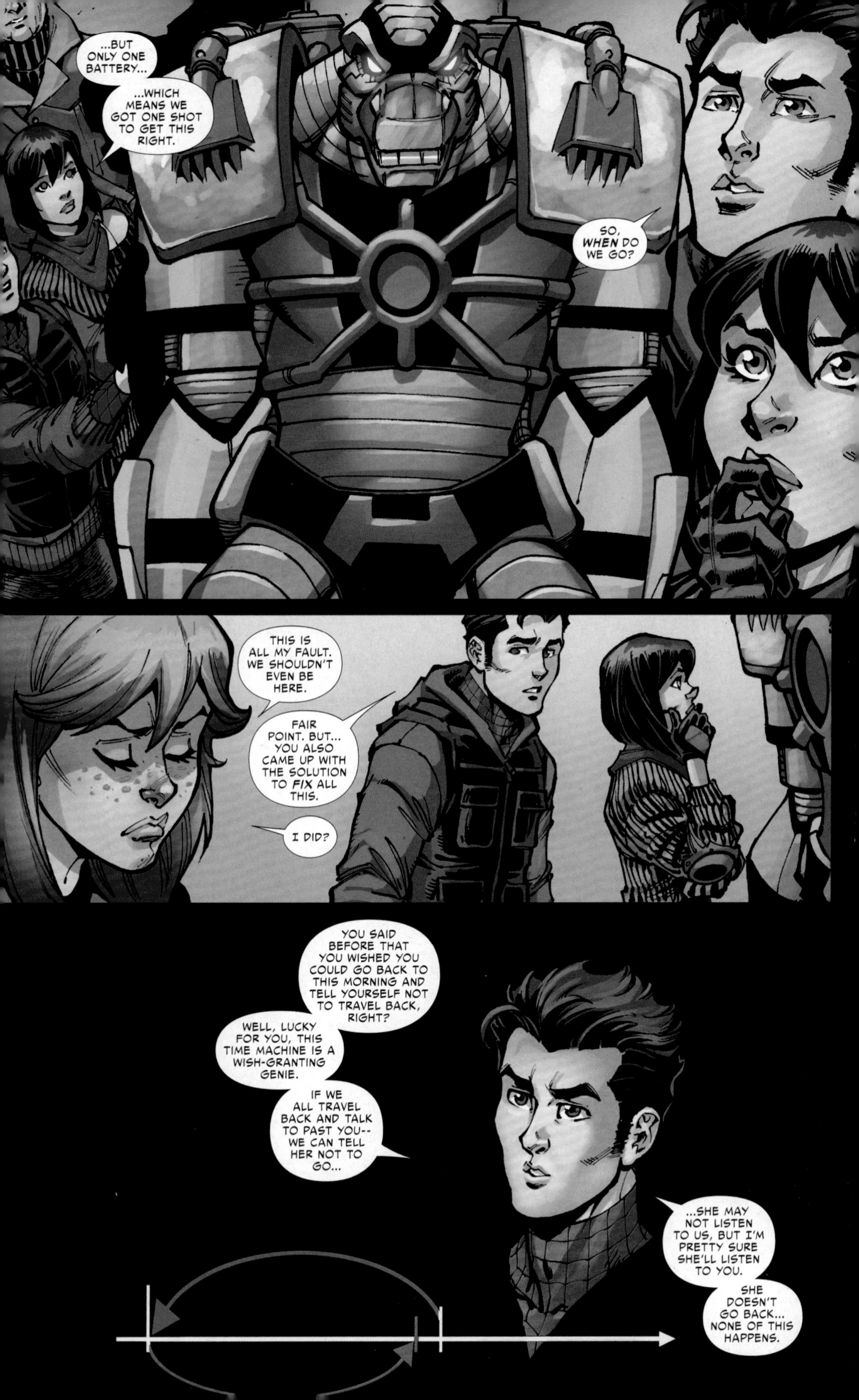
...BUT ONLY ONE BATTERY...
...WHICH MEANS WE GOT ONE SHOT TO GET THIS RIGHT.
SO, WHEN DO WE GO?
THIS IS ALL MY FAULT. WE SHOULDN'T EVEN BE HERE.
FAIR POINT. BUT... YOU ALSO CAME UP WITH THE SOLUTION TO FIX ALL THIS.
I DID?
YOU SAID BEFORE THAT YOU WISHED YOU COULD GO BACK TO THIS MORNING AND TELL YOURSELF NOT TO TRAVEL BACK, RIGHT?
WELL, LUCKY FOR YOU, THIS TIME MACHINE IS A WISH-GRANTING GENIE.
IF WE ALL TRAVEL BACK AND TALK TO PAST YOU-- WE CAN TELL HER NOT TO GO...
...SHE MAY NOT LISTEN TO US, BUT I'M PRETTY SURE SHE'LL LISTEN TO YOU.
SHE DOESN'T GO BACK... NONE OF THIS HAPPENS.

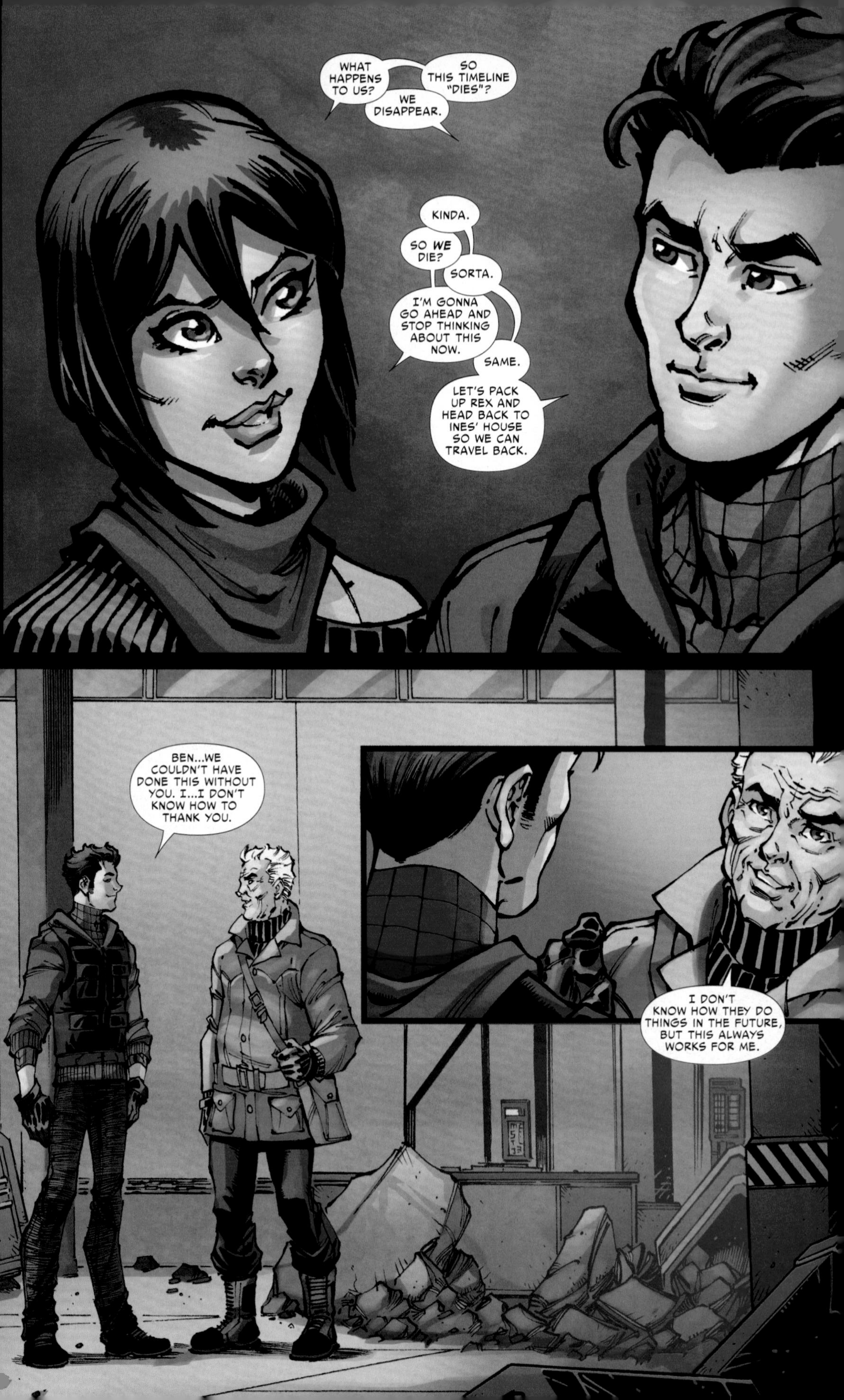
WHAT HAPPENS TO US?
SO THIS TIMELINE "DIES"?
WE DISAPPEAR.
KINDA.
SO WE DIE?
SORTA.
I'M GONNA GO AHEAD AND STOP THINKING ABOUT THIS NOW.
SAME.
LET'S PACK UP REX AND HEAD BACK TO INES' HOUSE SO WE CAN TRAVEL BACK.
BEN...WE COULDN'T HAVE DONE THIS WITHOUT YOU. I...I DON'T KNOW HOW TO THANK YOU.
I DON'T KNOW HOW THEY DO THINGS IN THE FUTURE, BUT THIS ALWAYS WORKS FOR ME.

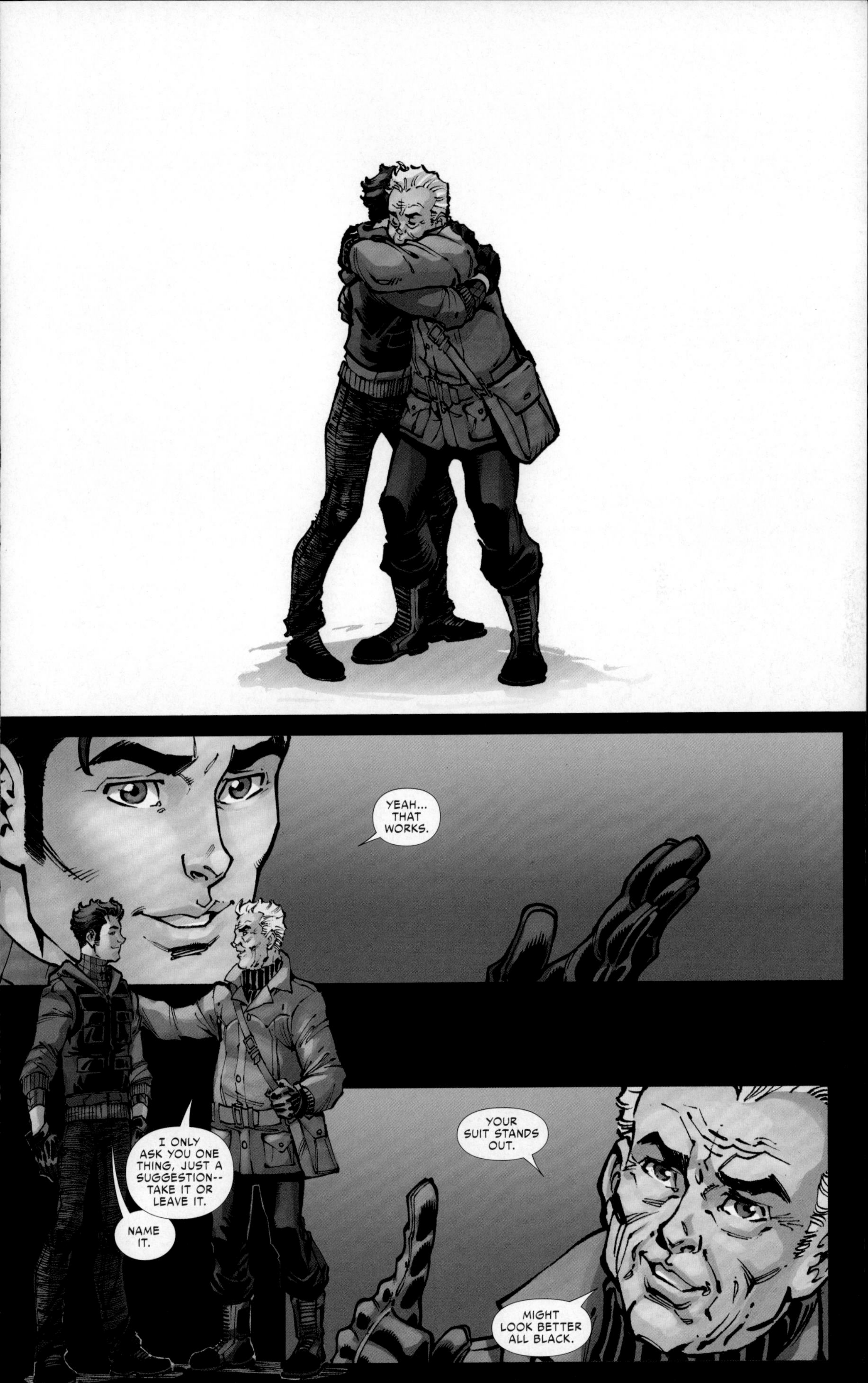
YEAH... THAT WORKS.
I ONLY ASK YOU ONE THING, JUST A SUGGESTION-- TAKE IT OR LEAVE IT.
NAME IT.
YOUR SUIT STANDS OUT.
MIGHT LOOK BETTER ALL BLACK.

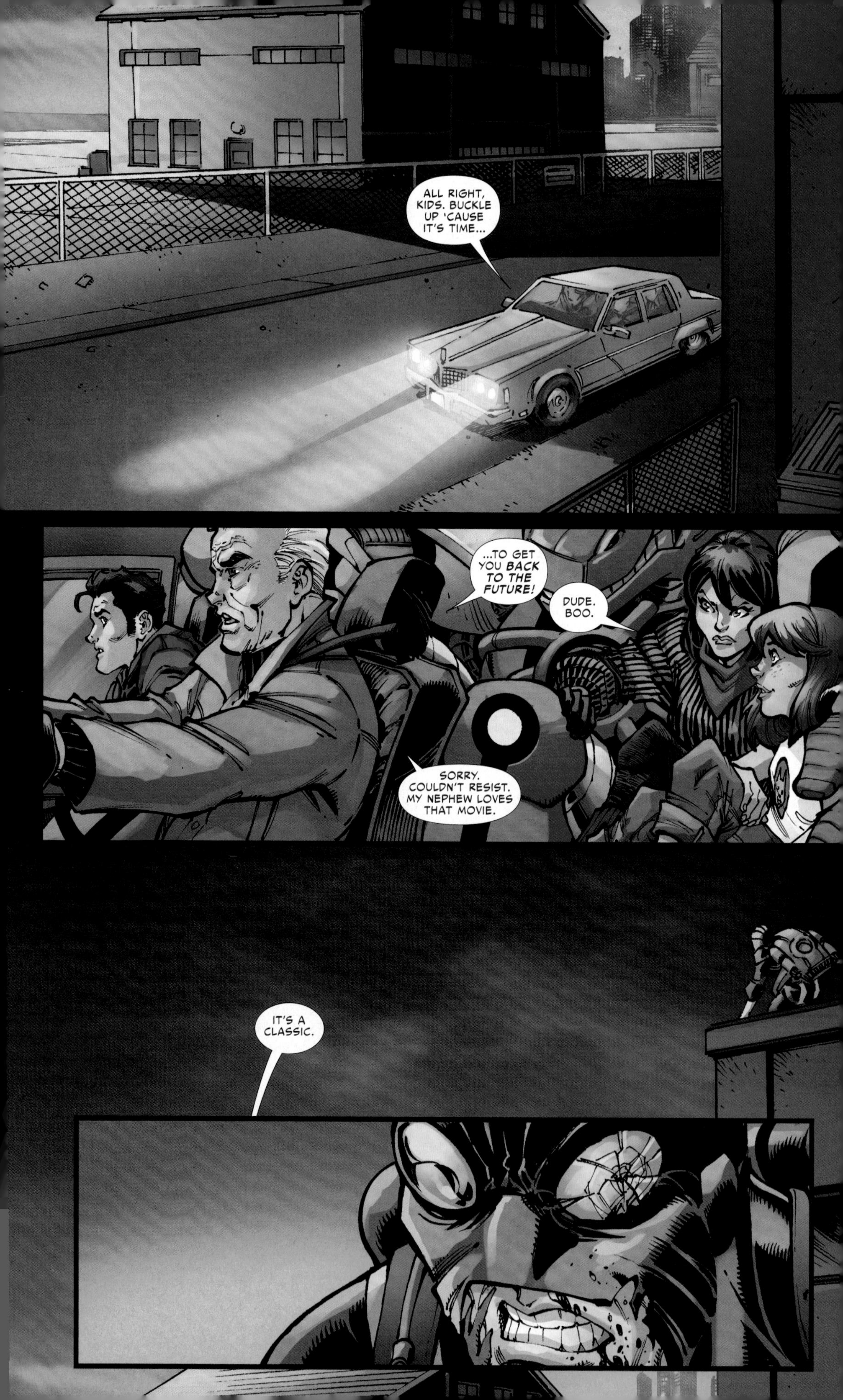
ALL RIGHT, KIDS. BUCKLE UP 'CAUSE IT'S TIME...
...TO GET YOU BACK TO THE FUTURE!
DUDE. BOO.
SORRY. COULDN'T RESIST. MY NEPHEW LOVES THAT MOVIE.
IT'S A CLASSIC.

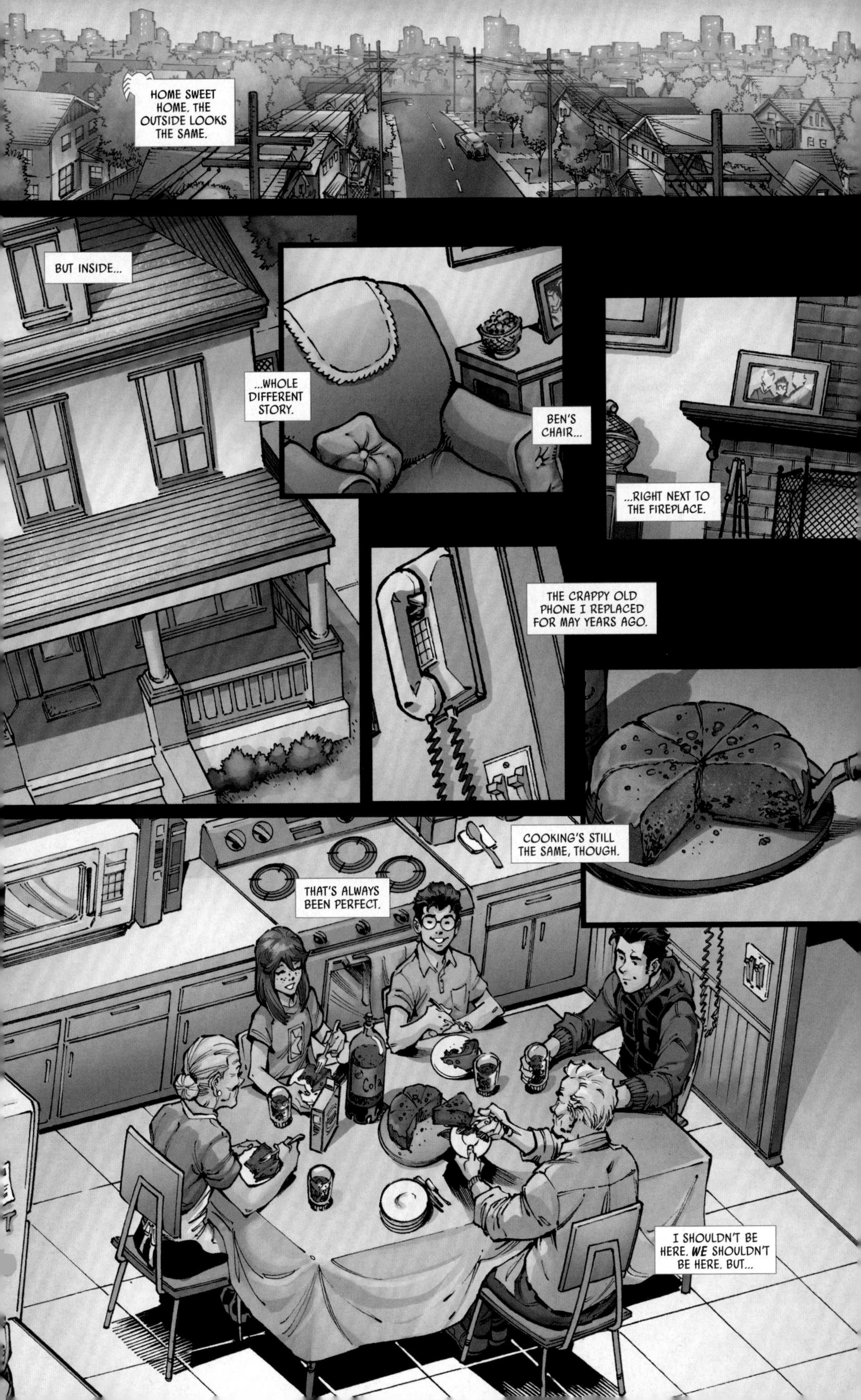
HOME SWEET HOME. THE OUTSIDE LOOKS THE SAME.
BUT INSIDE...
...WHOLE DIFFERENT STORY.
BEN'S CHAIR...
...RIGHT NEXT TO THE FIREPLACE.
THE CRAPPY OLD PHONE I REPLACED FOR MAY YEARS AGO.
COOKING'S STILL THE SAME, THOUGH.
THAT'S ALWAYS BEEN PERFECT.
Cola
I SHOULDN'T BE HERE. WE SHOULDN'T BE HERE. BUT...

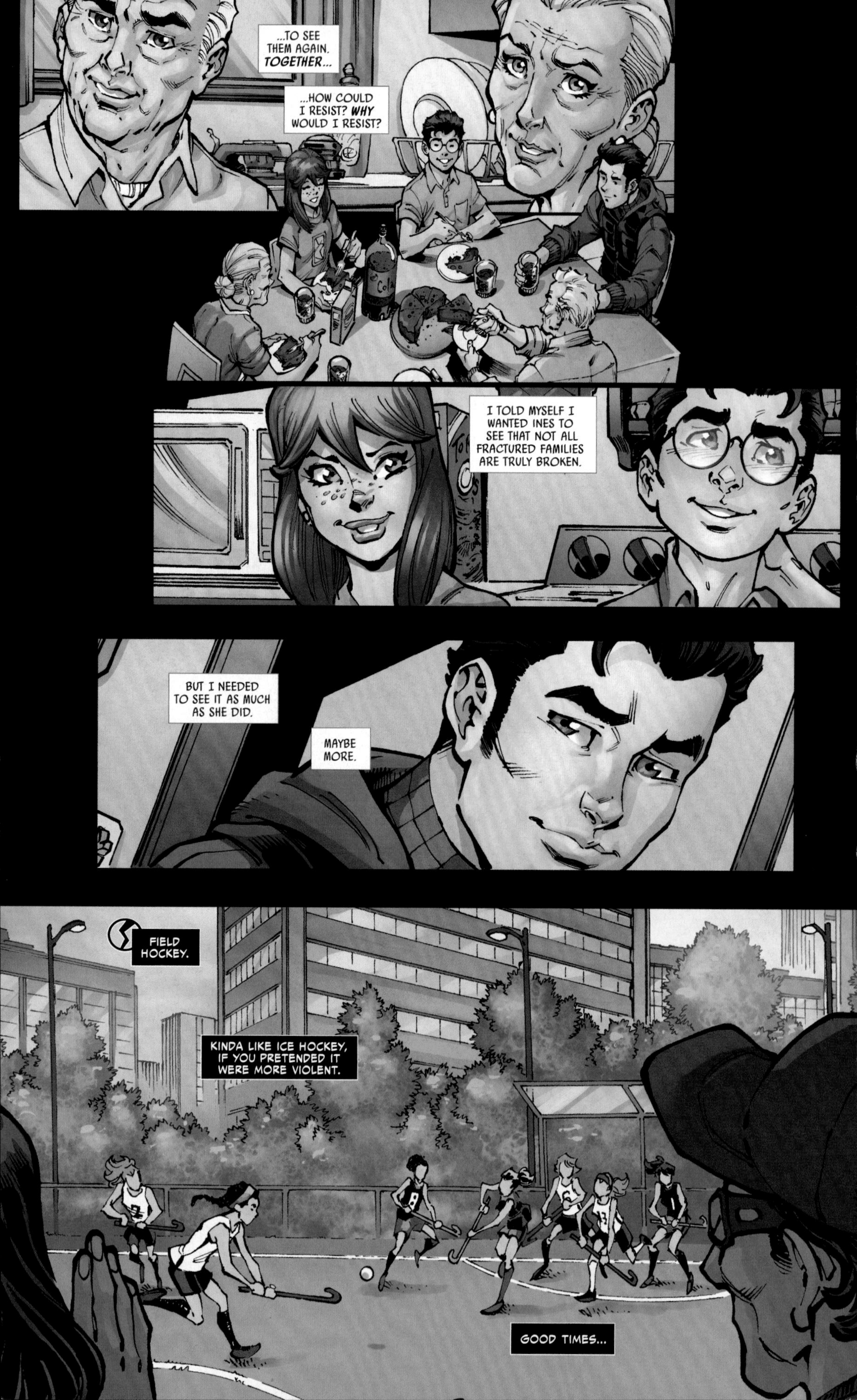
...TO SEE THEM AGAIN. *TOGETHER*...
...HOW COULD I RESIST? *WHY* WOULD I RESIST?
I TOLD MYSELF I WANTED INES TO SEE THAT NOT ALL FRACTURED FAMILIES ARE TRULY BROKEN.
BUT I NEEDED TO SEE IT AS MUCH AS SHE DID.
MAYBE MORE.
FIELD HOCKEY.
KINDA LIKE ICE HOCKEY, IF YOU PRETENDED IT WERE MORE VIOLENT.
GOOD TIMES...

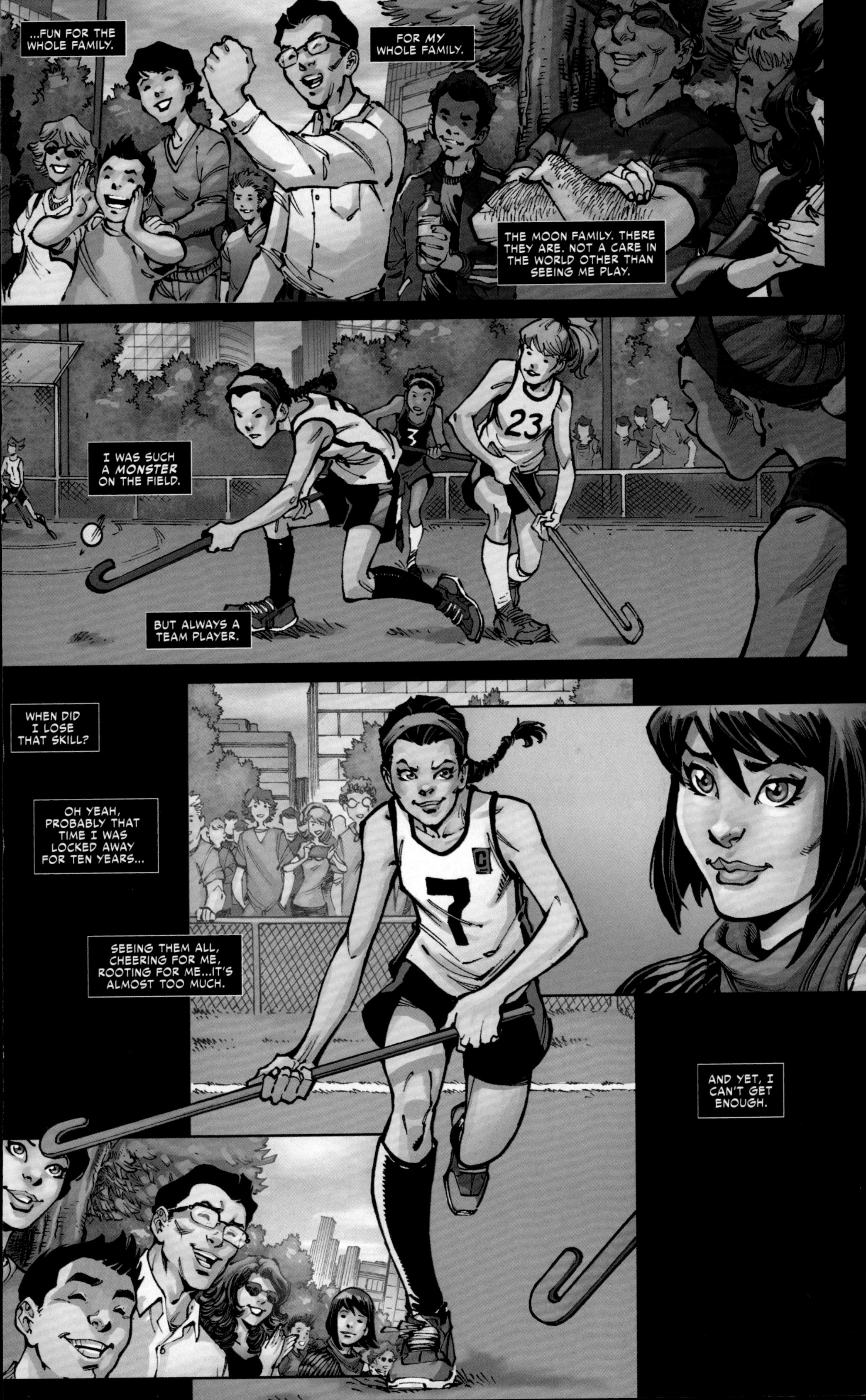
...FUN FOR THE WHOLE FAMILY.
FOR MY WHOLE FAMILY.
THE MOON FAMILY. THERE THEY ARE. NOT A CARE IN THE WORLD OTHER THAN SEEING ME PLAY.
23
3
I WAS SUCH A MONSTER ON THE FIELD.
BUT ALWAYS A TEAM PLAYER.
WHEN DID I LOSE THAT SKILL?
OH YEAH, PROBABLY THAT TIME I WAS LOCKED AWAY FOR TEN YEARS...
C
7
SEEING THEM ALL, CHEERING FOR ME, ROOTING FOR ME...IT'S ALMOST TOO MUCH.
AND YET, I CAN'T GET ENOUGH.

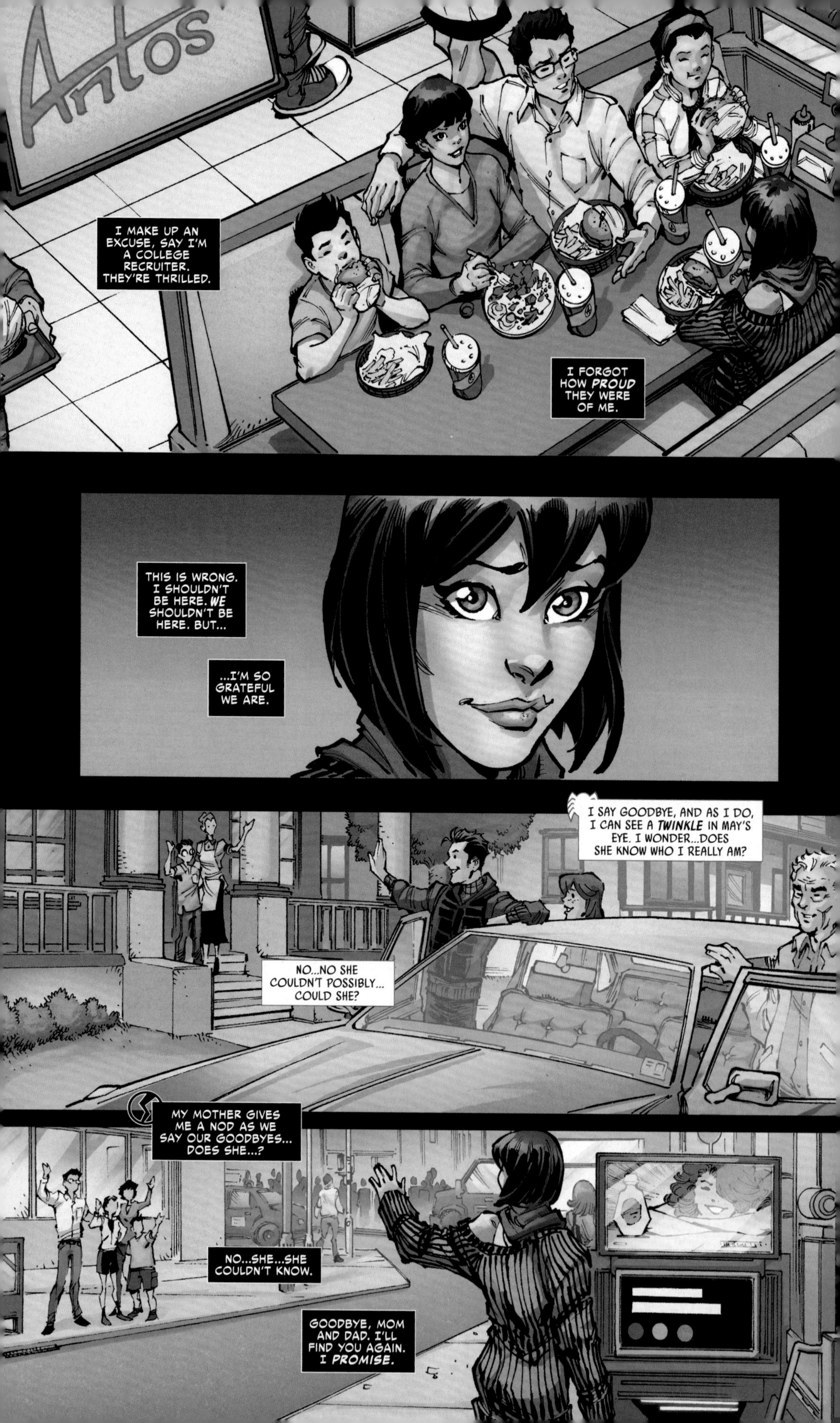

Antos
I MAKE UP AN EXCUSE, SAY I'M A COLLEGE RECRUITER. THEY'RE THRILLED.
I FORGOT HOW PROUD THEY WERE OF ME.
THIS IS WRONG. I SHOULDN'T BE HERE. WE SHOULDN'T BE HERE. BUT...
...I'M SO GRATEFUL WE ARE.
I SAY GOODBYE, AND AS I DO, I CAN SEE A TWINKLE IN MAY'S EYE. I WONDER...DOES SHE KNOW WHO I REALLY AM?
NO...NO SHE COULDN'T POSSIBLY... COULD SHE?
MY MOTHER GIVES ME A NOD AS WE SAY OUR GOODBYES... DOES SHE...?
NO...SHE...SHE COULDN'T KNOW.
GOODBYE, MOM AND DAD. I'LL FIND YOU AGAIN. I PROMISE.

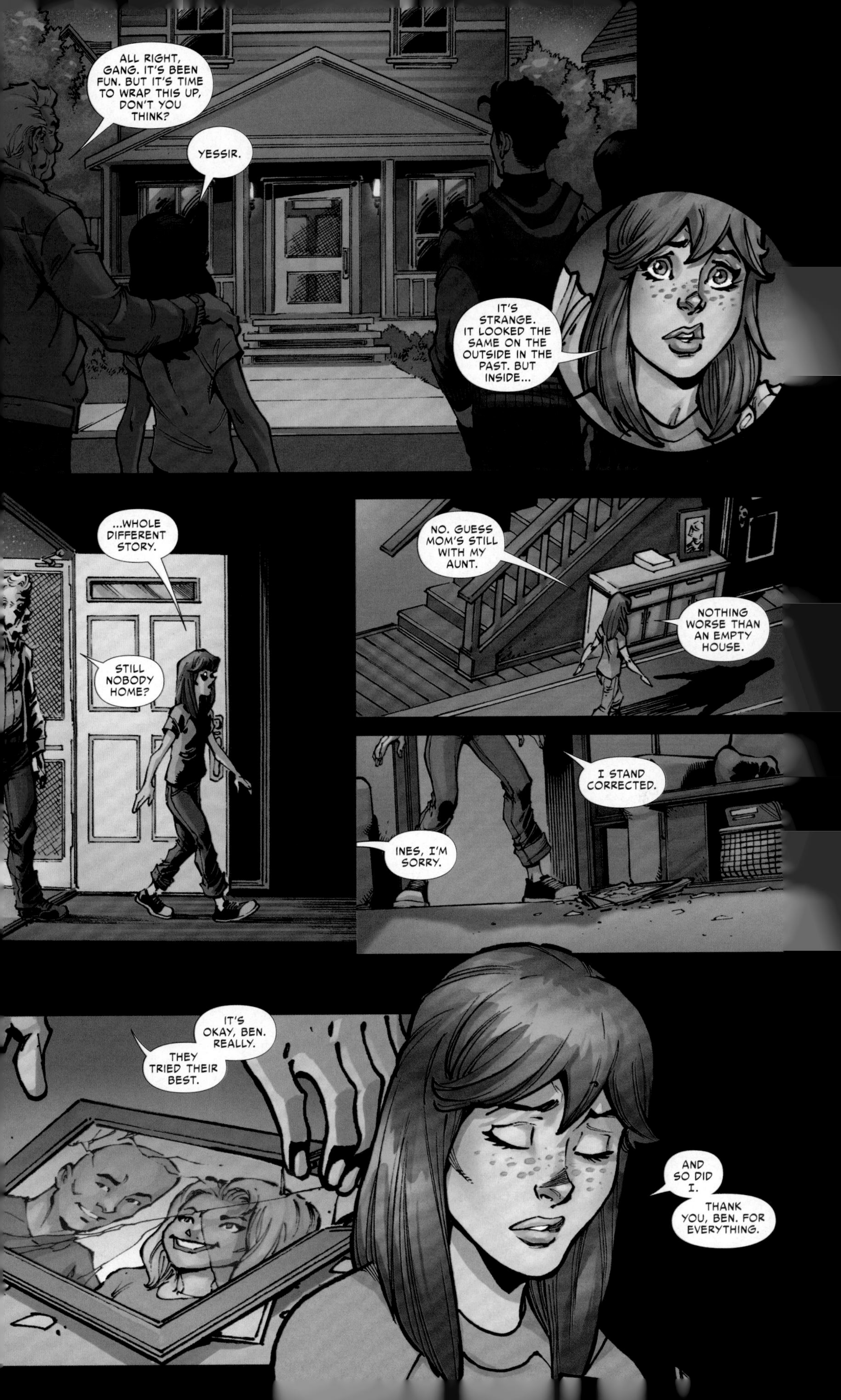
ALL RIGHT, GANG. IT'S BEEN FUN. BUT IT'S TIME TO WRAP THIS UP, DON'T YOU THINK?
YESSIR.
IT'S STRANGE. IT LOOKED THE SAME ON THE OUTSIDE IN THE PAST. BUT INSIDE...
...WHOLE DIFFERENT STORY.
STILL NOBODY HOME?
NO. GUESS MOM'S STILL WITH MY AUNT.
NOTHING WORSE THAN AN EMPTY HOUSE.
I STAND CORRECTED.
INES, I'M SORRY.
IT'S OKAY, BEN. REALLY.
THEY TRIED THEIR BEST.
AND SO DID I.
THANK YOU, BEN. FOR EVERYTHING.

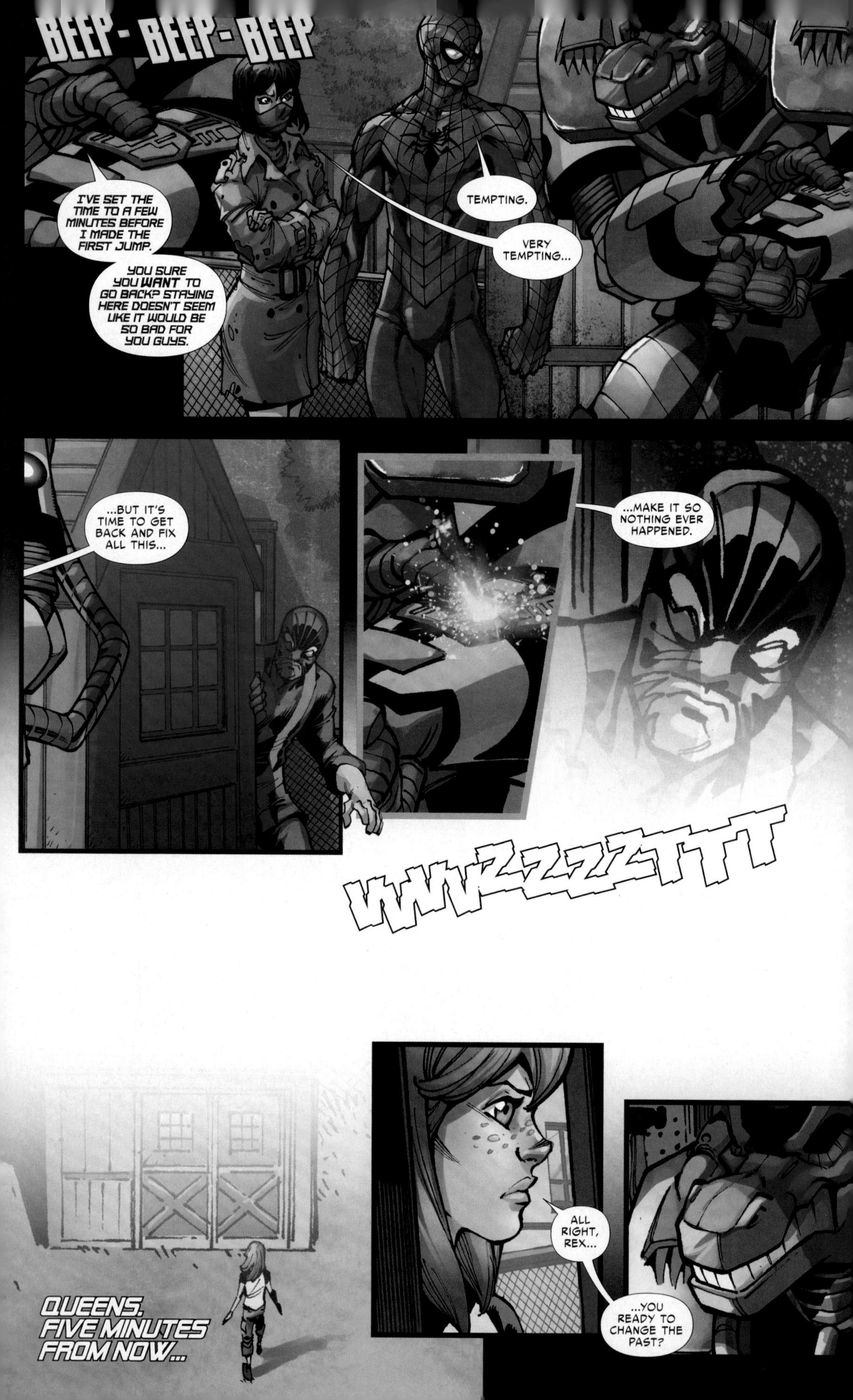
BEEP-BEEP-BEEP
I'VE SET THE TIME TO A FEW MINUTES BEFORE I MADE THE FIRST JUMP.
YOU SURE YOU WANT TO GO BACK? STAYING HERE DOESN'T SEEM LIKE IT WOULD BE SO BAD FOR YOU GUYS.
TEMPTING.
VERY TEMPTING...
...BUT IT'S TIME TO GET BACK AND FIX ALL THIS...
...MAKE IT SO NOTHING EVER HAPPENED.
VVVVZZZZTTTT
QUEENS. FIVE MINUTES FROM NOW...
ALL RIGHT, REX...
...YOU READY TO CHANGE THE PAST?

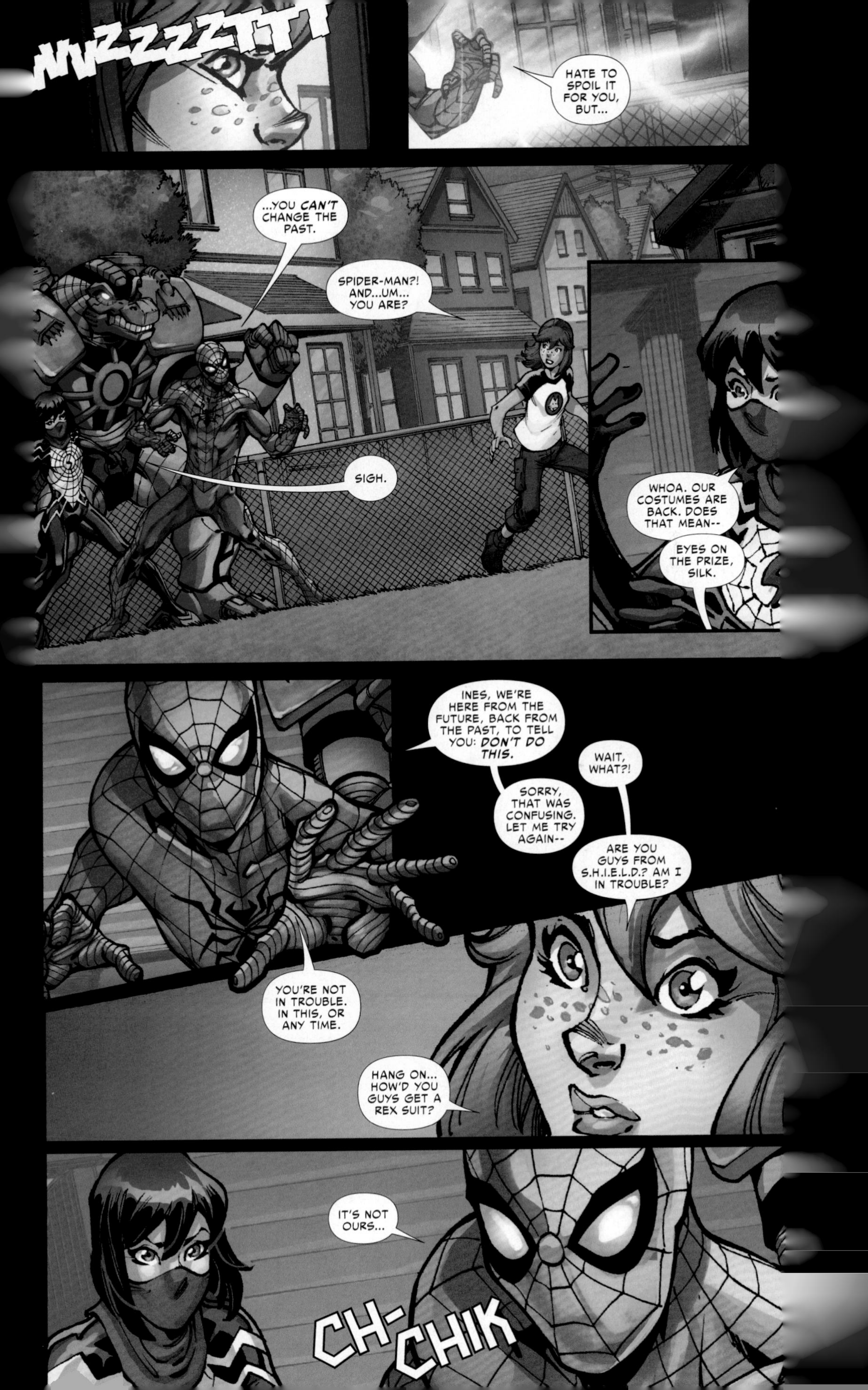
NVZZZZTTT
HATE TO SPOIL IT FOR YOU, BUT...
...YOU CAN'T CHANGE THE PAST.
SPIDER-MAN?! AND...UM... YOU ARE?
SIGH.
WHOA. OUR COSTUMES ARE BACK. DOES THAT MEAN--
EYES ON THE PRIZE, SILK.
INES, WE'RE HERE FROM THE FUTURE, BACK FROM THE PAST, TO TELL YOU: DON'T DO THIS.
WAIT, WHAT?!
SORRY, THAT WAS CONFUSING. LET ME TRY AGAIN--
ARE YOU GUYS FROM S.H.I.E.L.D.? AM I IN TROUBLE?
YOU'RE NOT IN TROUBLE. IN THIS, OR ANY TIME.
HANG ON... HOW'D YOU GUYS GET A REX SUIT?
IT'S NOT OURS...
CH-CHIK

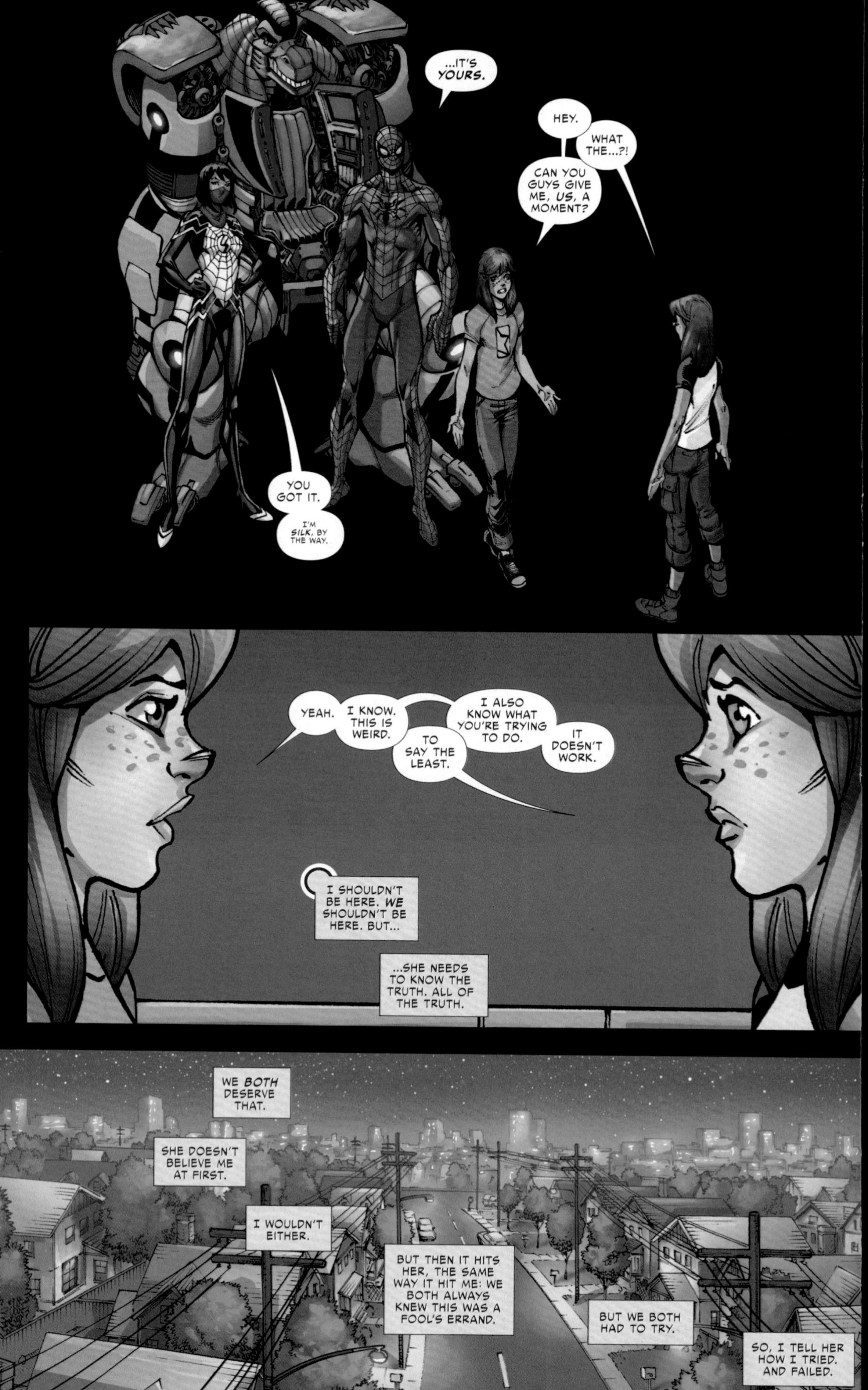

...IT'S *YOURS.*
HEY.
WHAT THE...?!
CAN YOU GUYS GIVE ME, *US*, A MOMENT?
YOU GOT IT.
I'M *SILK*, BY THE WAY.
YEAH.
I KNOW. THIS IS WEIRD.
TO SAY THE LEAST.
I ALSO KNOW WHAT YOU'RE TRYING TO DO.
IT DOESN'T WORK.
I SHOULDN'T BE HERE. *WE* SHOULDN'T BE HERE. BUT...
...SHE NEEDS TO KNOW THE TRUTH. ALL OF THE TRUTH.
WE *BOTH* DESERVE THAT.
SHE DOESN'T BELIEVE ME AT FIRST.
I WOULDN'T EITHER.
BUT THEN IT HITS HER, THE SAME WAY IT HIT ME: WE BOTH ALWAYS KNEW THIS WAS A FOOL'S ERRAND.
BUT WE BOTH HAD TO TRY.
SO, I TELL HER HOW I TRIED. AND FAILED.

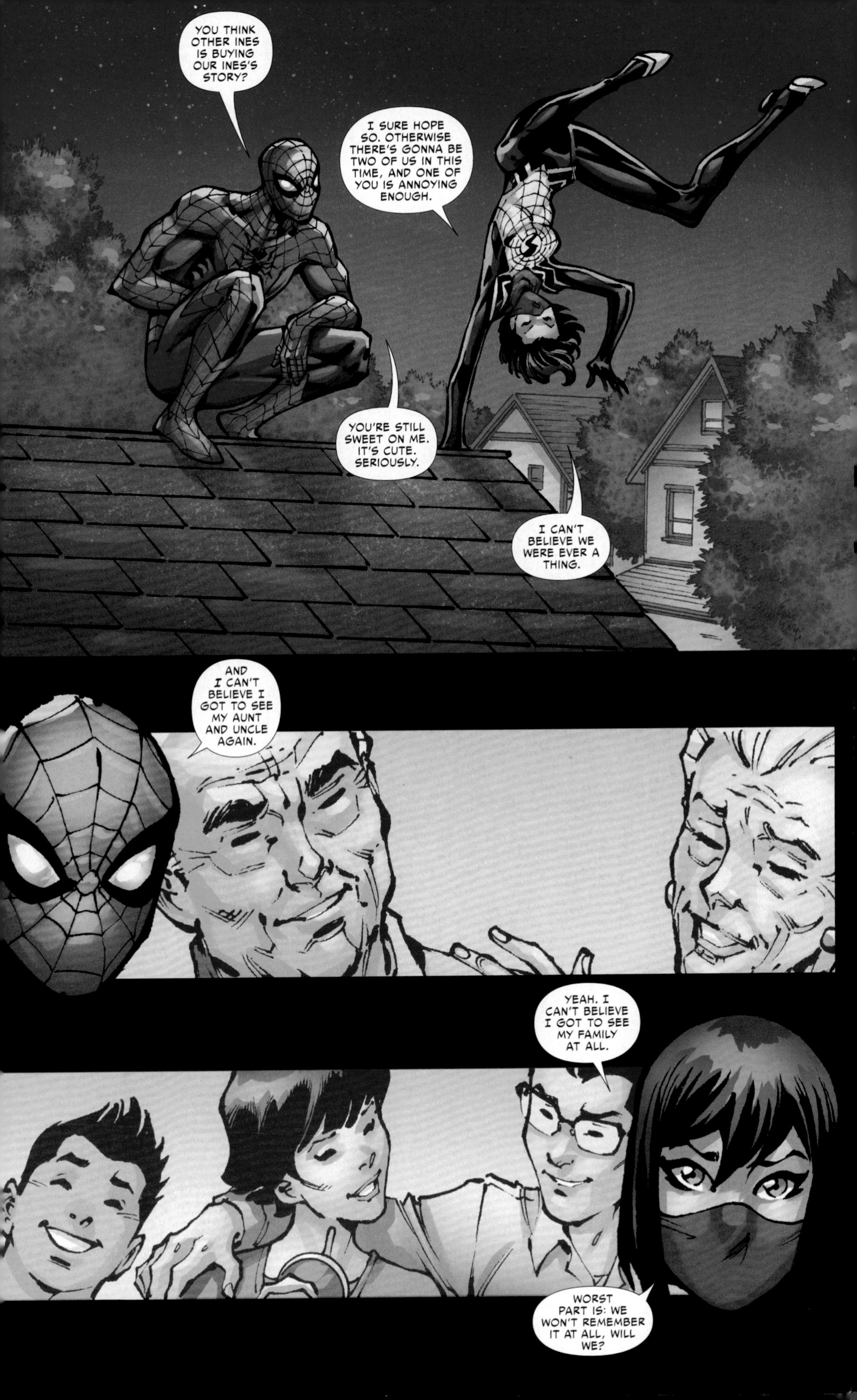
YOU THINK OTHER INES IS BUYING OUR INES'S STORY?
I SURE HOPE SO. OTHERWISE THERE'S GONNA BE TWO OF US IN THIS TIME, AND ONE OF YOU IS ANNOYING ENOUGH.
YOU'RE STILL SWEET ON ME. IT'S CUTE. SERIOUSLY.
I CAN'T BELIEVE WE WERE EVER A THING.
AND I CAN'T BELIEVE I GOT TO SEE MY AUNT AND UNCLE AGAIN.
YEAH. I CAN'T BELIEVE I GOT TO SEE MY FAMILY AT ALL.
WORST PART IS: WE WON'T REMEMBER IT AT ALL, WILL WE?

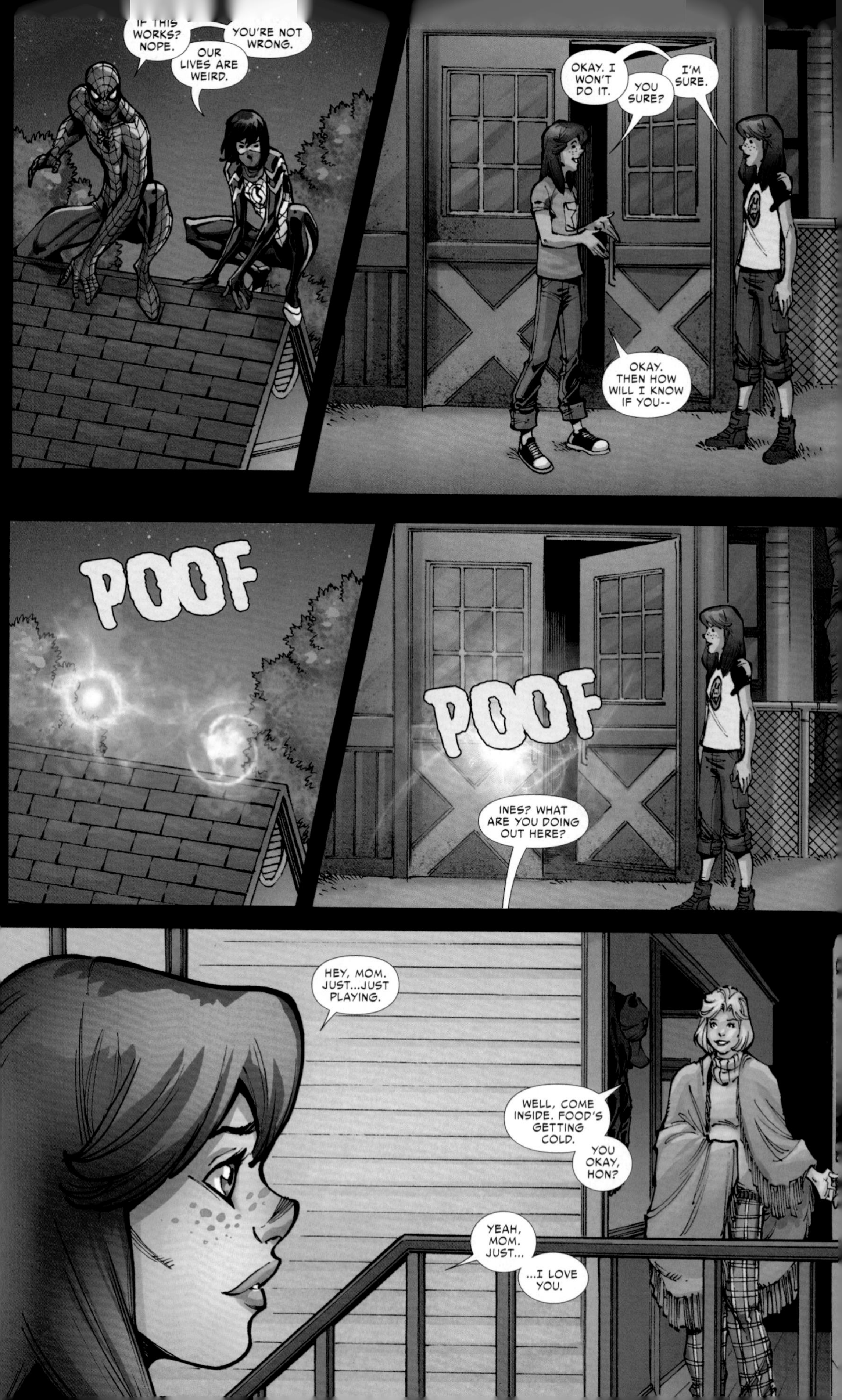
IF THIS WORKS? NOPE.
YOU'RE NOT WRONG.
OUR LIVES ARE WEIRD.
OKAY. I WON'T DO IT.
I'M SURE.
YOU SURE?
OKAY. THEN HOW WILL I KNOW IF YOU--
POOF
POOF
INES? WHAT ARE YOU DOING OUT HERE?
HEY, MOM. JUST...JUST PLAYING.
WELL, COME INSIDE. FOOD'S GETTING COLD.
YOU OKAY, HON?
YEAH, MOM. JUST...
...I LOVE YOU.

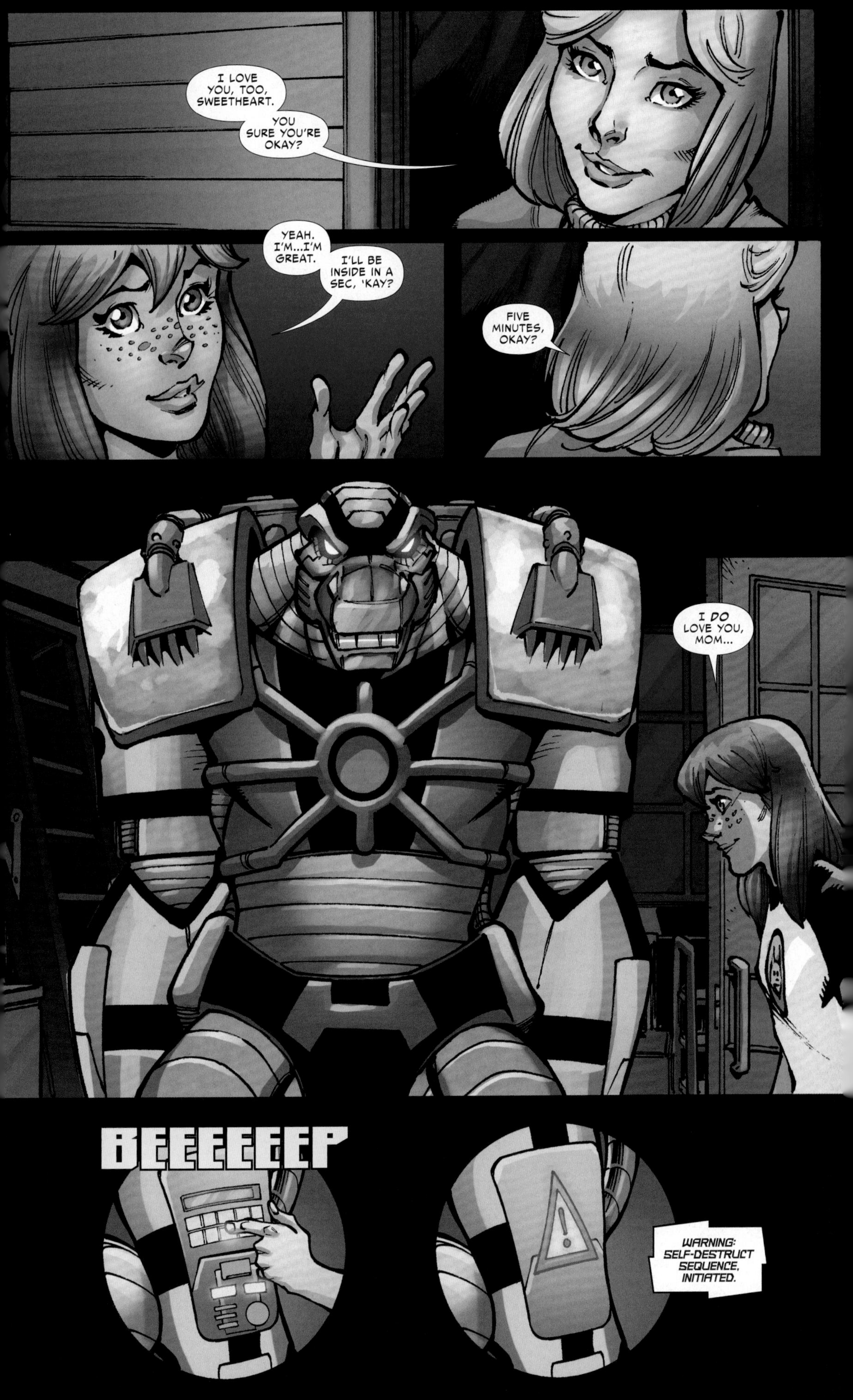
I LOVE YOU, TOO, SWEETHEART.
YOU SURE YOU'RE OKAY?
YEAH. I'M...I'M GREAT.
I'LL BE INSIDE IN A SEC, 'KAY?
FIVE MINUTES, OKAY?
I DO LOVE YOU, MOM...
BEEEEEEP
WARNING: SELF-DESTRUCT SEQUENCE, INITIATED.

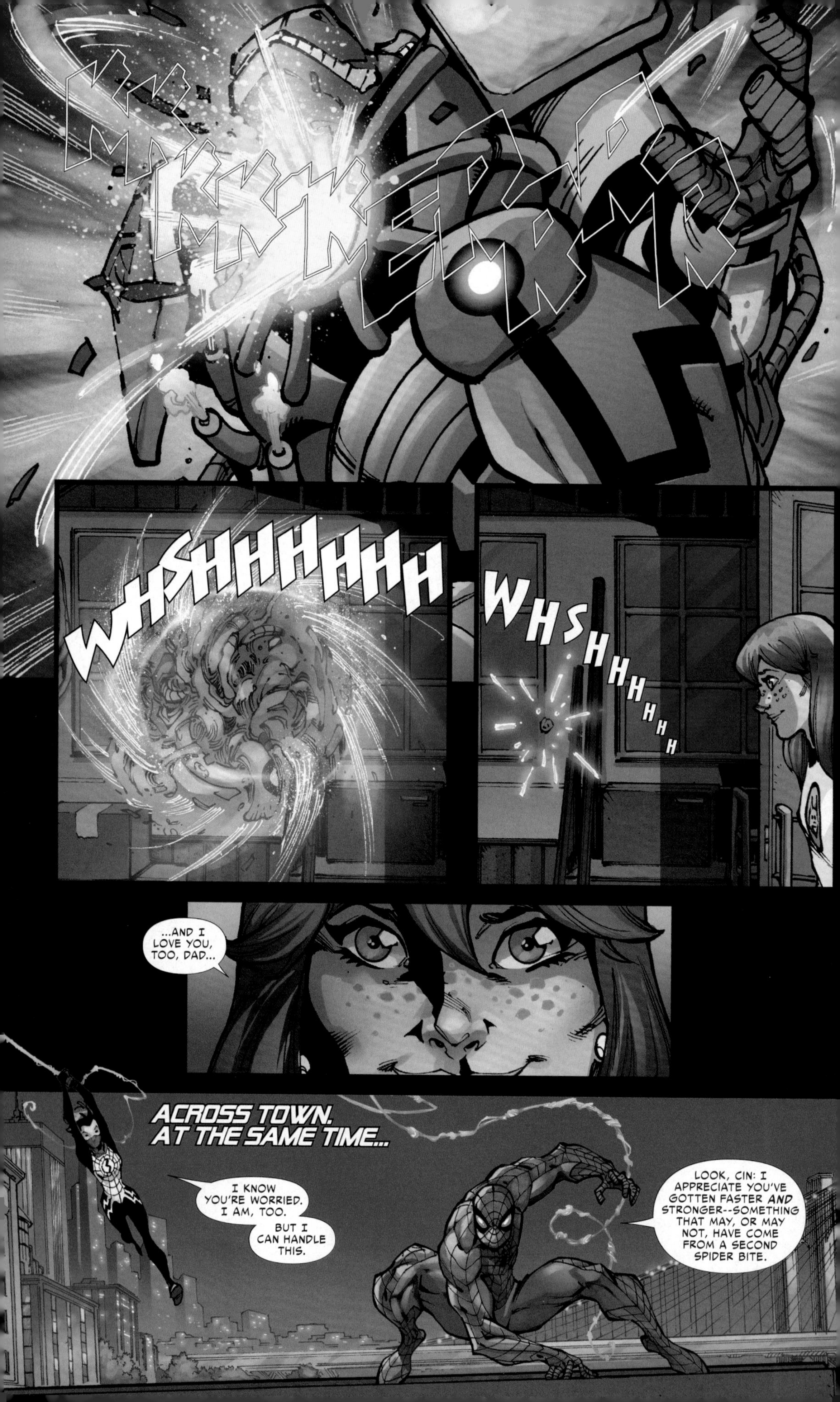
WHSHHHHHHH
WHSHHHHHHH
...AND I LOVE YOU, TOO, DAD...
ACROSS TOWN. AT THE SAME TIME...
I KNOW YOU'RE WORRIED. I AM, TOO.
BUT I CAN HANDLE THIS.
LOOK, CIN: I APPRECIATE YOU'VE GOTTEN FASTER AND STRONGER--SOMETHING THAT MAY, OR MAY NOT, HAVE COME FROM A SECOND SPIDER BITE.

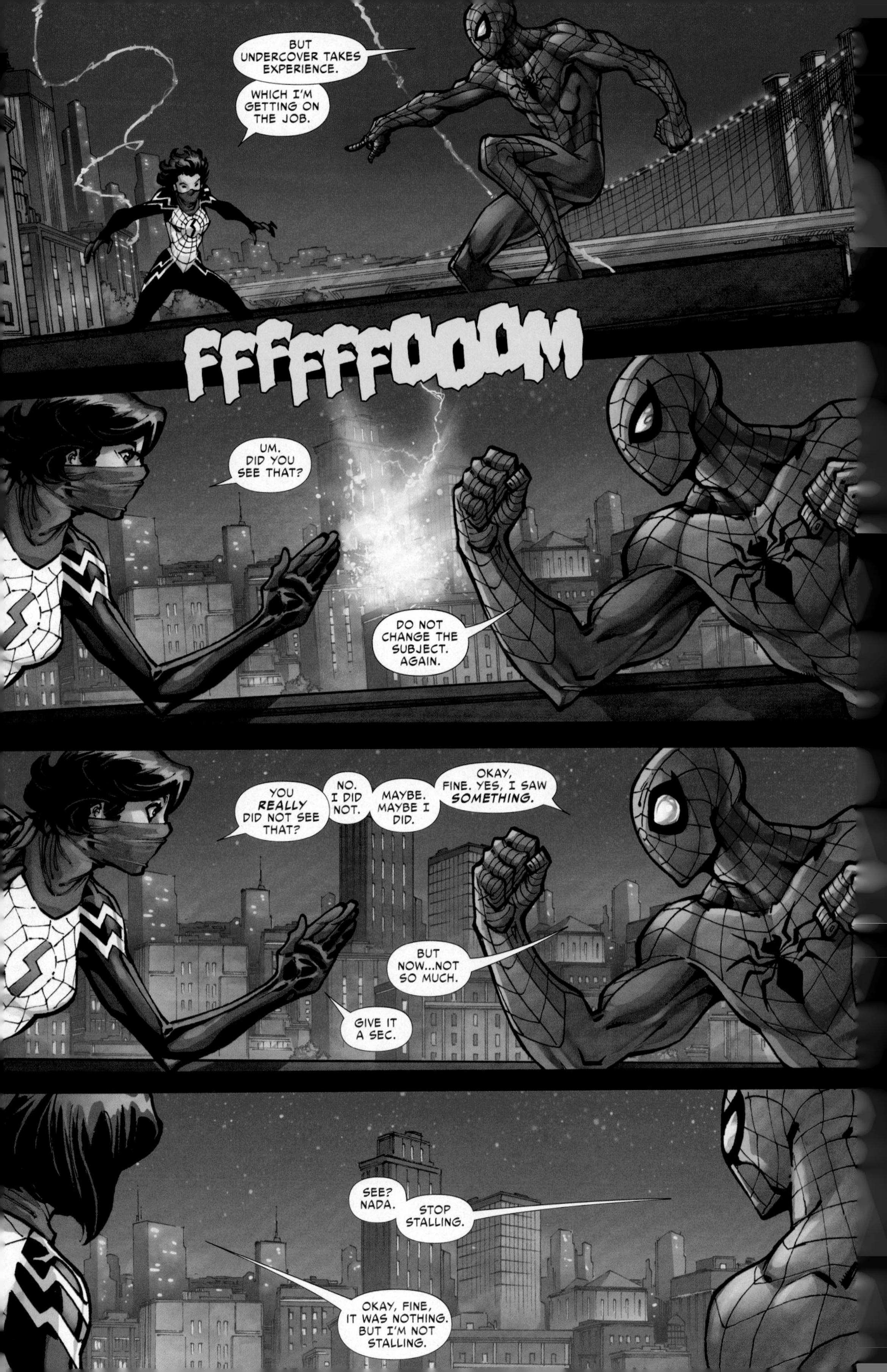
BUT UNDERCOVER TAKES EXPERIENCE.
WHICH I'M GETTING ON THE JOB.
FFFFFFOOOM
UM. DID YOU SEE THAT?
DO NOT CHANGE THE SUBJECT. AGAIN.
YOU REALLY DID NOT SEE THAT?
NO. I DID NOT.
MAYBE. MAYBE I DID.
OKAY, FINE. YES, I SAW SOMETHING.
BUT NOW...NOT SO MUCH.
GIVE IT A SEC.
SEE? NADA.
STOP STALLING.
OKAY, FINE, IT WAS NOTHING. BUT I'M NOT STALLING.

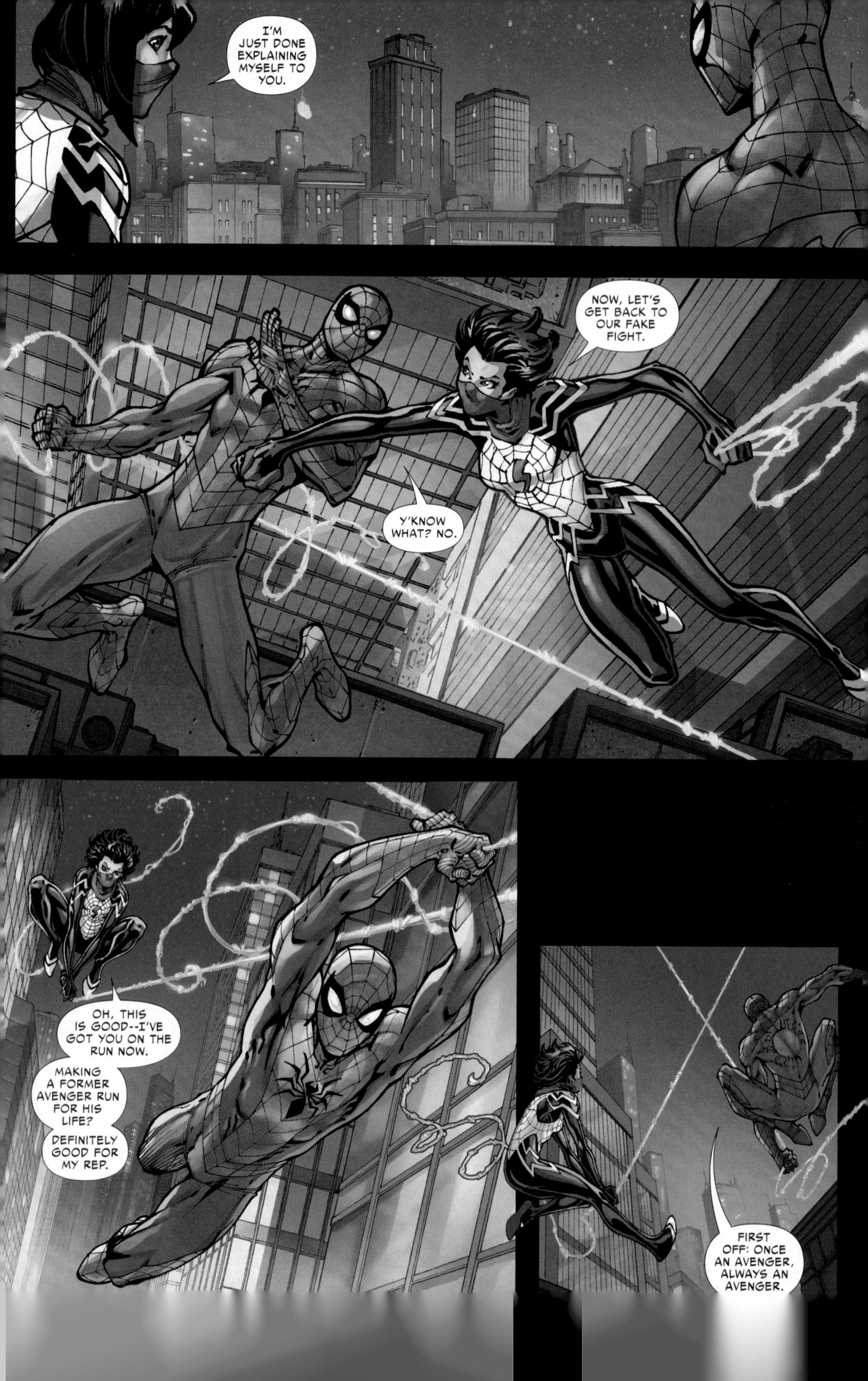
I'M JUST DONE EXPLAINING MYSELF TO YOU.
NOW, LET'S GET BACK TO OUR FAKE FIGHT.
Y'KNOW WHAT? NO.
OH, THIS IS GOOD--I'VE GOT YOU ON THE RUN NOW.
MAKING A FORMER AVENGER RUN FOR HIS LIFE?
DEFINITELY GOOD FOR MY REP.
FIRST OFF: ONCE AN AVENGER, ALWAYS AN AVENGER.

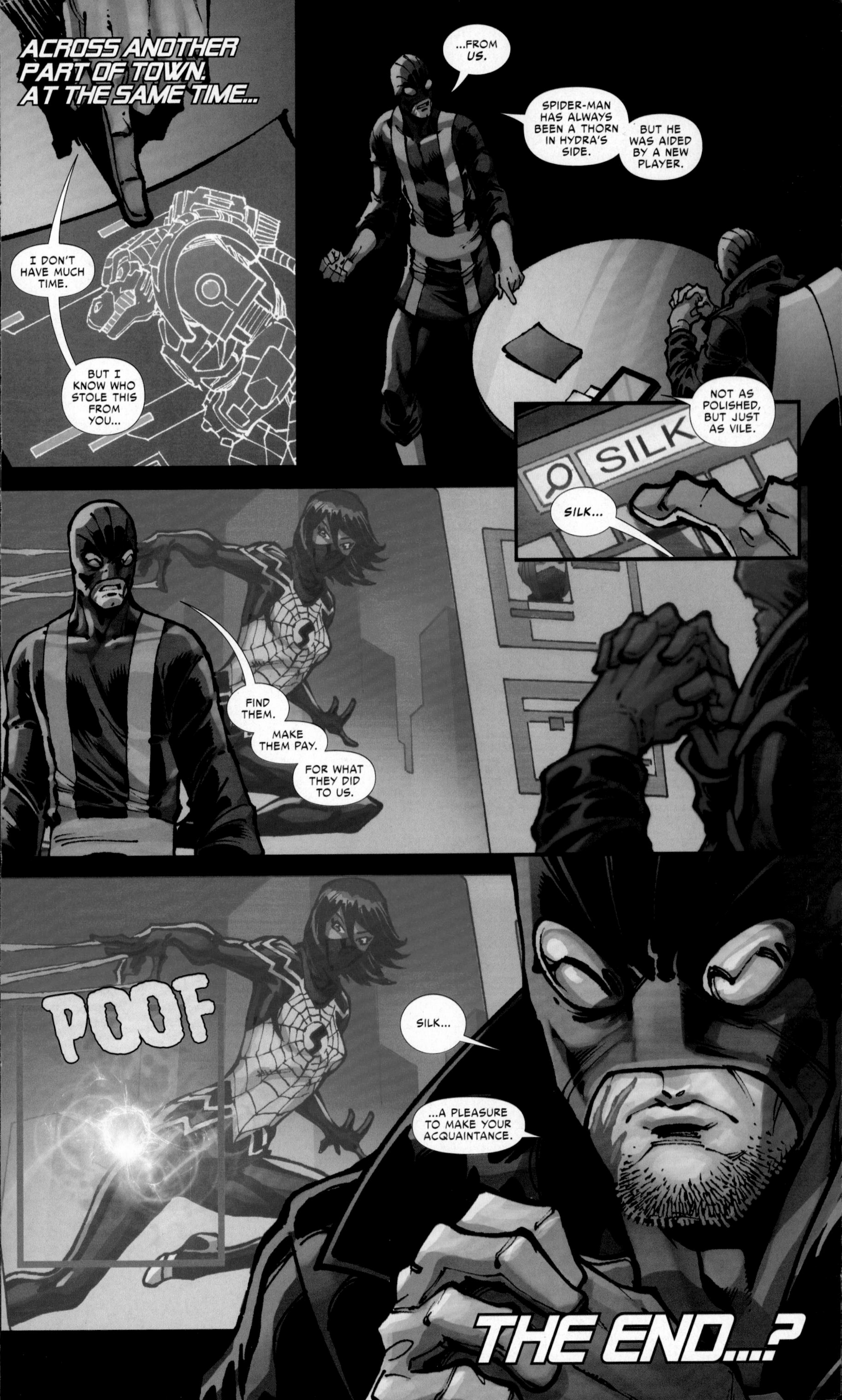
ACROSS ANOTHER PART OF TOWN. AT THE SAME TIME...
I DON'T HAVE MUCH TIME.
BUT I KNOW WHO STOLE THIS FROM YOU...
...FROM US.
SPIDER-MAN HAS ALWAYS BEEN A THORN IN HYDRA'S SIDE.
BUT HE WAS AIDED BY A NEW PLAYER.
NOT AS POLISHED, BUT JUST AS VILE.
SILK
SILK...
FIND THEM.
MAKE THEM PAY.
FOR WHAT THEY DID TO US.
POOF
SILK...
...A PLEASURE TO MAKE YOUR ACQUAINTANCE.
THE END...?